Altruism, Morality, and Economic Theory

Altruism, Morality, and Economic Theory

Edited by Edmund S. Phelps

Russell Sage Foundation New York

PUBLICATIONS OF RUSSELL SAGE FOUNDATION

Russell Sage Foundation was established in 1907 by Mrs. Russell Sage for the improvement of social and living conditions in the United States. In carrying out its purpose the Foundation conducts research under the direction of members of the staff or in close collaboration with other institutions, and supports programs designed to develop and demonstrate productive working relations between social scientists and other professional groups. As an integral part of its operation, the Foundation from time to time publishes books or pamphlets resulting from these activities. Publication under the imprint of the Foundation does not necessarily imply agreement by the Foundation, its Trustees, or its staff with the interpretations or conclusions of the authors.

Russell Sage Foundation
230 Park Avenue, New York, New York 10017

Library of Congress Catalog Card Number: 74-79448
Standard Book Number: 87154-659-0
Printed in the United States of America.

The Contributors

Kenneth J. Arrow
Professor of Economics
Harvard University

William Baumol
Joseph Douglas Green '95 Professor of Economics
Princeton University

Bruce R. Bolnick
Assistant Professor of Economics
Duke University

James M. Buchanan
Professor of Economics
Virginia Polytechnic Institute & State University

Guido Calabresi
John Thomas Smith Professor of Law
Yale University

Peter Hammond
Lecturer in Economics
University of Essex

Edward F. McClennen
Professor of Philosophy
University of Western Ontario

Roland N. McKean
Professor of Economics
University of Virginia

Thomas Nagel
Professor of Philosophy
Princeton University

Wilfried Pauwels
Lecturer in Economics
University of Antwerp

Edmund S. Phelps
Professor of Economics
Columbia University

Amartya K. Sen
Professor of Economics
London School of Economics

Karl Shell
Professor of Economics
University of Pennsylvania

William S. Vickrey
McVickar Professor of Political Economy
Columbia University

Burton A. Weisbrod
Professor of Economics
University of Wisconsin

Contents

Preface

The self-interest model has had sweeping success over recent decades in the study of both economics and politics. Yet the inner ambiguities and limitations of that model could not indefinitely escape notice and examination. Self interest in some interpretation is some of the story some of the time, never the whole story. On March 3 and 4, 1972, a number of social scientists met at Russell Sage Foundation to speculate and theorize on the roles that altruism and morality in a society may play in shaping human behavior and institutions within it.

The nine papers presented at the conference are by economists. The commentaries on them were drawn from representatives of other disciplines, primarily philosophy and law. This volume is a rough approximation to the proceedings of the conference. An introduction by the editor has been added to announce some of the main themes and to bring out some of the interrelations among the papers.

The contributors are grateful to Russell Sage Foundation for its sponsorship of the conference and of this volume. Particular thanks go to Orville Brim, Jr., former president of the Foundation, to Eleanor Bernert Sheldon, now president of the Social Science Research Council, and to Hugh F. Cline, now president of Russell Sage Foundation. The editor is also grateful to William Baumol for allowing the use of his paper in place of one of the original conference papers subsequently withdrawn.

E.S.P.

New York
May 1974

Introduction

Edmund S. Phelps

The compartmentalizing of the study of human behavior and human knowledge into separate fields of inquiry, and the segregation of scholars into these compartments, seems to be a widely acknowledged fact of scientific life. However, the separations have never been airtight, and the leakages and seepages have often been as important as the walls limiting them. Men of great talent like Hume, Mill, Pareto and Ramsey commuted comfortably from economics to philosophy, or to politics or sociology, with their talents evidently conserved in the process. Just as successful nuclear physicists have felt licensed to share with us their views on the theory of knowledge, the distinguished economic theorist in the autumn of his career has often enjoyed visits to the interface of his subject with other fields. When Sir Dennis Robertson lectured at the bicentennial celebrations for Columbia University, it was therefore expectable that he would address a question of grandeur: "What Do Economists Economize?" His unexpected answer: They economize on love.

In recent years there have been leakages from the economics compartment springing more from a curiosity to try the methods of economic analysis in other fields than from the restless talents of a versatile few. We have witnessed excursions into the theory of national defense, the axiomatics of neo-utilitarianism, the economics of crime and punishment—and it has seemed to some that the leaks from economics threaten to inundate the compartment of political science. Because the areas of competing wants within a person and conflicting desires between persons go beyond the marketplace, it is natural that economists should check to see to what extent the techniques for analyzing the market mechanism (its successes and failures) as a means of resolving such wants and desires carry over to these other areas.

One (only one) mission of the present volume is an expedition of that kind, this time into the area of altruism, of behavior actuated by a sense of others, their desires and expectations. Several of the authors here have brought the concepts of economic theory, including game theory, and sometimes the theory of other disciplines as well, to bear on the analysis of the altruistic use of scarce resources. The range of altruistic behavior, or what we commonly interpret as such, is impressive. It is sometimes exhibited (for good or ill) by sellers and buyers in the marketplace. The presence of altruistic behavior, as economic activity in general, is even more pronounced away from commercial settings. More than one half of the American population depend for their security and material satisfactions not upon the sale of their services but rather upon their relationships to others. Altruism is expressed in varied forms. It may be individual, interpersonal, and unilateral, as within the family. It may also be cooperative and multilateral, being institutionalized in agencies of government, voluntary associations or private philanthropies. If a task of economists is to illuminate the allocation of resources, then the analysis of altruistic resource use is a bridge to be crossed.

The wonderment over the phenomenon of altruism has led to several questions. Can altruistic behavior be fit into some version of the economist's beloved model of utility maximization subject to constraints? Or must that model be importantly modified and hooked up to some complementary body of analysis to yield a satisfactory product? More specifically: why, when and how do some persons behave in a way that is apparently altruistic—for what motives, under what circumstances, through what channels?

In such an analysis, it would seem important to classify the various kinds of motives behind the collection of acts that are called altruistic. Possibly some acts called altruistic are interpretable as an investment, a *quid* for some implicit and conjectured *quo*. Another polar case in the typology is the altruistic act which is an unrequited transfer; the giving provides its own gratification. There should be room too in the taxonomy for acts of altruism in which there is "nothing personal," only a generalized regard for human rights, social codes, business "ethics," and so on. This last type of altruistic behavior is perhaps best thought of as the result of additional, moralistic constraints on utility maximization rather than the result of a compulsive or superstitious utility function (in a manner of speaking).[1]

---

[1] Why? Presumably a moral constraint could and might cause the consumer to fail to obey the law of "compensated" consumer demand in some neighborhoods of the (amoral) choice set. To say this, however, is not to suggest that a particular morality may not be driven out if the costs of adhering to it should come to exceed some threshold level.

There is also the where and how, the study of the occasions and vehicles for altruism. Why do we often find a good being supplied altruistically, without charge or at less than maximum gain to the supplier, while another good in the same society is supplied at the market price? What accounts for the success of some voluntary associations of potential "free riders" in providing certain goods without charge, especially when governmental mechanisms for providing like goods exist alongside? May the provision of some goods by the market or by the government spoil the reserves of altruism, as GNP may pollute water and air, a hypothesis suggested by Titmuss? Or was Robertson right that the use of competitive market processes wherever the technical requirements for their functioning are met, like the use of perfect capital markets in an economy of certainty to ration privately owned exhaustible resources over time, will really economize our limited reserves of love for uses in the ways we care about most?

These are difficult questions, and full answers to them are a long way off. The place of this volume in relation to those questions is that of a starting place where they are thought about and, in some cases, where some tentative candidates in the way of partial answers are explored. Nor is it an assumption or conclusion of the papers here that economics alone can necessarily provide answers.

The impression should not be left that this volume is another essay in academic imperialism by the queen of the social sciences—a queen who need not (or cannot) learn anything new. Thinking about the economics of altruism has contributed to the rethinking of economics. Important as the recognition of altruistic behavior may be for the explanation of certain resource allocations, especially those outside the market, altruistic phenomena are equally crucial to the functioning of markets. The adherence to certain altruistic precepts and traditions by the participants in commercial markets makes a crucial contribution to the national income and thus, very likely, to Bentham-Bergson economic welfare. The price system would work less well, and would be less widely applied, were it not that the economic agents—portrayed by the Walrasian model of the price system as flint-hearted maximizers—in fact display a decent regard for the interests of those with whom they exchange and for society as a whole.

The other mission of this volume, then, is to inquire into the economic functions served by certain kinds of altruistic behavior in the society's "production" of economic welfare. That altruism can play an economic role is a theme heralded earlier by non-economists. It was a motif of the German Historical School, as in Sombart's *Capitalism*. Among recent studies, one may cite Banfield's *The Moral Basis of a Backward Society* and Titmuss's *The Gift Relationship*.[2] It has remained for economists to scrutinize and elaborate the proposition, and to reexamine accordingly the postulates of the Walrasian model. What sorts of altruistic behavior are productive, and for what reasons?

What sorts are not productive, or even counterproductive? What are the costs of altruistic conduct? If it sometimes substitutes for law and regulation, what are the costs of the responsibility and power it thus places in private hands?

Just as the builders of the pure theory of international trade developed the welfare-economics theorem that "some" international trade is unambiguously better than none, the authors here are groping towards the elements of a pure theory of altruism which says that, for economic welfare, some kinds and amounts of altruism are better than none. It should be remarked, perhaps, that the claims made here for some altruism, like the claim for some trade, hold for a conception of economic welfare of *arbitrary* distributive bias, that is, for *any* Bentham-Bergson welfare function, $W(U_1 U_2, \ldots, U_n)$. It is, of course, a triviality that the willingness of citizens to vote redistributive taxes or the generosity of a corporation in some social cause *may*, via the resulting redistribution of goods, increase economic welfare as measured by some Ideal Ethical Observer. It is also patent that the "altruism" of conniving oligopolists and the "ethical" codes of some business associations may, by their redistributive effects, decrease the level of welfare similarly measured. The claims for altruism developed here are that certain forms of it promote economic efficiency, so that everyone can be made better off—not just that some deserving folk will be made better off at the expense of others.[3]

The attribution of that sort of efficiency function to altruistic market behavior clashes with some tenets of classical economic liberalism still clung to in some quarters today. Smith pronounced that "It is not from the benevolence of the butcher . . . that we expect our dinner but from his regard to his own self interest," and the classic liberals apparently made no room, at least explicity, for altruism in the marketplace. In our own time, many conservatives decry the doctrine of corporate responsibility and see no useful role for altruism outside the voting booth and the nuclear family. If this classical position has any foundations in economic theory, it probably rests on the neoclassical analysis of atomistic and monopolistic markets under the Walrasian postulate of perfect information and perfect foresight. In that world there is no uncertainty of the sort arising from the costs of transmitting and acquiring information about current prices, wages, rentals, the characteristics of goods, jobs, factor services

[2] Not to mention literary works such as Ibsen's *Enemy of the People* with its examination of business responsibility or Traven's *Treasure of the Sierra Madre*. Undergraduates seeing the film version of the latter often note the lecture on the labor theory of value, but its lessons on the economics of trust are its main concern.

[3] Of course, any change in morals or conventions may require an investment cost for its realization, and once effected it may cause random casualties. A cautious theorist would prefer to defend this weaker version of the thesis: the resource saving permitted by (some) altruistic behavior helps every "type" of person "over life" and "on the average"—that is, raises expected remaining lifetime utility for persons in every broad impersonal class.

and the rest; taken literally, there is not even uncertainty as to the numbers and preferences and technologies of economic agents yet unborn so the future can also be known. It is for that Walrasian world that modern mathematical economists prove the "fundamental theorem of welfare economics": A decentralized perfectly competitive price mechanism will, under suitable technical conditions and the right tax-subsidy corrections, produce a Pareto efficient allocation of resources—without benefit of altruism.

Evidently the efficiency functions of altruism depend upon an unclassical view of the conditions under which markets operate in the contemporary world.[4] Some early steps have recently been taken toward the development of non-Walrasian models of economic behavior in which the participants have to make decisions without perfect information and perfect foresight. From that more realistic view of the economic environment one sees unsafe factories and unsafe products (beyond the economical danger point), labor unions and business associations, bad debts, discrimination (of the statistical sort), gouging, extortion, and short-weighing by Smithian butchers. But in that frightening world one is relieved to see also the prevalence of altruistic behavior: a producer may advertise his product truthfully when he need not, a labor union may refrain from breaking the law when it could do so for a net gain, a producer may resist contaminating a river when he could do so without detection, a firm may elect to pay "fair wage rates" when it could exploit some workers' ignorance of wage rates and job availability elsewhere with impunity, a benevolent butcher may abstain from short-weighing. These altruistic practices involve imperfections of information and foresight in a central way: they represent the refusal to deceive through false information (truthfulness) or the refusal to mislead through concealed information (disclosure), or the refusal to test the information costs for others of investigation and prosecution (lawfulness), or the refusal to let uncertainty that others will keep their bargain discourage one's own good faith (trustingness).

The prevalence of such altruistic conduct in non-Walrasian markets contributes to their economic efficiency. Certainly it reduces the risks and anxieties of being cheated or exploited. Beyond that, it tends to improve market resource allocation by lowering the transaction costs of an informational origin that society pays in doing business and running markets. Truthfulness and disclosure by others will often avert initial misallocations and subsequent search costs; there may result a reduction in the investment of resources in gathering information necessary to achieve a given resource allocation. Lawfulness reduces the costs of protection against crime, particularly the costs of enforcing market

---

[4] It is not being asserted that altruistic behavior itself requires imperfect information—whatever such a thesis might mean. And even in the classical economy, cooperation springing from mutual affection, say, might produce "economies" outside the market.

contracts and the tax system. Mutual trust in the adherence to some contract or obligation will often permit a resource allocation that is superior for everyone to any allocation reached by the noncooperative actions of distrustful individuals. Paradoxically, the presence of these altruistic virtues in the real non-Walrasian world, with its vast potential for damage and waste, may make the Walrasian perfect-information model a more accurate description than it could be if these virtues were absent. In any case, whatever the final verdict on the usefulness of altruism in economic life, as economic theorizing the efforts here belong alongside some recent developments in the pure theory of idle resources and the pure theory of money as evidence of the growing effort to build a welfare economics of the non-Walrasian economy.

The papers in Part 1 emphasize, though they do not wholly concentrate on, this second theme of the volume, the scope for altruistic codes and conduct in economic life as a means of raising economic efficiency. The applicability of the fundamental welfare theorem of neoclassical economics—the usability of markets as a decentralized allocation technique for maximizing some prescribed Bergson welfare function—rests on the neoclassical assumption that the government has perfect information and foresight from which to calculate needed corrective taxes, subsidies, etc. In the non-classical world of ignorance and uncertainty, the willingness of the public to abide by certain moral constraints permits the self-enforcement of some desirable resource allocations that could not be enforced by pecuniary incentives and legal sanctions of the government.

Kenneth Arrow considers some contributions of altruism to economic welfare, using Titmuss's investigation of the commercial system of blood distribution as a point of departure. He argues that truthfulness in exchanging goods of uncertain quality has the economic virtue of increasing the efficiency of markets when, in its absence, there would be a difference in knowledge between buyer and seller. Competitive markets for some goods would be unworkable, and indeed the whole price system would break down, were it not that these non-self-enforcing economic arrangements were supported by voluntary adherence to implicit or explicit social contracts.

Many examples of the cost savings that result from the ability to trust others to stick to rules, as well as what he calls non-rule-oriented altruism, are provided by Roland McKean. This leads him to a much-discussed question of the day, the reliance that should be placed on voluntary corporate responsibility instead of or in addition to detailed governmental regulation. If the willingness of physicians to be guided by ethical codes is a satisfactory way of reducing the information-gathering and decision-making costs we pay in the protection of our health, why may we not trust corporations to do the right things about product safety? Why not entrust them with the protection of our environment? McKean believes that the success of ethical codes has depended upon their reinforcement by enlightened self-interest—and the latter is of limited applicability. (A more sanguine tone is taken by Bruce Bolnick in Part 3.)

Even if a wholesale desire to do good in their every transaction were to sweep over the country's businesses, however, it might well do more harm than good if it were not channeled and confined to the right directions. William Baumol in his paper examines some of the dubious responsibilities that American businesses have recently been called on to assume. He concludes that the most important contribution that corporations can make in this regard is to reveal their interests and share their information in an open and forthcoming participation in the legislative process.[5]

A person's altruistic behavior may express his desire that others' welfare should be increased, or his gratification in making a gift to someone else, or his sense of obligation to others to behave that way, to use the classification suggested by Arrow. Even when these motivations can be fitted into persons' individual utility functions (the first two can), however, explaining the behavioral outcome of altruistic utility maximization is not a problem that is characteristic of neoclassical economics. There are typically strategical aspects to the interactions of altruists owing to the potential or actual uncertainty of each as to the conjectured responses of the others. In Part II James Buchanan discusses the situation of the samaritan who, if he acts pragmatically and nonstrategically, will obtain a result that is not the most desired by him. The samaritan may be able to do better in an intertemporal setting if for a while he plays to demonstrate his strategic courage. The members of society may all be able to do better if, recognizing the interdependence among behavioral patterns, they voluntarily adhere to certain rules of individual conduct or cooperate to impose such rules. But Buchanan suspects that short-sighted pragmatic utility maximization is on the ascendancy.

The other two papers in Part 2, by the present writer and by Peter Hammond, bring out somewhat differently the role that morals may play in certain game situations. My paper considers the process of game-equilibrium growth in which each generation wishes to bequeath some capital to the next generation in an amount that depends upon its conjecture of how the consumption of its bequest will be distributed over infinitely many future

[5] Without attempting to identify their various themes, I would like to call attention to the presence of the extensive commentaries by Guido Calabresi and Thomas Nagel at the end of Part I, and the comments of the other discussants that follow the papers in Parts 2 and 3. It is presumably unnecessary to add that the remarks on each of the papers in this introduction are selective, sometimes arbitrarily so, thus not a full account or summary of them.

generations. To any given assumption that all generations commonly make about the rest point which the economy approaches, there corresponds a game-equilibrium fixed-point solution that describes the bequest behavior of any generation as a function of its current capital. But there is a multiplicity of such game solutions corresponding to the multiple assumptions that can be entertained, with internal consistency, as to the rest point the economy is headed for. The determinacy of the game-equilibrium growth path would appear therefore to require the existence of some restrictive convention, or the existence of a prevailing "ethic," that helps the players calculate what to expect of other players.

Peter Hammond studies possible cooperative solutions to somewhat different dynamic games when the infinitely many players are egoists, not altruists. The apparent charitableness of B to A and of C to B cannot be explained as a noncooperative game solution of rational egoists if C will rationally take no account of whether B was charitable before when C is deciding whether to be charitable; then B has no incentive to be charitable. Hammond shows, however, that in his "pension game" charitable behavior would be shown even by total egoists provided they share the appropriate expectations. Further, by "agreeing" to form expectations that are in their mutual interests they can achieve a solution to the game that is better for every player than the noncooperative solution.

Part 3 deals with the motives and mechanisms that underlie certain institutions of cooperative altruism. William Vickrey considers the role that public policy can play in situations where A would spend more on his pet charity if B were taxed some matching (or fractionally matching) amount for the same purpose and B would spend more on his pet charity if, reciprocally, he could force A to match (or match fractionally) his spending; it may result, then, that A and B will agree to a certain tax deductibility for their gifts to certain types of philanthropic and religious agencies. The merits of such decentralization of governmental support include savings in information costs and, as Vickrey emphasizes, the avoidance of any discriminatory "establishment of religion" such as to contravene the Constitution. The same "externalities in giving" may cause every shareowner of a corporation to vote his stock in favor of a certain sum of corporate donations despite the sacrifice of individual control over the amount and distribution of the corporate contribution.

The other two papers in Part 3 take up the explanation of the voluntary organization, particularly as a provider of public goods to its members. The "demand" for such voluntary organizations as a residual supplier of public goods not provided by the various layers of government is studied by Burton Weisbrod. He views the governmental production of certain public goods as leaving some voters undersupplied and some voters oversupplied with each public good because voters cannot arrange the lump-sum surtaxes and compensations envisioned in classically pure theory. The undersupplied are thus motivated to attempt to provide some public goods to themselves through voluntary quasi-governmental organizations.

Bruce Bolnick tackles the "free-rider dilemma" that the individuals desiring to have such a voluntary organization must overcome if the organization and its public good is actually to be supplied. It may be that each individual prefers that only the others give their efforts and money to the organization so that he can receive the benefits at no cost. However, if everyone acts in accordance with this preference the organization will not succeed. Bolnick believes that role expectations and the psychic satisfactions from heeding them may permit the formation of an organizational core. But once the organizational core is formed, who will be willing to pay to it the needed revenues? The author discusses the manner by which social influences are transmitted by the leaders to create new social costs and rewards that re-shape individual preferences even if the underlying preference orderings away from the social context are left unchanged.

According to the pure theory of altruism, prefaces like any advertisement ought to have the virtues of truthfulness and disclosure. But the limitation of space, if nothing else, ensures that many features of the papers here have been neglected or distorted. The fretful prefacer conquers this worry with the trust that the readers he may interest will want to see for themselves what the papers say.

Part 1

*Gifts and Exchanges**

Kenneth J. Arrow

Richard Titmuss is justly distinguished for his devotion to the welfare of society at large and particularly to those who have received the least of society's benefits. He has not rested content with the moral satisfaction of advocating the good but has immersed himself in the detailed factual analysis and speculative thinking needed if good intentions are to become good deeds. The gift he has made of his talents has now found an appropriate embodiment in his latest and much-noticed study, *The Gift Relationship: From Human Blood to Social Policy.*[1] The study focuses specifically on the workings of a particular supply system, that by which blood is made available for transfusions in the United States and in the United Kingdom, with some reference to other nations. But this close study is intended as something of a searchlight to illuminate a much broader landscape: the limits of economic analysis, the rival uses of exchange and gift as modes of allocation, the collective or communitarian possibilities in society as against the tendencies toward individualism. Most of the discussion takes place in the precise and objective language of empirical sociology: surveys and tables are presented, the limits of the data are stated with the utmost care, but every now and then the strength of Titmuss's convictions shines forth.

---

*Presented at the Conference on Altruism and Economic Theory held by the Russell Sage Foundation, and prepared with the partial support of NSF Grant GS-28626X, Harvard University. This paper was first published in *Philosophy and Public Affairs*, Vol. I, no. 4 (Summer 1974), 343-362. Reprinted by permission of Princeton University Press.

[1] (London: George Allyn & Unwin, 1971.) All page references in the text are to *The Gift Relationship*.

Perhaps the flavor of the lessons he wants us to learn can best be suggested by a somewhat lengthy quotation of his final two paragraphs:

> From our study of the private market in blood in the United States, we have concluded that the commercialization of blood and donor relationships represses the expression of altruism, erodes the sense of community, lowers scientific standards, limits both personal and professional freedoms, sanctions the making of profits in hospitals and clinical laboratories, legalizes hostility between doctor and patient, subjects critical areas of medicine to laws of the marketplace, places immense social costs on those least able to bear them—the poor, the sick, and the inept—increases the danger of unethical behavior in various sectors of medical science and practice, and results in situations in which proportionately more and more blood is supplied by the poor, the unskilled, the unemployed, Negroes and other low-income groups, and categories of exploited human populations of high blood yielders. Redistribution in terms of blood and blood products from the poor to the rich appears to be one of the dominant effects of the American blood-banking systems.
>
> Moreover, on four testable non-ethical criteria the commercialized blood market is bad. In terms of economic efficiency it is highly wasteful of blood; shortages, chronic and acute, characterize the demand-and-supply position and make illusory the concept of equilibrium. It is administratively inefficient and results in more bureaucratization and much greater administrative, accounting, and computer overheads. In terms of price per unit of blood to the patient (or consumer), it is a system which is five to fifteen times more costly than voluntary systems in Britain. And, finally, in terms of quality, commercial markets are much more likely to distribute the contaminated blood; the risks for the patient of disease and death are substantially greater. Freedom from disability is inseparable from altruism.

The present essay is a series of reflections on the descriptive and prescriptive issues raised by Titmuss's evidence and assertions. It is obvious on the most superficial observation that the allocation of goods and services is not accomplished entirely by exchange, as standard economic models would hold. Clearly this is true for such impalpable goods as respect, love, or status, but even when we confine ourselves to goods whose allocation the economist believes himself capable of analyzing with his tools, the donation of blood for transfusions is only one example of a large class of unilateral transactions in which there is no element of payment in any direct or ordinary sense of the term. Formal philanthropy has always been a prominent element of all economic systems and has shown no signs of diminution. Long ago Kropotkin pointed out the vast amount of informal and irregular mutual help given in times of need.[2] Of course, the whole structure of government expenditures is a departure from the system of mutual exchange. It is true that it has its own logic of coercion, so that it is not quite an example of pure altruism, but in a democratic society the voting of expenditures for the benefit of others plainly constitutes an institutionalization of giving. Nor are gifts solely in the form of money. The contribution of personal services, services which may well involve significant personal costs or which could command a considerable market value, for voluntary cooperative efforts of one kind or another remains a prominent feature of social life, even—or perhaps especially—in the United States, a country that Titmuss holds up as the very model of a society atomized by excessive reliance on the dictates of the marketplace.

There is another and very important sense in which a more subtle form of giving affects the allocation of economic resources. It can be argued that the presence of what are in a slightly old-fashioned terminology called *virtues* in fact plays a significant role in the operation of the economic system. Titmuss calls attention to the great value of truthfulness on the part of blood donors. The most serious risk in blood transfusion is the possible transmission of serum hepatitis from donor to recipient. Since no adequate test has yet been devised for the presence of hepatitis in the blood, its detection depends essentially on the willingness of the donor to state correctly whether or not he is suffering from that disease. This is a prototype of many other similar situations in economic life. Many of us consider it possible that the process of exchange requires or at least is greatly facilitated by the presence of several of these virtues (not only truth, but also trust, loyalty, and justice in future dealings). Now virtue may not always be its own reward, but in any case it is not usually bought and paid for at market rates. In short, the supply of a commodity in many respects complementary to those usually thought of as economic goods is not itself accomplished in the marketplace but rather comes as an unrequited transfer.

Finally, there is a broader set of issues raised by Titmuss. The picture of a society run exclusively on the basis of exchange has long haunted sensitive observers, especially from the early days of the capitalist domination. The ideas of community and social cohesion are counterposed to a drastically reduced society in which individuals meet only as buyers and sellers of commodities. Of course, giving is not the only alternative to a system of pure exchange. Authority and hierarchy constitute one alternative system, rational bureaucracy with place determined by merit another; but certainly the role of free giving in producing a more humanitarian social order is worth considering.

---

[2] Petr A. Kropotkin, *Mutual Aid: A Factor of Evolution* (London, 1902), chap. VIII.

The points raised above determine the organization of the rest of this discussion. I shall consider in turn the role of giving as an expression of individual volition, as a contribution to economic efficiency, and as a determinant of social cohesion.

One further remark. As Titmuss indicates very clearly, the giving of blood is giving not to specific individuals but to an anonymous recipient. The motives for such giving are regarded as more definitely altruistic than those for giving to individuals. In what follows the discussion is therefore confined to impersonal giving. I shall take for granted in most cases that Titmuss's empirical analysis is correct and concentrate rather on setting it in other contexts, though some comment on the evidence is unavoidable. I shall conclude with a further, though still cursory, examination of the extent to which in fact the empirical evidence he advances proves or at least strongly supports his various theses.

I. THE INDIVIDUAL'S DESIRE TO GIVE

The starting point of Titmuss's analysis and reflections is the basic fact that in the United Kingdom the supplying of blood for transfusions is completely voluntary and unpaid, while in the United States there is a mixed system with both commercial and noncommercial blood banks and with payments of various kinds. According to Titmuss's estimates, based on admittedly unsatisfactory surveys, about one-third of the United States supply (including derivatives such as plasma, plasma fractions, and red blood cell concentrates) comes from paid blood donors. Nor are the rest considered to be truly voluntary; by Titmuss's standards a donor is considered to be voluntary only if the recipient is unknown to him and there are no social sanctions enforcing the donation. Thus only 9 percent of the United States donors are regarded as voluntary. About one-half give blood free of charge, but in most cases they are in effect replacing blood given to relatives.

These figures, needless to say, are subject to a wide margin of error (the categories above are not completely exhaustive; I omit a few minor ones for the sake of simplicity). In the United Kingdom there are, of course, no paid donors. However, Titmuss has not attempted to classify the British donors in a comparable way, though in fact he has better evidence (mainly the results of a questionnaire survey which he himself developed). It does turn out that in the case of 28 percent of the British donors either they or their families have received blood transfusions.

As might be supposed, the distribution of blood donations between paid and unpaid donors influences the distribution of blood-giving among socio-economic categories. A rough impression of the fragmentary United States data together with that for the United Kingdom suggests that unpaid donations are distributed among socio-economic classes more or less in proportion to the relative size of each class. Paid donors, on the contrary, are drawn almost exclusively from the lower-income categories, including the unemployed.[3]

Even in the United Kingdom the percentage of the eligible population that gives blood is actually very small, only 6 percent according to Titmuss's estimates. Titmuss does not comment on this fact. The picture of a broadly altruistic society seems somewhat blurred when we realize what a small fraction of the population is in fact functioning altruistically.

It may be inferred from Titmuss's presentation that the motives for giving blood can be divided into three types: a generalized desire to benefit others, a feeling of social obligation, and a response to personal social pressures, as in the case of donations to known recipients or responses to institutional blood drives. I suggest here a reformulation of the first two of these motives in the language of utility theory. I find three classes, which do not correspond precisely to those of Titmuss:

(1) The welfare of each individual will depend both on his own satisfaction and on the satisfactions obtained by others. We here have in mind a positive relation, one of altruism rather than envy.

(2) The welfare of each individual depends not only on the utilities of himself and others but also on his contributions to the utilities of others.

(3) Each individual is, in some ultimate sense, motivated by purely egoistic satisfaction derived from the goods accruing to him, but there is an implicit social contract such that each performs duties for the other in a way calculated to enhance the satisfaction of all.[4]

This classification is not exhaustive, or even exclusive.

In (1) and (2), one is to distinguish between two levels of utility: each individual may be regarded as deriving satisfaction from the goods he receives, but his overall aim is to maximize welfare, a function of the satisfactions of all; he derives a utility from seeing someone else's satisfaction increased. The second version differs from the first only in that welfare is derived not merely from an increase in someone else's satisfaction but from the fact that the individual himself has contributed to that satisfaction. The first hypothesis has been used occasionally by economists in trying to explain why people give to others or why they vote for redistribution of income. But it does not seem very appropriate for the case of giving blood, especially with anonymous recipients. The utilities of all others would have to enter the welfare function in a completely symmetrical fashion. It does appear necessary to supplement this

[3] One curious piece of data is that in the United States blood donors are overwhelmingly male, even among unpaid groups, while in the United Kingdom the donors are distributed between the sexes in the same proportion as that of men to women in the general population. Titmuss does not remark on this, and I have no explanatory hypothesis.

[4] I am indebted to Thomas Nagel for some illuminating comments on these points.

motivation with the additional measure of satisfaction derived from the fact that I, rather than someone else, have brought about the improvement in social welfare. Put another way, under the first hypothesis I would prefer that you rather than I give to a third individual, but in the second case I might well prefer to give myself, because I would have the satisfaction of personal participation in social welfare.

The third possible hypothesis is, according to my understanding, in the spirit of Kant's categorical imperative or Rawls's theory of justice. In real life, however, emphasis must be put on the implicit nature of the social contract. One might be thought of as giving blood in the vague expectation that one may need it later on. More generally, perhaps, one gives good things, such as blood, in exchange for a generalized obligation on the part of fellow men to help in other circumstances if needed. Some of the subtleties of the social contract theory are seen when the anonymous recipients in question are future generations or indeed the sick and poor of the present generation. Actual behavior, as reflected in decisions of democratic governments, shows that individuals are in fact willing to sacrifice present satisfactions for future generations, as in the case of public investments, or even for others living in the present, as evidenced by willingness on the part of middle-class citizens to vote for county hospitals while they themselves in fact use voluntary hospitals. Similarly, in voting for educational expenditures, there must be many advocates of greater expenditure who do not have children who will benefit. One can try to rationalize their behavior either in terms of one of the first two hypotheses or in terms of the social contract made with previous and future generations. How such a social contract is in fact carried out is another matter. There are, of course, cultural institutions which reinforce it; Kropotkin argued that there is a built-in evolutionary mechanism to this end, for altruism aids in the survival of the species, a thesis repeated more recently by Wynne-Edwards.[5]

Titmuss makes explicit a feeling held by many, I think, in his discussion of what he calls in a chapter title "The Right to Give." Economists typically take for granted that since the creation of a market increases the individual's area of choice it therefore leads to higher benefits. Thus, if to a voluntary blood donor system we add the possibility of selling blood, we have only expanded the individual's range of alternatives. If he derives satisfaction from giving, it is argued, he can still give, and nothing has been done to impair that right. But this is emphatically not the view held by Titmuss. On the contrary, he states, "as this study has shown comparatively, private market systems in the United States and other countries . . . deprive men of their freedom to choose to give or not to

[5] V.C. Wynne-Edwards, *Animal Dispersion in Relation to Social Behavior* (New York: Hafner Press, 1962).

give" (p. 239). Shortly thereafter he continues: "In a positive sense we believe that policy and processes should enable men to be free to choose to give to unnamed strangers. They should not be coerced or constrained by the market. In the interests of the freedom of all men, they should not, however, be free to sell their blood or decide on a specific destination of the gift. The choice between these claims—between different kinds of freedom—has to be a social policy decision; in other words, it is a moral and political decision for the society as a whole" (p. 242). I can find no support in the evidence for the existence of such a dilemma. Indeed, it is not easy to see what kind of evidence would be relevant. Presumably the best that could be done would be to show that the amount of blood given in the United States is less than it would be if commercial blood-giving were prohibited. In turn, this might be inferred from a comparison of the number of donors in the United States and in the United Kingdom. Titmuss nowhere makes any explicit comparison of this kind. I would in fact gather from his figures that the percentage of donors in the United States *is* lower than that in the United Kingdom, but since the figures are not presented in comparable form I am not at all sure of the accuracy of my inferences. In any case, there is so much in the way of historical development that is not covered that one cannot arrive at any relevant answer. It may be that the spread of commercial services in the United States was itself due to the failure of the voluntary services to supply enough blood, to give one simple hypothesis. The comparison might indeed indicate that the United States is a less altruistic society than the United Kingdom, but it would not show that commercial blood-giving was a cause rather than an effect.

In any case the empirical evidence can only be made meaningful with at least a minimum of theoretical analysis. *Why* should it be that the creation of a market for blood would decrease the altruism embodied in giving blood? I do not find any clear answer in Titmuss. He does make the following statement: "In not asking for or expecting any payment of money, these donors signify their belief in the willingness of other men to act altruistically in the future, and to combine together to make a gift freely available should they have a need for it. By expressing confidence in the behavior of future unknown strangers, they were thus denying the Hobbesian thesis that men are devoid of any distinctive moral sense" (p. 239). The statement does indeed imply that individuals will be willing to give without payment. But it does not explain why this willingness should be affected by the fact that other individuals receive money for these services, especially when the others include those whose need for financial reward is much greater. Evidently Titmuss must feel that attaching a price tag to this activity anywhere in the system depreciates its value as a symbolic expression of faith in others. But note that this is really an empirical question, not a matter of first principles. Do people in fact perceive the signals as Titmuss suggests? Would they, were the moral questions expounded with greater clarity?

II. GIVING AND EFFICIENCY

The aspect of Titmuss's work that will probably have the most striking effect both immediately and in the long run is his argument and evidence that a world of giving may actually increase efficiency in the operation of the economic system. This is on the face of it a dramatic challenge to the tenets of the mainstream of economic thought. Since the time of Adam Smith, economists have preached the virtues of the price system in enforcing efficiency and penalizing waste. To be sure, there has grown up a tradition, stemming from Alfred Marshall and developed by A. C. Pigou, Allyn Young, F. H. Knight, and more recent writers, which emphasizes that the price system does not always work satisfactorily. There are, in the language of welfare economics, "externalities," benefits and costs transmitted among individuals for which compensation in price terms is not and perhaps cannot be obtained. The problem of pollution has always been a standard example; the costs to others of the emission of noxious substances from smokestacks is not usually paid for. No self-enforcing price system would be feasible.

When we introduce externalities into the picture of resource allocation, we are really implying a very broad concept of efficiency. Efficiency is here measured with reference to a wide class of goods and evils, whether they are marketable or not. A system is inefficient if there is another way of allocating these goods, all the goods that we consider relevant, such that everybody is better off according to appropriate criteria. These criteria might be clean air or the availability of blood when needed as well as automobiles or steak.

Titmuss presents a powerful indictment of the efficiency of blood-giving in the United States. The inefficiencies he finds are of three sorts: the imposition of unnecessary risks on recipients, the imposition of unnecessary risks on certain classes of donors, and the prevalence of waste and shortage in the distribution of blood.

With regard to the first, dramatic evidence has been advanced by Titmuss. The essential problem is that the use of infected blood in transfusions can lead to serum hepatitis in the recipient (as well as certain other diseases of much lower incidence). Not only Titmuss but a number of American investigators have shown that there is a remarkably high rate of post-transfusion serum hepatitis, an incidence which may reach 3 to 4 percent. Hepatitis is a serious illness and occasionally fatal. Out of those over age forty who receive transfusions, about one in one hundred and fifty die of it. Most striking of all, there seems to be very clear evidence that it is the commercial blood that is the primary source of hepatitis. Titmuss cites statistics showing that the risk of infection from blood given by prison and skid row populations is over ten times as great as from the population in general. One highly controlled study yielded very convincing evidence. The subjects underwent cardiac surgery, in which large amounts of blood were used, an average of eighteen to nineteen pints per person. Half the group was given blood from commercial sources, half from unpaid sources. The incidence of hepatitis in the first group was 53 percent, that in the second zero percent (the figure of 53 percent is not as far out of line with the 3 to 4 percent incidence as might be supposed; the eighteen or nineteen units of blood represent a corresponding number of individual opportunities to become infected, any one of which would suffice). On the other hand, the incidence of post-transfusion serum hepatitis in the United Kingdom is apparently less than 1 percent.

Further evidence comes from such comparisons as are possible with other countries. In West Germany, where evidently most of the blood is supplied commercially, post-transfusion hepatitis is estimated at 14 percent; in Japan, where virtually all the blood is commercial, the incidence is between 18 and 25 percent.[6]

The basic problem here is one that has many parallels. The commodity or service offered has uncertain characteristics. The buyer is not really in a position to know what it is that he is buying. In many circumstances buyers can protect themselves by testing the product in one way or another. If the product is one that is frequently used, then past experience can serve as a guide, particularly if the consequences of a defective performance are not especially severe. In other circumstances buyers are able to protect themselves by formal tests of not too great expense. This solution is unfortunately not available here. There is at the present time no test that can accurately detect whether a given blood donor is capable of transmitting hepatitis. The recently developed Au antigen test can detect only about 30 percent of potential infectors.

Now a situation in which the quality of a service is uncertain is not in itself an especially difficult situation to analyze. Every case of major surgery involves exactly the same considerations, the possibility of a large benefit weighed against some possibility of failure or even death. No doubt there are special considerations attached to high risk, but there is a further and very important distinction to be made in the case of blood donors. Usually the donor will know that he has had hepatitis, and therefore his truthfulness in recording his past history is of the utmost importance. At the same time, at least if the blood is to be collected in large quantities at relatively low cost, there is little or no opportunity to check the donor's word.

The situation is precisely the one alluded to earlier, that the virtue of truthfulness in fact contributes in a very significant way to the efficiency of the economic system. The supplying of truthful information is an example of an

[6] According to such data as Titmuss could locate, commercial blood was very common in most countries and overwhelmingly so in the U.S.S.R., where about 50 percent of the blood is paid for at a very high rate. In Sweden, usually regarded as a society oriented toward collectivism, all of the blood is paid for. It is gathered by the state, not by commercial blood banks. The percentage of commercial blood in East Germany exceeds that in West Germany.

externality, if you like, but that classification does not really help us in deciding how truth is to be obtained. A voluntary donor system is from this point of view self-enforcing. Anyone whose motive for giving is to help others, but who suffers from hepatitis and is aware of the implications of this, will of course refrain from giving. On the other hand, a commercial blood donor, especially one driven by poverty, has every incentive to conceal the truth.

To repeat, the two key features of the situation are uncertainty about the quality of the service and a difference between the degrees of knowledge possessed by buyer and seller. The situation here is exacerbated by the severity of the risks involved. One can think of many parallels, and these have given rise to significant questions about the nature of responsibility in economic life. A good example is the question of automobile safety. The seller is supplying a complex machine. The details of both design and construction are inevitably better known to the seller than to the buyer. Further, if the risk of disastrous consequences is relatively low, no buyer can hope to acquire the relevant information from experience. In these circumstances it seems clear to me that the price system is no insurance of efficiency in all respects. The qualities of the product are simply not well defined from the buyer's point of view. Some alternative system of determining quality and providing assurance for buyers is needed. One such candidate is a sense of social responsibility on the part of the seller. This may indeed be easier to create in the case of the large organization than in that of the individual seller, for the obligation may then fall upon the individual members of that organization. In this context, ethical behavior can be regarded as a socially desirable institution which facilitates the achievement of economic efficiency in the broad sense.

I should add that, like many economists, I do not want to rely too heavily on substituting ethics for self-interest. I think it best on the whole that the requirement of ethical behavior be confined to those circumstances where the price system breaks down for the reasons suggested above. Wholesale usage of ethical standards is apt to have undesirable consequences. We do not wish to use up recklessly the scarce resources of altruistic motivation, and in any case ethically motivated behavior may even have a negative value to others if the agent acts without sufficient knowledge of the situation. In the case of medical practice and elsewhere, it might be plausibly argued that ethical codes serve as an instrument for increasing the economic advantage of one segment of the population at the expense of the rest.

It also appears that commercial blood-giving leads to unanticipated risks to the donors, though much less serious than those to the recipients. Commercial blood donors have some incentive to give blood more frequently than is desirable from the point of view of their health. This in and of itself is something of a gray area, because presumably the individual has some freedom of choice in such cases; but there is the possibility of a much more acute problem with respect to something like 20 percent of the blood collected. For many purposes, particularly the treatment of anemia, only the red blood cells are needed. There has been developed a new process called plasmapheresis. Here the red blood cells are separated from the plasma in which they float and the plasma is then reinjected into the body of the donor. Under these conditions donations can be, and are, made much more frequently. Several donations a week can be made, or so it is held. The collection of red blood cells for plasmapheresis is almost exclusively commercial, being carried out by or on behalf of the pharmaceutical companies. The fact that a very substantial income can be had through frequent donations means at least the potentiality of serious risk to the donors. There is, however, very little evidence of any damage actually having taken place.

A third apparent inefficiency in the United States system, according to Titmuss, is a very substantial amount of wastage of the blood collected; persistent shortages are also observed. Blood deteriorates after being drawn from a donor, and for most purposes it must be used within twenty-one days of collection. If the figures for collection and transfusion are compared, it appears that about 30 percent of the blood is wasted (the figures, as Titmuss notes, are far from adequate). Titmuss does not present any exactly comparable data for the United Kingdom. If one compares the number of bottles "issued" with the number collected as given in one of his tables, there would seem to be about 10 percent wastage. However, there is a further possibility of wastage of bottles issued but not actually used in transfusions. The evidence for the existence of shortages is largely confined to several quotations from American authors (pp. 66–67). He notes that elective surgery is occasionally postponed because of the shortage of blood. It is asserted that no such shortages exist in the United Kingdom; a study by two economists that arrives at the opposite conclusion is abruptly dismissed by Titmuss as having been badly designed.[7] How supply and demand in the United Kingdom happened to balance so well over a period of twenty years in which the demand per capita has been rising steadily (due to new surgical techniques requiring much more blood) is left unexplained by Titmuss. Economists are accustomed to the idea of explaining the balance of supply and demand by the movement of prices. In the absence of prices something else must do the job. Perhaps there has been an expansion of the facilities for taking blood, but nothing in the book explains this remarkable parallel growth.

Although Titmuss links wastage of blood to the commercial system, he really gives no theoretical explanation of this link. I cannot conceive what it is. One would be much more tempted to explain a greater wastage of blood in the

[7] M.H. Cooper and A.J. Culyer, *The Price of Blood*, Hobart Paper No. 41, The Institute of Economic Affairs (London, 1968).

United States, if such exists, by the generally decentralized nature of the American blood collection system.[8] It should be noted that the voluntary system is quite chaotic as far as its organization is concerned. It is possible that, in the absence of a clear system of meeting shortages of a perishable commodity in one place with surpluses from another, such a system would perform much less efficiently than the British National Health Service. I find no clear evidence that commercialism per se is the key factor here.

In concluding this discussion of the relation between giving and efficiency, it strikes me that the essential point is the great importance of such a virtue as truthfulness in widely prevalent circumstances of economic life. I have remarked on the responsibility for truthfulness in economic life, but the issue goes even further. Virtually every commercial transaction has within itself an element of trust, certainly any transaction conducted over a period of time. It can be plausibly argued that much of the economic backwardness in the world can be explained by the lack of mutual confidence; see Banfield's remarkable study of a small community in southern Italy.[9]

I have considered the situation in which the quality of the commodity or service may be unknown to one side or the other in a transaction. It may also be that the price is unknown, that is, the price that could be commanded in some alternative market. Taking advantage of a situation where the other party in a transaction is ignorant of the potential price of a commodity or service might be regarded as a classic definition of "exploitation."

More basic yet, I will say, is the idea that the price system, in order to work at all, must involve the concept of property (even in the socialistic state there is public property). Property systems are in general not completely self-enforcing. They depend for their definition upon a constellation of legal procedures, both civil and criminal. The course of the law itself cannot be regarded as subject to the price system. The judges and the police may indeed be paid, but the system itself would disappear if on each occasion they were to sell their services and decisions. Thus the definition of property rights based on the price system depends precisely on the lack of universality of private property and of the price system. This ties in with the third hypothesis put forward in section I. The price system is not, and perhaps in some basic sense cannot be, universal. To the extent that it is incomplete, it must be supplemented by an implicit or explicit social contract. Thus one might loosely say that the categorical imperative and the price system are essential complements.

---

[8] Just after these lines were written, President Nixon called for a study of the blood bank systems; the lack of coordination of the system was particularly noted (*New York Times*, 3 March 1972, p. 1).

[9] Edward C. Banfield, *The Moral Basis of a Backward Society* (New York: Free Press, 1958).

III. GIVING AND THE SOCIAL ORDER

Titmuss here and throughout his work is interested in still broader issues. For him the marketplace is basically subversive of the ideal social order. Some of his chapter titles are suggestive: "Blood and the Marketplace," "Economic Man: Social Man," and "Who is My Stranger?" He appeals to Tönnies' familiar dichotomy between *Gemeinschaft* and *Gesellschaft*. He greatly fears that "the myth of maximizing economic growth can supplant the growth of economic social relation" (p. 199).[10]

It is worthwhile to summarize a genuinely horrifying case which serves Titmuss as an empirical springboard for his general attack on the commercialization of society. In the mid-1950s the blood supply in Kansas City was essentially completely in the hands of commercial blood banks, whose quality is described as very unsatisfactory. As a result a community blood bank was organized on a volunteer basis, and the hospitals insisted on drawing their blood only from this source. The commercial blood banks attacked the hospitals for violation of the antitrust laws, and after long and expensive testimony before the Federal Trade Commission the hospitals were forbidden to discriminate against commercial blood. It should, however, be added that this decision was subsequently overturned by the courts.

The key issue here as Titmuss sees it is the fact that this case was regarded as subject to the antitrust laws because blood was treated as a commodity. It is the latter point that disturbs Titmuss and arouses his ire. He generalizes from this to the whole treatment of medical care as a commodity. He notes, with appropriate statistics, that malpractice suits have become increasingly prevalent in the United States. The cost of malpractice insurance is rising, the settlements are growing in size as well as in number. All this is contrasted with the British situation, in which malpractice suits are apparently quite negligible in number and seriousness. What do these observations in fact tell us? Titmuss, without giving a detailed theoretical explanation, suggests in a general sort of way that the commercialization of medical practice is accompanied by a legitimization of doctor-patient hostility.

One can, it seems to me, look at this matter somewhat differently. The ideal of Titmuss could be interpreted as that of a world where doctors and hospitals

[10] His antagonism to at least some economists is stated strongly a few lines below this quotation. "In saying this we recall that Keynes once expressed the hope that one day economists 'could manage to get themselves thought of as competent people on a level with dentists.' This day has not yet dawned for some of the order who, after taking strong oaths of ethical neutrality, perform as missionaries in the social welfare field and often give the impression of possessively owning a hot line to God." The reference is clearly to those laissez-faire economists, of whom there is an organized group in the United Kingdom, who have favored placing the blood supply and indeed the whole medical system in private hands.

are protected from the consequences of their errors, at least as far as legal proceedings are concerned. After all, there is one very important relevant question: Are the malpractice suits justified? I have no reason to believe that the courts have any biases against physicians. If anything, one would suppose the opposite. There may conceivably be biases in the procedure as such, but these have not been demonstrated, and in the absence of evidence to the contrary I think we can trust the courts to have made a much more detailed inquiry in each case than the social scientist can do. If this is so, then we have to reckon with the idea that there is a lot of malpractice in the United States. To discourage suits, then, would simply be a way of denying compensation to legitimate victims for the costs imposed upon them, and of minimizing a method of exerting pressure on doctors who perform badly. Titmuss views the latter contingency positively. He refers to the increased costs due to what is frequently termed defensive practice, the excess of precautions necessary to prevent future claims of malpractice; but after all, it may well be true that a little more care might be good rather than bad. In any case, the assertion that malpractice suits induce excessive care rather than better care should not be presumed sound without further evidence.

Titmuss quite candidly agrees that there may well be trouble with patients' claims in the United Kingdom: "All in all, the scales are weighted in favor of the doctor" (p. 170). He urges that there are remedies other than litigation but does not specify them. What is disturbing, in this case as in many others, is that an appeal against the marketplace and its coldness has a way of slipping into a defense of privilege. The *Gemeinschaft-Gesellschaft* dichotomy can be couched in different language; Maine spoke of the difference between status and contract.[11] It is very easy indeed for "community" to slip over into "status."

Indeed, there is something of a paradox in Titmuss's philosophy. He is especially interested in the expression of impersonal altruism. It is not the richness of family relationships or the close ties of a small community that he wishes to promote. It is rather a diffuse expression of confidence by individuals in the workings of a society as a whole. But such an expression of impersonal altruism is as far removed from the feelings of personal interaction as any marketplace. Indeed, the small number of blood donors in the United Kingdom suggests, if I were to generalize as freely as Titmuss does, the idea of an aristocracy of saints. I suppose this idea is indeed in the Fabian tradition; at any rate, it is certainly expressed with great clarity by Shaw in *Man and Superman*. This is a way of social life that seems to have worked remarkably well in the British context, while proving capable of catastrophic consequences in the Soviet Union.

The pervasive fear in Titmuss's thinking that commercialism may increas-

[11] Henry Maine, *Ancient Law* (London, 1861).

ingly damage the entire social system is in many curious ways a mirror image of Hayek's.[12] Hayek and Titmuss seem to agree that a mixed economy is necessarily unstable. But whereas Hayek believes that a little bit of collectivism is likely to lead to a total dictatorship, Titmuss is concerned rather with the insidious nature of a price system. Both arguments have a resemblance to some of those connected with abortion. If you allow abortion, how can you argue against homicide?

The first thing about the argument of instability is that it is, after all, strictly an empirical one. It simply may not be true. It is very hard to believe that the use of commercial blood in the United States has any important effect on the general doctor-patient relationship. That relation is governed essentially by the same principles as always; if anything, the spread of medical insurance has weakened rather than strengthened the commercial link between doctor and patient. In the United Kingdom, of course, the relation is different, but I wonder if malpractice suits were any more common in the period before the National Health Service was instituted.

The second difficulty with this argument is that it has a rather elitist flavor. Presumably, the high value of altruism or whatever other virtue is threatened by the growth of commercialization will still hold even after the price system has spread somewhat. What Titmuss would be afraid of, I take it, is that other, weaker souls would somehow succumb. In the present context, perhaps individuals will cease to give blood when they see that other people are being paid for it. Now, the argument that we should therefore not permit a commercial system amounts to saying both that I am more foresighted than my contemporaries and that my virtue is less assailable. Perhaps these propositions are really true, but I find them at any rate uncomfortable.

IV. REMARKS ON EMPIRICAL VALIDITY

At the beginning of this discussion I quoted Titmuss's final paragraphs, a statement which embodies a remarkably large number of empirical conclusions. It cannot really be maintained that most of them have been established. The most dramatic and best sustained is unquestionably the relation between the commercial blood supply and post-transfusion hepatitis. This indictment alone is fully worth the entire investigation. The evidences of inefficiency in the United States are also clear, though I find their causes less well established.

Indeed, with respect to empirical methodology there is much to be desired. Titmuss gives no consideration to the role of theory in empirical research. He seems to regard the argument *post hoc, ergo propter hoc* as infallible. At any rate, in most instances the comparisons used involve two cases between which

---

[12] Friedrich A. Hayek, *The Road to Serfdom* (Chicago: University of Chicago Press, 1944).

there are many differences. The commercialization of the blood supply can certainly not have all the consequences that he apparently ascribes to it.

Even by the least stringent rules for evaluating empirical evidence, many of Titmuss's points are not in any way established. I see, for example, no real evidence that the presence of a commercial blood supply decreases the amount of altruism. This is not to say that it may not do so; but the data for the two countries is not presented in forms sufficiently comparable to allow any statement whatever. Compensating factors are never considered; thus the point Titmuss makes about the redistribution of blood from the poor to the rich is not in any way offset by the fact of a corresponding flow of money from the rich to the poor, a point which should at least be taken into consideration.

Despite Titmuss's careful use of data in some places, he is very loose in others. On several less important points he makes statements about the United States without even bothering to compare the situation with that in the United Kingdom, although without such comparison there is no evidence of any kind. For example, as an evidence of the shortage of blood in the United States he observes that if hemophiliacs were given blood without restraint they would consume an amount equal to one-eighth of the blood used in the United States. Presumably the incidence of hemophilia is the same in the United Kingdom as in the United States, yet Titmuss does not bother to tell us whether hemophiliacs are in fact treated as fully there as he would have them treated here.

Again, as evidence of the corruption introduced into the United States medical system by commercialization he includes several damaging anecdotes about unethical medical experiments. No statement whatever is made about the ethics of experimentation in the United Kingdom. In fact, the United States today probably has the most stringent rules regarding such practices of any country in the world, requiring informed consent of the subject. Finally, for all Titmuss's strictures on the dangers involved in plasmapheresis, he does not have anything to say about this practice in the United Kingdom. Possibly it is unknown there, but the book is not clear on this point.

Despite—and in part because of—its flaws, Titmuss's book is a resonant evocation of central problems of social value. His blithe disregard of the usual epistemological strictures against confusion of fact and value permits him to raise the largest descriptive and normative questions about the social order in a highly specific and richly factual context. This is not a systematic, abstract work on the foundations of ethics. It is not a meticulous descriptive and causal analysis of the functioning of social systems. But by suggestively combining a passionately informed commitment to an ideal social order and an illustration of problems within the context of a concrete situation, it has greatly enriched the quality of social-philosophical debate.

*Economics of Trust, Altruism, and Corporate Responsibility**

Roland N. McKean

Greater ability to trust each other to stick with agreed-upon rules would save many costs and make life much pleasanter. It would economize on locks and keys, safes and vaults, guards, monitoring devices and procedures, some of the fine print in contracts, and, perhaps most important of all, time and anguish for everyone. It might make life still less costly (or more pleasant) if, in addition, concern for others was more prominent in our utility functions—that is, if we were less selfish. These are different phenomena—trust and altruism; the former means trusting each other to adhere to relatively specific written, oral, or tacitly understood agreements ("keeping one's word"), while unselfishness means concern for others without reference to any agreement governing specific behavior. Selfishness is not the same thing, incidentally, as pursuing self-interest or maximizing utility, for the latter merely means purposeful behavior to achieve *whatever* yields preferredness.

Whether or not less selfishness would yield greater well-being has to be conjectural. Conceptually, we can think of a utility frontier taking into account not only people's tastes for conventional goods but also their tastes for helping (or injuring) each other. If there were zero transaction costs, people would hire each other to behave as if they had the optimal degree of concern for each other. Hiring people to like one gets into seemingly paradoxical questions, though:

---

*The author is indebted to the NSF grant to the Thomas Jefferson Center Foundation for studying the implications of different resource rights. Thanks are due also to Russell Sage Foundation, the sponsor of the Conference on Altruism, and, for criticisms and suggestions, to John H. Moore and Roger Sherman of the University of Virginia, and to James M. Buchanan of Virginia Polytechnic Institute and State University.

"How much must I offer to get you to love me for myself quite apart from my offer?" If people felt that way to begin with, this degree of concern would exist even with real-world transaction costs. In this real world, however, the optimal degree of unselfishness cannot be determined, though it seems almost certain that the extremes,[1] complete selfishness or complete unselfishness, would yield horrible spillovers (maybe non-survival). Extreme altruism, for instance, would mean either ceaseless misguided meddling or enormous information costs in finding out what other people wanted (yet what they would want in turn would be to help other meddlers). I myself judge, however, that somewhat more altruism, or more evenly dispersed altruism, would be an improvement.[2] To me it appears non-optimal and downright discouraging when people are unwilling to give up a few seconds of their time in order to take up one parking space instead of two or when one man's unremitting concern for himself alone can make an entire organization miserable. (When I speak of "optimal concern or non-optimal selfishness, I have to consider altruism as a process or means for achieving other things. If I count different degrees of altruism as different utility functions, I have no basis for saying that one degree can yield Pareto optimality while some other degree cannot.)

Maybe one should stress, however, that the glass is half full instead of half empty, for the roles now played by both trust and unselfishness are remarkable, when one stops to think about it.

ROLES PLAYED BY TRUST, ALTRUISM

Life would be nasty, brutish, and poverty-stricken indeed, if there were no mutual trust and voluntary compliance at all. Even their short-run self-interest must have caused most persons to recognize this during the earliest history of man. It must have been apparent to almost everyone that it was economical (better) if each person could have considerable confidence in the other's word regarding exchanges, division of tasks in hunting (or warfare), information about hunting grounds, appointments, or promises of any sort. At some point, traditions and rules of etiquette arose—presumably to reduce external costs that were being inflicted on each other or to increase external benefits that would otherwise be withheld from each other (Charnovitz). Parents taught their offspring to follow these rules, and thus each person could (usually) expect certain kinds of behavior from the other, i.e., trust the other to adhere to the

[1] Selfishness is not the real extreme. As Boulding says, "The real world is so shot through with a complex network of benevolence and malevolence that selfishness has to be seen as a most unlikely case—merely the zero on the malevolence-benevolence scale" (p. 168).

[2] We know tragically little about how to produce some of the most important goods in life—mutual respect, friendliness, cohesiveness, a sense of belonging, peace of mind. With either private or public property rights we are apparently unable to perceive how to manufacture such valuable commodities.

agreed-upon rule. Indoctrination with maxims like "honesty is the best policy," and social pressures during adult life, served as relatively inexpensive monitoring or enforcement devices.

Unwritten agreements and trust (that is, confidence in each other's voluntary compliance) eventually played pervasive roles in business and social intercourse. Written contracts in business hit only the highspots of agreements; like the bulk of an iceberg, an enormous portion of such mutual understandings is unseen (MacCaulay). It would be extremely expensive to pin down in writing every aspect of an agreement—the *precise* quality of workmanship in every task, the *exact* quality of materials, the precise nature of every dimension of performance, the conditions under which goods can be returned or exchanged, the degree of pleasantness that is to prevail in business relationships the exact nature of working conditions to be provided by employers, and so on. Competition for repeat customers makes much dishonesty unprofitable in the private sector, of course, making it easier for businessmen to trust each other, and for customers to trust businesses, to a certain extent. Court and legal systems, too, bolster the honesty of people in their dealings. People value these reinforcements partly because they recognize, at least unconsciously, how costly life would be without trust, even if the basis has to be created in part by such enforcement mechanisms. Many small, yet in the aggregate highly significant, instances of trust exist, however, without the pressure of competition or the threat of a lawsuit. Perhaps some trust in others is an instinct or a product of family relationships or some other sort of element having positive value in our utility functions. Or perhaps there is widespread unconscious recognition that other desirable things can be accomplished more efficiently if there is some minimal amount of trust without special enforcement mechanisms.

The idea of a private enterprise, market-exchange system is almost absurd unless there is a good deal of mutual trust. Most exchanges are a little like the "silent trade," in which "foreign" islanders left goods on the beach and returned later to pick up whatever the "domestic" islanders left in exchange. Rarely can both parties in a trade fulfill their obligations simultaneously. Even at a baseball game, one of the two—either the vendor with the peanuts or the fan with the money—is likely to throw first. And exchange systems work better if people can trust credit instruments, stock certificates, bank checks, advertisements, reputations, quality indicators or inspection certificates, oral statements, and tacitly understood rules.

In social intercourse, too, a good deal of trust is essential to any sort of cooperation, social exchange, satisfying verbal exchange, or significant relationship. A church, a play-reading group, a Scout troop, a basketball team, a family, an oratorio society—no social organization or relationship is useful or capable of survival if individuals can *never* be depended on to do what they say they will. Even accomplishing undesirable ends—fighting duels, waging war, conducting the

Mafia's activities—requires considerable trust among a subset of persons. Just as the idea of a private enterprise exchange system is absurd without considerable trust, any kind of society would be grim and rather hopeless without customs and considerable trust in social intercourse.[3]

Altruism too is apparently a significant factor in our lives. It is almost impossible to separate (1) concern for others as an element in our utility functions from (2) enlightened selfish interest which recognizes that one collects rewards (or escapes retaliation) if one helps others (or does not damage them). Even anonymous assistance to complete strangers that one would never see again could be explained as part of a tradition which, in effect, trades A's aid to strangers for other strangers' aid to A.[4] For some purposes it doesn't matter which is the explanation: people often act *as if* they are altruistic. One does observe numerous acts of kindness and consideration acts which often (though not always) make life pleasanter for everyone affected. Even stockholders tolerate, and competition permits, a certain volume of charitable contributions by corporations. Managers could hardly exercise spontaneous kindness of unpredictable magnitude, though, for even if preference surfaces gave more weight than at present to generalized kindness, stockholders would still differ in the particular kinds and sizes of charitable actions which they condoned, and the relatively generous managements would fail or be replaced. Indeed, most of us would probably object to motley *promiscuous* actions that individual business managers felt were "kind" or "socially responsible."

Businesses do engage in some philanthropy, of course, and *generally* adhere to tacitly accepted minimal standards in their activities, e.g., in providing pleasant work conditions for personnel or safety in products. These standards probably do not arise from altruism, however, but rather from fairly specific trends that evolve from enlightened self-interest or public demand. Such standards may be enforced partly by competition, partly by the threat of lawsuits or governmental intervention; and they come under the previous heading of widespread acceptance of rules or traditions.

THE CREATION OF RULES OR ALTRUISM

Rules

Like other institutions, these "social contracts," including the custom of being honest, evolved from the process of individuals groping for better ways of living together. Changes probably occurred when conflicts became serious, and people weighed the alternative ways of resolving the conflicts. In a sense any

---

[3] Banfield's study of a community in Southern Italy suggests that a pervasive lack of trust can indeed lead to poverty in both a materialistic and spiritual sense.

[4] When people risk their lives to help strangers, however, it suggests that there is at least some simple concern for other creatures in our preference surfaces. (Also, at least *part* of our uneasiness about cloning, and using duplicates of people for experiments, may stem from genuine empathy for fellow creatures.

conflict stems from an externality–from a cost inflicted on someone, or a potential benefit denied to someone, without his voluntary agreement.[5] (For some of the not-so-obvious and pervasive impacts of each individual's behavior on others, usually without purchase of their consent, see Schelling, 1971.) Such conflicts leave some individual or group with a "desire on the part of the externally benefited (damaged) party (A) to modify the behavior of the party empowered to take action (B) through trade, persuasion, compromise, agreement, convention, collective action, etc." (Buchanan and Stubblebine, pp. 373–74). The dissatisfied persons ask themselves what they can do. They can fight, but that is costly, and they may try to get others to agree to a change in the rules. Nobody advocates a change, of course, on grounds that it would be Pareto optimal; but the changes that are easiest to sell are often ones that would yield mutual advantage or at least advantages to most of the population and no big disadvantages to large numbers of persons.

It has been suggested that tribal and individual property rights arose among certain Indian tribes from rising external costs imposed on each other with common ownership (Demsetz). Instead of incurring the costs of further violence, the individuals may have decided, "Let's assign rights, enforce them by means of tradition (or force, if trust is violated), and trade goods with each other wherever desirable." Similarly, assignment of certain "amenity rights" (Mishan) may have evolved when "common" ownership of resources like pleasantness or queuing privileges led to costly quarrels or shoving. Thus "rights" to courteous treatment and orderly queuing were created and assigned by the development of behavioral rules or traditions. Enforcing such rights by means of legislation and the courts would have been too expensive, but acceptance became so widespread, at least in some cultures, that trust and social pressures were sufficiently effective to yield pervasive mutual advantage.

Modifications of *private* property rights kept emerging too when some kind of transaction cost made it uneconomic to create or enforce rights to unpriced resources. (Transaction costs are those of making markets work, embracing costs of defining rights, acquiring information about the market or product, negotiating agreements, monitoring performance, enforcing the claims.) In the Middle Ages fraudulent practices were extremely common; and liability for fraud and injuries, and various restrictions on what one could do with his resources, emerged. For example, there was a restriction on the ability to sell a horse in 16th century England: *only* "if he [the horse] be tame and have ben rydden upon, then *caveat emptor*" (Fitzherbert, quoted by Hamilton, p. 1164). More recently, as populations have increased and interdependencies have multiplied, governmental interventions and regulations have modified private property rights extensively.

---

[5]Here I use the term "externality" in its broadest sense to include pecuniary and potentially pecuniary spillovers as well as all potentially Pareto relevant externalities.

As for unwritten rules, social contracts sometimes arose, for instance, to cope with littering, e.g., in England; one could not do whatever he pleased with paper and trash. Such traditions were evidently accepted generally enough, with each new generation being indoctrinated, that by and large gentle social pressure was the enforcement mechanism, and people could often trust each other to do little littering. It seems to be highly economical to have informal rules wherever they work and people can trust each other to observe them.

What are the conditions for the emergence and successful operation of informal rules or ethical codes? When can people have confidence in each other to carry out their respective parts of such informal agreements? Needless to say, the specific rules that survive will vary from one culture and era to the next and will depend upon the stage of development of a society. Also, numerous variables, e.g., religion, other than those that I will discuss can influence the effectiveness of unwritten regulations. The following seem to be key factors, however, in the evolution and survival of such social contracts.

Perceived gains to most persons.[6] One necessary condition appears to be that almost everyone receive and perceive net advantages not necessarily in the short run but at least in the longer run. Consider the rules concerning politeness and courtesy. Almost everyone benefits, and no one suffers much. If anyone experiments with being persistently rude, he can readily perceive, even in the short run, that the quality of life deteriorates for him as well as for others. Life would be much more expensive if most people were surly and said "Drop dead" instead of "Good morning."

Consider the custom of making a few cheerful though inane remarks about such things as the weather when one encounters another person. It's partly a way of touching base with reality intermittently. Some people have serious identity problems, and all of us occasionally wonder, "What am I doing up here on the moon?" This small-talk custom helps most people, and, unless it's overdone, causes nobody much suffering.

For numerous examples of rules that are to almost everyone's advantage—setting our clocks on the same time, using the same typewriter keyboard, agreeing on weights and measures—see Schelling (1971). Note that each person need not benefit each time or in the very short run in order for social contracts to be viable. It is important, though, for each person to anticipate that his turn will come and that he will receive a stream of net benefits during, say, the years in which he is fairly sure of being alive. If the advantages do not accrue to all, numerous individuals will be tempted to violate the custom, and people cannot trust each other to adhere to it. "Why should I take the trouble if others cannot be depended upon to reciprocate?" Without a high degree of adherence and trust, the advantages begin to melt away, and the custom is eroded.

[6] This point is closely related to the "perceived interdependence" stressed, for example, by Loomis and Deutsch.

Opportunities for application of social pressure. Another condition appears to be that the custom be bolstered by occasional opportunities for the application of social pressure (or for retaliation if the rule is violated). In a large city, for example, the chances of encountering a given individual again are much smaller than they are in a small town. If one does not keep his word or adhere to behavioral rules when dealing with strangers in a large city, the possibilities for retaliation during future relationships are limited. If one violates customs or his promises in a small town, the probabilities of incurring penalties or of sacrificing rewards are much greater.[7] Similarly, lack of courtesy on a freeway brings an angry look for a fraction of a second; rudeness in a sidewalk encounter may invite a right cross.

The evidence is, in my view, consistent with these notions. Lack of warmth or courtesy seems to be greater in large cities and on freeways than in small towns and on sidewalks. (The cause can perhaps be viewed as either smaller perceived advantages or weakened enforcement mechanisms.)

Stability and certainty. A corollary condition that helps customs (including honesty) to function is stability and a reasonable degree of certainty. Rapid change of conditions, associates, acquaintances, or locations makes tradition or ethical codes less effective, because rapid change, like a move from a small town to a large city, reduces the perceived gains from customs and honesty, makes them less certain, and/or attenuates the enforcement mechanism. Unfortunately, many aspects of modern industrialized society undermine the basis for such informal traditions. *Future Shock* describes the factors that make for transience—the throw-away, mobile, impermanent nature of our recent life style—and these factors may increase the difficulty of relying on the informal low-cost constraints on individual behavior. (I don't quite believe that man's inherent morality is changing, but altered conditions clearly affect the *specific* moral codes that are followed.) *Lord of the Flies* also suggested how fragile ethical codes are and how altered conditions can shake up the rules.[8]

Ambiguity of rules. A fourth and also related condition for effective ethical codes is that they be relatively unambiguous.[9] There is comparatively

---

[7] And this argument has a close relationship to that in Buchanan.

[8] Charnovitz has some interesting analyses of ways in which changing transaction costs may cause informal rules to be transformed into written laws and vice versa.

Certain periods in history also suggest the fragility of ethical codes and the general brutality that ensues when they break down.

[9] This notion is similar to Schelling's "conspicuous focal point"—apparently an essential condition for successful tacit bargaining. Schelling once used the following example: Suppose all members of a group sitting in a room are told that each will receive a prize if each, without any communication, writes down the same amount of money on his slip of paper. The prize will be the amount written down. The persons in the group get nothing if any one fails to select the same amount. If nothing else happens as they proceed, they will presumably try to guess which round number (e.g., $10, $100, $1000) the others are likely to pick. If, however, an outsider suddenly marches through the room and says in a loud voice, "Nine dollars and seventy-three cents," all members of the group will now surely choose to name that amount! (On tacit bargaining, see Schelling, 1957.)

little ambiguity about being honest or keeping one's word. Some fuzziness creeps in as one grows up, for one learns that there are social occasions when most people tell "white lies" or alter emphases by omitting part of the truth. In these ways the rule becomes "tell the truth most of the time," and erosion can more easily set in. Even so, it is a relatively specific ethical standard that so far commands considerable support. Many other traditions are quite specific—to remove one's hat when indoors, to shake hands when meeting someone, to return borrowed books, to keep appointments. Because they are clear-cut, these precepts are less likely to be eroded, other things remaining the same, than comparatively vague rules like "Play fair" or "Treat customers justly." With an ambiguous rule, one does not know exactly what he is supposed to do or exactly what he can depend on others doing. In short no one knows with any precision what the social contract is or what gains can be expected from it, and it is comparatively vulnerable to erosion. Traditions that survive while appearing to be vague usually turn out to comprise a set of fairly unambiguous rules applying to rather specific situations—rules that can therefore be taught to youngsters. British "fair play," for example, breaks down (in my opinion) into a number of *relatively* clear-cut guidelines. Note too that "Do not commit adultery" is more specific in content and is more likely to be effective than "Do not covet another man's wife."

In addition, as stressed above, uncertainty or lack of information in general can make applications of rules unclear (or obscure the gains from adherence and the penalties from violations). To repeat, the clearer the rule and the consequences, with other variables held constant, the more effective it is likely to be and the more confident each person can be that others will follow the behavioral rule.

Altruism

What are the conditions for producing incremental amounts of non-rule-oriented unselfishness? I don't believe we know any satisfying answers to this question. If, on the one hand, altruism is an element in our preference surfaces, it could conceivably be manipulated, but it seems likely to be a more basic element, and less manipulable, than a taste for Grape Nuts. There is no evidence, as far as I can see, that a more structured society like the U.S.S.R., in which there may be fewer ways to compete, reduces selfishness or even competitiveness; though a new cost-reward structure of some sort might, after several generations, alter basic tastes and behavior. Exhortation would probably not be effective; maybe generations of indoctrination, or of living in a culture in which unselfishness brought higher rewards, would have some influence. If, on the other hand, unselfishness derives merely from long-run selfish interest, the way to encourage it would be to educate people concerning their long-run interests—provided that incremental altruism really would yield net long-run payoffs to most people. Again, however, one would surely be stymied: we presumably do not know how to do more than at present—e.g., to promote free discussion of the future consequences of our procreational and environment-affecting activities—to help people perceive their long-run interests. (Either source of altruism can explain the great concern of most persons about their children's well-being. As a pessimistic digression, though, it seems extremely unlikely to me that large numbers of people will develop either altruistic attitudes or long-run notions of self-interest that entail great sacrifices to themselves or their children for the sake of benefits to later generations.)

CORPORATE BEHAVIOR AND RESPONSIBILITY

Many have urged that the large corporations exercise more social responsibility[10]—that they either adhere to informal rules and ethical codes regarding such things as pollution or show more generalized altruism. People have urged stockholders to push corporate management in this direction and have criticized universities and churches for holding stock in companies that contribute to pollution, do business in South Africa, or produce defense material. If voluntary compliance by stockholders and executives could bring about the right (or an improved) amount of air pollution, solid wastes, product safety, environmental protection, or defense capability, it would of course be an economical means of accomplishing these things. And, as mentioned earlier, voluntary shouldering of responsibility works to a certain extent for fraud prevention, working conditions, politeness, and unwritten portions of contracts; why not for these other matters? Voluntarily enforced ethical codes also guide physicians' conduct to a certain extent (Arrow, pp. 965–67); to reduce our information and decision-making costs, we hire them to make many decisions for us, trust them since we cannot evaluate their actions; and (up to a point) they do try to make choices that protect our health, even though the choices are not *always* in the physicians' narrow self-interest. Why can't we trust corporations to do the right things about these other problems?

Let us examine these situations that we would like corporations to improve, and see if they meet the conditions for reliance on informal rules or on increased altruism. To express the question in a different way, can we expect corporate ethical codes to enforce the additional amenity rights that we would like to assign to existing and future individuals? Can we rely on voluntary compliance, which requires each corporate manager to trust or confidently expect that other managers will carry out their part of such social contracts?

---

[10] See, for example, Holden's "Corporate Responsibility Movement Is Alive and Well," a discussion of a fairly recent Washington, D.C., conference on the subject; or see Committee for Economic Development in Reference section.

Outlook for Rules, Responsibility, and Trust in Chemical-Product Industries

Ambiguity of rules. As discussed earlier, one of the conditions for the effective use of informal rules is that the rules be comparatively unambiguous. Unfortunately, if we design clear-cut rules regarding environmental impacts, they would strike many persons as being unreasonable and would not command wide support. For instance, rules such as "Inject *no* pollutants into the water or air" or "Do not use *any* PCB's or hexachlorophene or DDT" are unambiguous but would probably yield more cost than gain, and most people would not be enthusiastic about such sweeping behavioral codes. Even the rule "Release all toxicity data promptly" has drawbacks, since it might curtail the production of toxicity data and might in any event generate undesirable hysteria when the data were extremely uncertain and inconclusive.

On the other hand, if we think of more reasonable rules, they become vague and open to varying interpretation. Consider "Do not pollute too much" or "Do the appropriate amount of testing before marketing new substances" or "Release toxicity data whenever it is socially desirable to do so." These rules are much less clear-cut than "Tip your hat when meeting someone" or "Drive on the right side of the road" (which, despite its unambiguous and mutually advantageous nature, has to be enforced partly by policemen).

Also (I assert) most environmental rules that might be widely supported are less clear-cut than physicians' ethical codes. "Always do things that are beneficial to your patient's health" calls for judgment, yet it gives somewhat specific guidance to a doctor. This Hippocratic code is not wholly reasonable, for it tends to ignore the social cost of treatments (prescribing X rays, putting patients on dialysis machines, making transplants, sending patients to other specialists), and it ignores the fact that some patients may prefer to die; but the point is that most people have thus far *regarded* this rule as being reasonable, and it has received widespread support. And it is less ambiguous than most environmental rules that might receive similar support.

Perceived gains to most persons. Unlike customs regarding politeness or honesty, the various possible environmental rules would not distribute perceived gains to most persons and would indeed impose severe short-run penalties on many individuals. If violations of certain rules would clearly bring catastrophe, then long-run gains to all from adherence could easily be perceived. But the risks are by no means that plain. What we seem so far to face are minute risks of utter disaster; low risks of several hundred thousand deaths; medium risks of a few fatalities or of skin disorders for several million; high risks (almost certainty) of growing congestion, ugliness, inconvenience, and minor ailments for billions. But except for the minute risks, the hazards, e.g., lung cancer, bladder tumors, eczema, or environmental deterioration, are not evenly distributed among the population.

Moreover, most chemical products convey significant benefits to some, so that restrictions, voluntary or otherwise, would impose severe costs on certain groups. For instance, isoniazid has turned out to be carcinogenic, but is invaluable in the treatment of tuberculosis (and its use led to the development of the anti-depressants). To prohibit such a chemical would yield disadvantages as well as reduced risks of cancer. The ban on cyclamates inflicts at least short-run disadvantages on diabetics, and restricted use of DDT releases the gypsy moth's attacks on forests and orchards and could cause a resurgence of malaria. In addition, of course, selected sets of stockholders and laborers face losses or non-trivial adjustment costs when restrictions are introduced. Or consider oral contraceptives. They may be carcinogenic and, unlike most drugs, are being used by at least nine million younger individuals over a period of many years. The disaster, if it materialized, would be a large one. Yet restrictions reduce the profitability of research and development and the chances of discovering new safer male or female contraceptives (even with supplementary government R & D), and lack of such contraceptives may also be a disaster. Hard value judgments as well as judgments about uncertain consequences are involved. Even "experts" cannot decide what kind of restrictions would bring net gains. How can one expect most laymen and rival corporation executives to perceive gains to themselves and to most others? Yet perceived gains to most persons are probably essential to voluntary compliance with informal rules. Note in particular that the very persons expected to take action—corporation managers, stockholders, and employees—are among those who would perceive large losses rather than gains. Even if some common action would be Pareto-optimal, it would not yield reciprocal gains to all the actors. Yet it is usually actions that promise reciprocal gains, i.e., gains to all participants, that generate social contracts.

This uncertainty about net gains is especially striking if one appreciates how little we know about the interpretation of animal tests. Sometimes a substance will produce malignancy or tumors in one species of mouse or dog, yet not in another. Because of statistical (sampling) problems, test dosages have to be heavy, and as a consequence, even aspirin has proved to be teratogenic in animal tests. Cyclamates were supposedly banned on the basis of a ten-rat study; and, because of some fragmentary animal tests, the FDA is about to restrict (perhaps ban entirely) the use of Red-1—a food coloring that has been in use for many years and constitutes about 50 percent of all the food coloring used. I am *not* saying that we should ignore animal tests or that regulation is inappropriate. I am merely pointing out that, in the face of such uncertainties about the gains, it is unlikely that informal behavioral rules, enforced voluntarily or by social pressure, can evolve or be effective.

Consider the gains from adverse reaction reporting. The paucity of our knowledge about adverse reactions from chemical substances is startling. Except for dramatic instances like the teratogenic effects of thalidomide, we have few data on adverse reactions that would enable scientists to discover what substances cause what ailments. Even the experts learn mostly by following up hunches, hearing rumors about special groups such as workers in enzyme-using factories, encountering minor disasters, or discovering correlations fortuitously. One might think therefore that better reporting of adverse reactions would bring easily perceived gains for almost everyone and that an effective ethical code might evolve in this instance. And, it must be admitted, such voluntary reporting did occur to at least a moderate extent in England. Yet the benefits from any one doctor's reports are actually quite uncertain, given sketchy reporting by others, non-random samples, and the unsystematic methods of interpretation that prevail. Without systematic recording of other variables that might cause the reaction (e.g., other drugs taken recently, other substances to which the patient has been exposed, various facts about the patient's condition or vulnerability), a report may not have much meaning. Without knowledge of much earlier events, a report may not yield much benefit: long exposure to asbestos fiber can apparently cause cancer as much as 40 years later. Complicated interactions among substances cannot be disentangled on the basis of simple reports. (Azo dyes and methycholatrene are both carcinogens, yet a combination of the two is not. Chemicals often have synergistic effects, sometimes because one affects the metabolism of the other, e.g., exposure to and inhalation of radon apparently increases the carcinogenic effects of cigarette smoking.) Without the use of refined statistical techniques and follow-ups, even systematic and thorough adverse reaction reports may not yield much knowledge. In the light of all these uncertainties about the benefits, why should physicians (or corporation executives) voluntarily undertake to report reactions (quite costly to the reporter if done carefully) and risk extra malpractice suits, liability suits, and loss of clientele? Again, because the gains are unclear and are not distributed with some evenness over the population (let alone being reciprocal), it is doubtful that a new "tradition" and mutual trust can do the job.

Opportunities for application of social pressure. The possibilities of applying social pressure to corporate executives in these situations are extremely limited in comparison with the possibilities of villagers ostracizing a rude person or townspeople frowning upon an erring local builder or buisnessmen retaliating against another's violations of tacitly understood contracts. Who knows a producer of PCB's or hexachlorophene if he meets him on the street? Who should be frowned at anyway—the stockholders, the Board of Directors, or various managerial echelons? In large firms, big cities, and big societies, there is much arms-length impersonality that impairs the effectiveness of personally applied social pressures (though it may make people more responsive to pressures for other types of conformity). Where there is organized pressure for some unambiguous action, e.g., the non-production of napalm or NTA, there will probably be some response as long as the pressure continues. Mere picketing of Dow Chemical *by itself*, however, is probably not as painful to executives and other personnel as *personal* retaliation against the man who fails to keep appointments. In any event, who, by and large, will persistently give paper-mill executives pats on the back for voluntarily installing costly waste-treatment plants? Who will bestow social favor on the managers who quit producing saccharin, which may be hazardous, or coffee, which now appears to be a cause of bladder cancer? What *personal* approval will be given to executives who release toxicity data and perhaps lose out to competitors? What *personal* disapproval is heaped upon distillers, who produce what is probably today's most hazardous chemical product?

Stability and uncertainty. A related condition for social responsibility regarding rules is stability, and here, too, the circumstances do not appear to be propitious with respect to environmental standards. In chemical products, for instance, change is pervasive. One month phosphate detergents seem to be the villain; a little later it appears that eutrophication would occur anyway or that an inexpensive way of treating sewage to eliminate phosphates has been developed. One month NTA is touted as a substitute for phosphates, but later its accessibility turns out to cause fatalities among children.[11] In other words, not only are the net gains from such rules unclear, but our knowledge and perception of them keeps changing. Also the shortcomings of social pressure as a method of enforcement are aggravated by today's mobility. Neighbors, employees, executives, and plant locations keep changing. How many participants in the process stick around long enough to apply or receive social pressures?

In general, these factors produce uncertainties, and imperfect information further undermines all the conditions for reliance on unwritten rules and uncoerced responsibility. Uncertainty aggravates the ambiguity of rules, the hazy perception of benefits, and the obstacles to social pressure as an enforcer.

Outlook for Responsibility through Altruism of Chemical Producers

As indicated previously, little is known about how to change the degree of selfishness, whether it is a basic taste or simply a means of working toward the satisfaction of other tastes. I see no evidence that one could now rely on such generalized altruism to regulate chemical products, and I can't visualize concrete steps that people or governments could take to make such reliance possible in the future.

---

[11] Or consider the recent shifts in attitudes and guidelines concerning hexachlorophene, with the reappearance of hospital staph infections (which I understand had nearly vanished in recent years).

Conclusions

Thus, while it would be economical if appropriate behavioral rules to guide management could evolve or be established and if voluntary responsibility could enforce them, it seems most unlikely that these things can happen with respect to business behavior affecting health and environment. It seems even less likely that generalized altruism, or increased altruism, can be relied on (or that it would produce *appropriate* behavior). Hence I fall back on a commonly held position: if we wish to alter business behavior affecting health or environment, we must turn to legislation and formal means of enforcement[12]—as shaped by the political process. Alternative mechanisms for establishing more "amenity rights" include (1) implicit modification of existing rights by regulations restricting usage of products or requiring certain actions, and (2) explicit reassignment of rights, e.g., by sale of pollution rights (Dales) or stepping up producers' or damagers' liability to protect amenity (property) rights. This might include expanding physicians' liability, though in designing any reforms the disadvantages should be carefully weighed against the advantages.

It might be noted that transaction costs (including enforcement costs) are crucial in choosing the preferred form of intervention. Some economists have become impatient with property-rights-transaction-cost analysis (Kneese, pp. 153–55, and Boulding, p. 167) but all the above-mentioned actions reassign rights, and transaction costs determine their effectiveness and the outcome. If we tax or charge fees for effluents or other external costs generated, the results depend upon monitoring and enforcement costs. If regulations restrict production processes or the use of products, enforcement costs are decisive in shaping what really happens to amenity rights. If pollution rights are created and sold, negotiation and enforcement and other transaction costs determine how it will really work out. If producers' liabilities are increased, what actually happens depends upon the costs of lawsuits and producer adjustments. The best way to analyze any proposal, in my own view, is to see what happens to effective rights and the appropriability of rewards from the standpoint of various participants. In fact, one way to sum up the deficiencies of informal rules, altruism, and corporate responsibility—as devices for regulating activities affecting health and environment—is to say that the transaction (especially enforcement) costs appear to be almost infinite.

---

[12] According to *Time* magazine, Al Capone summed up such matters thus: "You can get so much farther with a kind word and a gun than with a kind word alone."

REFERENCES

Kenneth J. Arrow, "Uncertainty and the Economics of Medical Care," *American Economic Review* LIII, December, 1963, pp. 941–73.

Edward C. Banfield, *The Moral Basis of a Backward Society* (New York: Free Press, 1958).

Kenneth E. Boulding, "The Political Economy of Environmental Quality: Discussion," *American Economic Review* LXI, May, 1971, pp. 167–69.

James M. Buchanan, "Ethical Rules, Expected Values, and Large Numbers," *Ethics* LXXVI, October, 1965, pp. 1–13.

James M. Buchanan and W. Craig Stubblebine, "Externality," *Economica*, November, 1962, pp. 371–84.

Committee for Economic Development, *Social Responsibilities of Business Corporations*, CED, 1971.

Diane W. Charnovitz, "Economics of Etiquette and Customs," M.A. Thesis, University of Virginia (unpublished).

Harold Demsetz, "Toward a Theory of Property Rights," *American Economic Review* LVII, May, 1967, pp. 347–59.

Merton Deutsch, "Trust and Suspicion," *Journal of Conflict Resolution* 2, September, 1958.

Fitzherbert, *Boke of Husbandrie,* 1534, quoted by Walton Hamilton, "The Ancient Maxim *Caveat Emptor*," *Yale Law Journal* 40, 1931, p. 1164.

William Golding, *Lord of the Flies* (New York: Coward-McCann, 1954).

Constance Holden, "Corporate Responsibility Movement Is Alive and Well," *Science* 172, May 28, 1971, p. 920.

Allen V. Kneese, "Environmental Pollution: Economics and Policy," *American Economic Review* LXI, May, 1971, pp. 153–66.

James L. Loomis, "Communication, the Development of Trust, and Cooperative Behavior," *Human Relations* 12, No. 4, 1959, pp. 305–15.

Edward [Ezra J.] Mishan, *The Cost of Economic Growth* (New York: Praeger, 1967).

Thomas C. Schelling, "Bargaining, Communication, and Limited War," *Journal of Conflict Resolution* 1, March, 1957, pp. 19–36.

Thomas C. Schelling, "On the Ecology of Micromotives," *Public Interest*, Fall, 1971, pp. 61–98.

Alvin Toffler, *Future Shock* (New York: Random House, 1970).

*Business Responsibility and Economic Behavior**

William J. Baumol

Under pressure from many sides, corporate managements have been quick to assert their agreement in principle to the proposition that the firm should concern itself with the ills of society, particularly as those ills have begun to seem increasingly threatening. After all, the modern firm has shown itself to be one of the most efficient economic instruments in history. Since the beginning of the industrial revolution it has increased real per capita incomes perhaps twenty-fold, incredible though that may seem. It has doubled and redoubled and redoubled again the energy placed at the service of mankind, and has achieved an increasing productivity of human labor which is astonishing both in its magnitude and its persistence. With such a record, what other institution can be better adapted to deal with the difficult economic problems that underlie so many of our social issues?

I will argue that this line of reasoning is fundamentally valid, but not if interpreted and implemented in the obvious manner which generally seems to be proposed by both business and its critics. The proposal seems to be that industry should exhibit a massive outburst of altruism, modifying its goals to include in addition to the earning of profits, improvement of the environment, the training of the unskilled, and much more. As John Diebold has put the matter in a recent address: "[There is the danger that] . . . business as 'good corporate citizen'

---

*This paper originally appeared in *Managing the Socially Responsible Corporation*, edited with commentaries by Melvin Anshen, Project for Studies of the Modern Corporation (Macmillan, New York, 1974). Reprinted by permission of the Trustees of Columbia University.

[will] start to view itself, or be viewed by others, as an all-purpose institution that should right all social wrongs. (If you added together the rhetoric in this field you wouldn't fall far short of business being called upon to do just this!)."[1]

I will argue that any such undertaking is undesirable even if it were achievable. Moreover I will give reasons why it cannot be expected to work—why the task undertaken on such a basis is likely to be managed badly. Tokenism is the natural product of such a process. Indeed, not only is business likely to prove inefficient as a voluntary healer of the ills of society, but the attempt to play such a role may well have adverse effects on its efficiency in the fields where it now operates and in which its abilities have been demonstrated so strikingly.

I will argue that the primary job of business is to make money for its stockholders. This does not mean that the best way to do everything is as it is done now. On the contrary, society has every reason to ask business to be much more careful in its use of the environment, to do much more to protect the interests of consumers, etc. But we neither should nor can rely on "voluntarism" for the purpose.

If we want business to behave differently from the way it does today we must change the rules of the game so that the behavior we desire becomes more profitable than the activity patterns we want to modify. If pollution is made expensive enough, we will be treated quickly to a spectacular display of business efficiency in reducing emission rates. If the production of unsafe products is made sufficiently costly, one can be confident of a remarkable acceleration in the flow of innovations making for greater safety. Business will then do the things it knows how to do best and society will be the beneficiary.

Under the terms of such an approach, is there no role for "business responsibility"? Is the firm simply to pursue profits and no more? That is not quite enough. Responsibility on the part of business, from this viewpoint, has two requirements: (1) when appropriate changes in the rules are proposed by the duly constituted representatives of the community, responsible management must refrain from efforts to sabotage this undertaking; (2) business should cooperate in the design to these rules to assure their effectiveness in achieving their purpose and to make certain that their provisions interfere as little as possible with the efficient working of the economy. But, by and large, these are just the things businessmen have, in effect, refused to do.

DANGERS OF VOLUNTEER "SOCIAL RESPONSIBILITY"

The notion that firms should by themselves pursue the objectives of society is, in fact, a rather frightening proposition. Corporate management holds in its

[1] "The Social Responsibility of Business," Address at the conference on "An Economic Society for Man," June 21, 1972.

hands enormous financial resources. Voluntarism suggests, or rather demands, that management use these resources to influence the social and political course of events. But who is to determine in what way these events ought to be influenced? Who is to select these goals? If it is management itself, the power of interference with our lives and the lives of others that management is asked to assume is surely intolerable. The threat to effective democracy should be clear enough.

The point is made most clearly by recent demands that business firms exercise responsibility in their investments abroad, meaning specifically that firms should abstain from investment in countries whose governments draw the disapproval of the person who happens to advocate such a course. The firm may be asked to eschew investment in countries that repress or persecute particular ethnic groups, or whose governments trample civil liberties, or are aggressive militarily, or simply oppose United States foreign policy with sufficient vigor. I do not want to argue here either the efficacy or the desirability of boycotts. Nor do I wish to defend the countries which have been attacked by critics of corporate policies on overseas investment. I, too, am repelled by some of their governments. In sum, I am not arguing for isolation or for the ignoring of oppression. Rather, I deplore the notion that American business should attempt to arrogate to itself the determination of our foreign policy.

It may or may not make sense to boycott some particular foreign government. But I do not want a business management to decide what government should be boycotted. And certainly I do not want management to use the capital I have entrusted to it to impose its notions of international morality upon the world.

Again, in Diebold's words,

> I personally believe [the choice of social goals] is the job of the politician working in a democratic political process. The businessman as businessman should not be making essentially social decisions. The businessman should be the tool who responds to market demand by making what society shows it wants. Do not make him more mighty than that.

An increase in corporate power is probably the last thing that those who call for greater "corporate responsibility" would want. Yet that, paradoxically, is precisely where some of their prescriptions lead.

TOKEN ACTIVITIES

Predictably, there has been a considerable gap between business' glowing accounts of its own accomplishments and the actual magnitude of its achievements. Newspapers report many cases in which their public relations men have run far ahead of what companies have actually accomplished. *Newsweek* reported the case of a company with the

> ". . . only industrial mill in the U.S. to have been the subject of separate air and water pollution abatement hearings before Federal authorities whose advertising asserted 'it cost us a bundle but the Clearwater River still runs clear' . . . [W]hat [the firm] neglected to mention was that the picture [in the advertisement] had been snapped some 50 miles upstream from the . . . plant [where] it dumps up to 40 tons of suspended organic wastes into Clearwater and nearby Snake River every day."[2]

After citing several other such cases, the article goes on to report some more routine examples.

> Even without bending the facts, companies may inflate their ecological contributions with half-truths. FMC Corp. recently took out double-page spreads in national publications to boast of its participation in the $3.8 million Santee, Calif., water-reclamation project, which converts sewage into water fit for swimming and boating. Conveniently omitted was the fact the FMC did no more than sell the project some $76,000 worth of pumps and equipment. Nor was there any mention of the company's inorganic-chemical plant in West Virginia which daily dumps more than 500,000 pounds of wastes, mostly toxic, into a nearby river, according to the Federal Power Commission.
>
> Similarly, Union Carbide began an ad boosting its efforts to reduce auto pollution with the observation that 'Driving through this beautiful land of ours, you can get all choked up.' To the residents of the Kanawha Valley in West Virginia this is hardly news. So much smoke billows from the chimneys of Union Carbide's main ferroalloy plant there–28,000 tons of particulates a year–that a nearby Roman Catholic church had to encase an outdoor statue of St. Anthony in a fiber glass case to protect if from corrosion.

The conclusion to be drawn from this and the many other illustrations that can be cited is not that businessmen are particularly dishonest. Having associated with many businessmen over the years, I have come away with the impression that their personal integrity, their good will, and their distress at injustice does not differ notably from those of other groups. Of course, the honesty and the degree of concern with social issues will vary from one businessman to another,

[2] *Newsweek*, December 28, 1970, pp. 49–51.

as it does elsewhere.[3] But even with the best intentions, given the rules of the game as they are today, there is little the individual businessman can do.

It is the prime virtue of the competitive process that it leaves little up to the good will of individual managements. The firm that is inefficient or that does not provide the public with the products it wants is given short shrift by the market mechanism. It is a merciless process which has no pity for the weak, ineffectual businessman. The chiseller who undercuts an inefficient concern is the consumers' best friend, though he is anathema to the firms that long for the quiet life and its permissive mediocrity.

But that same competitive process which prevents laziness or incompetence also precludes voluntarism on any significant scale. The businessman who chooses voluntarily to spend till it hurts on the environment, on the training of the handicapped, or in support of higher education is likely to find that he, too, is vulnerable to the chiseller without social conscience who, by avoiding such outlays, can supply his outputs more cheaply.

In the words of Edward L. Rogers, general counsel of the Environmental Defense Fund, "If I were a company president right now, I wouldn't do any more than I had to on the pollution front, because that would hurt my company more than its competitors."[4]

The invisible hand does not work by inducing business firms to pursue the goals of society as a matter of conscience and good will. Rather, when the rules are designed properly it gives management no other option. Adam Smith was acutely aware of this. The famous invisible hand passage is often quoted, but, for some reason, the two critical sentences that conclude the paragraph are often omitted: "I have never known much good done by merchants who affected to trade for the public good. It is an affectation, indeed, not very common among merchants and very few words need be employed in dissuading them from it."

USE OF THE PRICE MECHANISM

Economists have long argued that when faced with mounting social problems one should not abandon the profit system or undermine its workings. Rather, if one is really serious about the social goals that are being urged upon business, one should use that powerful economic instrument, the price mechanism, to help attain them.

For example, it has been suggested that the reason industry (like others) has been so free in using the atmosphere as a dumping ground for its gaseous wastes

[3] Note that consumers' records of voluntary compliance in these areas are no better than those of business firms. It is easy to document cases in which there has been a response that is less than spectacular to voluntary programs for recycling of solid wastes, for the increased use of car pools, or for installation of inexpensive emission control kits in automobiles.

[4] *Newsweek*, December 28, 1970, p. 51.

is that clean air is a valuable resource available for use by anyone at a price far below its cost to society. Imagine what would happen if, say, coal or cloth or some other such resource were supplied free to anyone who wanted to use it, in any desired quantity and with no accounting for its manner of utilization. The resulting wastes and inefficiencies are all too easy to envision. But that is precisely what is encouraged when society, by virtue of long tradition, makes available on precisely those terms the use of its water, its air, and its other resources that are held in common.

Economists have, therefore, suggested that an appropriate remedial measure is to levy an adequate charge for the use of such resources. If made costly enough, their use will rapidly become more sparing and less inefficient.

There are many virtues to such a program which need not be gone into in any detail. Any such system of charges (e.g., a tax of x dollars per gallon on the discharge of certain types of effluents into waterways) is as automatic as any tax collection process. It does not involve the uncertainties of detection of violations and of the subsequent judicial process. It does not rely on the vigor of enforcement agencies, which seems so often to wane rapidly with the passage of time. It offers its largest rewards in the form of decreased taxes to the firms that are most efficient in reducing emissions. It thereby makes use of the full force of the market mechanism as an instrument of efficiency. It may be added that these are not all the virtues that can be claimed for such an arrangement. From the point of view of the businessman himself there is a great deal to be said for it.

First, it is a natural extension of the profit system, which he should welcome as a means to strengthen its workings and its social acceptability in the long run.

Second, it protects him from the notion that he is engaged in criminal activity when in the course of his productive operations wastes are unavoidably generated. By making him pay the full social costs of his activities, including all of the resources he utilizes in his operations, it becomes clear that he is engaged in a normal and commendable productive process, rather than the antisocial activity of which he is all too easily suspected under current arrangements.

Third, such a set of rules protects him against undercutting by competitors when he does behave in a manner consistent with social objectives—there is no room created for undercutting by the chiseller when everyone is subject to similar costs imposed for the protection of society.[5]

Finally, and this should in the long run be most important of all to the businessman, the proposal avoids completely the imposition of direct controls

[5] Of course, if such a rule applies only in a small geographic area, it does not protect the firm from the competition of suppliers located elsewhere. But this argues that such rules should cover as large a geographic area as possible, not that they should be avoided.

by the government. A management is not told how to run its business—whether to install taller smokestacks or to recycle or to adopt a higher-grade fuel. Rather, emissions are made highly unprofitable and the businessman is invited to decide for himself the most effective ways of reducing them or of eliminating them altogether. There need be no acceleration in the process of erosion of the freedom of enterprise. Changes in prices of inputs are a normal business phenomenon. Fuel can be expected to grow more expensive as its scarcity increases, and other inputs grow cheaper as innovation improves their productive technology, but neither of these changes undercuts the prerogatives of management. Similarly, the imposition of a charge corresponding to the social costs of the use of environmental resources does not interfere with the managerial decision process. It merely changes the structure of the economy's rewards to the company, increasing the profitability of the behavior desired by the community.

CHANGES IN RULES

This proposal is not, in itself, my central point. Rather, it illustrates what I mean by a change in the rules of the game. Many other types of changes in rules are possible.

The type most frequently talked about is direct controls: for example, quotas assigned to firms or to municipal treatment plants, specifying maximum quantities of emissions and standards of purity which they must meet before they can be discharged into waterways. All sort of things can be specified by direct controls. They can require the installation of specified types of devices which limit the emissions of automobiles; they can make mandatory the use of various safety devices. The range and variety of such regulations should be obvious enough.

Besides such direct controls, whose enforcement is left to government agencies, other changes in rules are also possible. For example, legislation authorizing legal suits by interested private citizens has often been advocated. Something intermediate between direct controls and the fiscal methods described above is represented by the construction of treatment facilities by governmental agencies, whose costs polluters are then required to bear.

The essential point is that all of these procedures involve changes in the rules themselves. The firm is not expected to do anything as a pure act of benevolence. Rather, it is faced with a new set of conditions under which it and its competitors must operate, and they must adapt themselves as effectively as they can. The two most important characteristics of such changes in the rules, as far as we are concerned, are that there is nothing voluntary about following them, and that it applies equally to all competitors. In this way, it frees management from pressures to undertake a role in the policy-making process which it has no reason to want and which society has every reason to fear. Moreover, it protects the firm from attacks by those who stand ready to undercut it at the first opportunity, an opportunity which would be opened were the firm to bow to social pressures for the voluntary pursuit of its social responsibilities.

THE RESPONSE OF BUSINESS

With such potential advantages to the firm, to the free enterprise system, and to society, one might have expected that at least a substantial segment of the business community would have welcomed such changes in the rules with open arms. After all, does not that constitute a true acceptance by business of its social responsibility, through an arrangement that elicits desirable behavior from everyone and avoids the ineffectiveness and inequities of voluntarism?

But nothing of the sort has in fact occurred. Only recently have there appeared a few breaks in the solid opposition of the business community, when one automobile manufacturer (Ford) and one gasoline distributor (Mobil) joined those who question the desirability of the Highway Trust Fund as currently constituted. However, such defections are still very much a rarity.

Let me illustrate the point. When I first undertook the preparation of this paper it seemed appropriate to see what might be suggested by the newspapers. For the next twelve days I searched the *New York Times* for relevant materials and encountered not a single example of industry support for anything that could be interpreted as a change in the rules designed to strengthen the protection of the public's interests. But I did find a profusion of pertinent cases in which industry took the opposite position. These are summarized in the following excerpts:[6]

Example 1. Consumer Protection

> Legislation to create a consumer protection agency which would represent consumers before federal courts and regulatory agencies died on the Senate floor, a victim of a filibuster. The bill, regarded as the most important consumer measure of the present Congress, commanded majority support in the Senate; but it ran into intensive opposition from industry.[7]

Example 2. Regulation of Phosphate Utilization

> Administration officials reported today that Governor Cahill will push next month for final legislative approval of a controversial measure

[6] I do not mean to suggest that this is a random sample, i.e., that this represents the number of such stories one would encounter in a representative two weeks. The period that happened to be chosen encompassed the adjournment of Congress and so the number of pieces of legislation whose fate was settled was unusually high.

[7] J.W. Finney, *New York Times*, October 8, 1972, Sect. 4, p. 1.

that would give New Jersey the power to ban phosphates from detergents and other cleaning agents. . . . State officials reported that the Senate's Republican leadership now favors the measure, which died last year in committee at the hands of the detergent industry and organized labor interests in the Legislature.[8]

Example 3. Control of Strip Mining

Legislation to provide for regulation of the strip-mining of coal and the conservation and reclamation of strip-mining areas was passed by the House today and sent to the Senate. The vote was 265 to 75.

The House measure would give the Interior Department authority to issue cease-and-desist orders against any surface-mining of coal when the health and safety of the public or employees is involved; to designate certain areas as unsuitable for strip-mining if lasting injury would be caused to the environment; and to issue and revoke permits for strip-mining.

Six months after enactment, no coal strip-mining could be conducted without a permit. Except for reclamation plans, any permit application would have to have the written consent of the owner of the surface of the land.

Carl E. Bagge, president of the National Coal Association, representing coal operators, said the bill was a punitive, unrealistic measure which would reduce the nation's production of coal by 25 percent almost overnight.

Mr. Bagge assailed the bill as an "arbitrary, simplistic solution" to a complex problem. He urged the Senate to reject it, contending that it was too late in the session to amend the House bill to one that was satisfactory.[9]

Example 4. Safety of Drug Products

In an effort to persuade the House to narrow the legal remedies in a pending product safety bill, Thomas G. Corcoran, a Washington lawyer who represents major drug interests, pointed out that the bill could overburden the Federal courts with new cases. The drug industry was leading the fight against the bill, which is now nearing enactment.[10]

Example 5. Inspection for Disease–Carrying Pets

When the polyethylene bag was invented, the tropical fish industry ballooned. Its bubble may burst, pet supply wholesalers say, because of a proposed Federal law affecting fish imports, modeled after other

[8] R. Sullivan, *New York Times*, October 11, 1972, p. 1.
[9] New York Times, *October 12, 1972*, p. 1.
[10] F. P. Graham, *New York Times*, October 14, 1972, p. 1.

regulations restricting the sale of turtles and banning the import of certain birds to prevent communicable disease.

"We recognize the need for inspection and regulation," says Richard Kyllo of Saddle River, vice president of the newly organized tropical Fish Institute of America. "But the new codes were enacted in a state of panic. They are so loosely worded that they leave an open road to any kind of interpretation."

New Jersey is among many states that recently passed restrictions on selling turtles unless they were found free of salmonella, a bacteria that causes intestinal disease. The regulations were a reaction to the death in 1969 of a 9-year-old turtle owner in Connecticut.[11]

Example 6. Information on Restaurant Sanitation

The New Jersey Public Health Council tonight ordered all restaurants in the state to post the results of their state sanitary inspection reports conspicuously near their entrance, in an effort to open heretofore confidential inspection files to public scrutiny.

"We have kept intact our promise to provide consumer health protection unequaled anywhere in the country," Dr. Cowan said.

As a result, the restaurant industry, which bitterly opposed the open posting of inspection reports at a public hearing here last month, is expected to contest the council's order in the courts.[12]

Example 7. Water Pollution Control

The Senate and House of Representatives overrode today President Nixon's veto of the Federal Water Pollution Control Act of 1972, which thus becomes law and authorizes $24.6 billion over three years to clean up the nation's lakes and rivers. During nearly two years of Congressional deliberation on the bill, the White House had supported industry's opposition to many of its provisions, particularly the goal of no discharges of industrial pollutants by 1985 and the setting of limitations on effluents for classes of industry.[13]

Other illustrations are easy enough to provide. The billboard industry, the manufacturers of plastics, of tetraethyl lead, and many others have all played the same game. The outcries have become familiar: proposed regulations are "punitive," "unworkable," "staggeringly expensive," and even "ruinous." Said a representative of the pet fish industry (in the October 15 article just cited): "if [the bill as it now stands] passes, I'll be completely wiped out and so will the industry."

---

[11] J. Marks, *New York Times*, October 15, 1972, p. 96.
[12] R. Sullivan, *New York Times*, October 17, 1972, p.1.
[13] E. W. Kenworthy, *New York Times*, October 18, 1972, p. 26

But we rarely hear of industry representatives who volunteer drafts of alternative regulations which really prove to be effective. Certainly I have never heard of an industry representative arguing that a proposed piece of legislation is not sufficiently strong!

RESPONSIBILITY AND VOLUNTARISM

We can only conclude that business still has a long way to go before it will have succeeded in a program of effective cooperation with the duly constituted authorities, the only bodies that do have any authorization to decide on social goals. Of course, the fault has not been entirely that of the businessman, but the illustrative cases of the preceding section suggest to me that so far he has done remarkably little to try to make such a process work, and that he has often effectively served as an accomplice to the undermining of any workable measures for the treatment of a number of the more pressing social ills.

I am aware that there is an element of inconsistency in my position. On the one hand I have argued that business should have no truck with voluntarism which, at best, offers the illusion of effective activity and, at worst, poses a threat to the democratic process. Yet at the same time I am urging businessmen to cooperate voluntarily in the design and implementation of effective legislative measures as the appropriate medium of social responsibility. However, though both processes call for voluntary acts on the part of managements, the two differ completely in their potential consequences.

The adoption of new rules differs in two fundamental respects from a regime of pure voluntarism. First, it involves no takeover by business management of powers of decision that belong more properly to others–government retains the final authority on matters of social policy. Second, because what is involved is a change in rules that applies equally to everyone, there is no reason why a well-designed action of the variety under discussion need turn out to be ineffective. For the market mechanism, instead of undermining such a program, certainly need not interfere with it, and in some cases will actually serve to implement it. With competitors all subject to the same regulations, competitive pressures will not forestall the program, and if the structure of rewards and penalties is so modified in the process as to make failure to cooperate highly unprofitable, then the profit motive becomes the automatic force behind this program.

Thus, in my view, the true social responsibilities of business can be met only by a new spirit which may be called "meta-voluntarism"–systematic cooperation in the design and implementation of measures which are basically involuntary.

Let me not be misunderstood. I am not suggesting that all companies call in their lobbyists and turn their instructions about by a full 180 degrees. Such a goal is neither particularly attractive nor achievable. It would surely be unreasonable to expect the representatives of industry to spearhead a drive to impose the costs of public interest programs on themselves. And I am not particularly attracted by political activity on the part of corporations, no matter what it may happen to favor.

Rather, I am suggesting that, once the issue has been raised, and once it seems clear that some sort of government action is about to be undertaken, the time is ripe for constructive participation by the business sector. That is the time for voluntary participation by the business sector. That is the time for voluntary cooperation in the design of more effective changes in the rules drawn up so that they are not unnecessarily burdensome to anyone. By concerning itself with the last of these matters, business will still look after its own interests as well as those of the general public, but then it will do so in a manner that is fundamentally constructive and that can help to lighten the clouds of suspicion that now hang over the business community.

Comment

Guido Calabresi

The three papers I am to discuss appear to alternate between viewing altruism as a commodity which has value in our individual preference functions, and as a tool or device which might be useful in achieving an efficient allocation of other goods. Let us assume that Taney is altruistic—that is, he gets pleasure from Marshall's well-being— or even that Taney gets pleasure from the existence of altruism in the world—that is, that he gets pleasure from Marshall's getting pleasure from Chase's well-being. One may view these preferences of Taney's as matters to be taken into account in determining which institutional structures are most likely to maximize total utility, or one may view them as of no consequences in themselves, but as useful devices for maximizing utility in relation to other goods.

In the first sense altruism is a good whose quantity directly affects the level of social welfare, but which, for reasons I shall advert to later, is hard to determine in ways we use to determine the production of other goods. In the second sense, altruism can be examined in the same way coercion, or trading among individuals with atomistic, independent, utility functions are treated, namely as devices which are costly to establish and whose relative desirability depends essentially on how efficiently they achieve, in comparison with alternative devices, something like an optimal allocation of resources in a given area. In fact, altruism, trust, and most of the other attitudes that have been discussed are both goods in themselves (in that individuals get pleasure from them and from having others have them) and devices for allocating other goods (in that their existence modifies or even substitutes for the workings of other methods of allocation). The point, then, is that both ways of approaching altruism are analytically useful, but one must be very careful as to which approach one is taking, for confusion is very easy.

It should be clear that altruism is not needed as a device to accomplish an optimal allocation of resources if one is prepared to accept an assumption of no transaction costs, using that phrase in the broad sense which Coase uses.[1] Similarly, altruism as a device is not needed if one accepts the presuppositions of a Walrasian general equilibrium model. It is also clear that the moment one drops some of these presuppositions, or assumes some impediments to transactions, theoretical situations can be described where the presence of altruism will make possible the achieving of a more efficient result than would its absence. Conversely, one can also describe theoretical situations where the existence of altruism would lead to a less efficient result.[2] The issue then is no more whether altruism is a good or bad device in the abstract than it is whether collective production is, in the abstract, desirable. It is rather in what real situations are the conditions which make altruism desirable likely to be present and when are they likely to be absent.

Similarly, the optimization of altruism, viewed as a good in itself, presents no problems if one assumes a Coasian perfect world. If instead, one drops such unrealistic assumptions, then the determination of how a society produces the optimal amount of altruism becomes very hard indeed. Here it is well to distinguish, as Kenneth Arrow does, several forms of altruism. In the first, Taney gets pleasure from helping Marshall. Taney cares only about his own act, not its actual effect. In the second, Taney gets pleasure from *choosing* to help Marshall but only if Marshall is thereby made better off and this, let us assume, requires that others help Marshall too. Taney cares about participating freely, but only given a beneficial result for Marshall. In the third, Taney gets pleasure from Marshall's being better off, but gets no pleasure from participating in making Marshall better off. Taney just cares about the result; participation in achieving it makes no difference. Finally, in the fourth, Taney gets pleasure from the fact that others get pleasure in helping Marshall.[3]

The first case presents few problems; Taney can decide for himself how much to benefit Marshall. The third presents typical public-good type

[1] See Coase, "The Problem of Social Cost," 3 *Journal of Law & Economics* 1 (1960). Cf. Calabresi, "Transaction Cost, Resource Allocation and Liability Rules—A Comment," 11 *Journal of Law & Economics* 67 (1968).

[2] I assume that the existence of altruism is not something we can turn on or off. That is, it is not simply an additional technique we can employ when its use is beneficial and discard when it would be harmful. If it exists, it affects decisions whether we want it to or not.

problems which are closely analogous to those discussed in the literature on Pareto optimal income redistribution and which are said by that literature to justify coercion. The second and fourth present problems which are rather more complex.

In the second case, Taney's pleasure is dependent both on achieving a result, which given public-good problems will not be achieved by the market, and on participating freely, which may not be possible given a coercive solution of the public-good problem. If Taney desires to give Marshall no more than 10, if he is not only willing to give that 10 freely but will only get pleasure from giving the 10 if he can give it freely, and if his pleasure also depends on a result for Marshall which can be achieved only if Marshall receives 10 from everybody, a coercive solution requiring all to give Marshall 10 will not suffice. For Taney is deprived of his pleasure in giving freely.[4]

Similarly, the fourth case, where Taney gets pleasure from the existence of altruism in third parties, may not be amenable either to traditional market or coercive solutions. This case presents starkly the problem which Roland McKean raised of the man who asked "how much must I pay you to love me only for what I am." The benefits to Taney stem from the existence of altruism in third parties, yet that altruism cannot be bought nor can it be coerced. How then can Taney's desire for it be taken into account in structuring society?

The third and fourth cases suggest, I think, a broader problem. There is a whole category of goods or characteristics whose production cannot be bought or coerced and yet whose presence in the society gives individuals pleasure.[5] These goods are often attitudes like trust, love and altruism whose value depends on their being freely given and which are therefore destroyed if they are bought or coerced. The fact that they cannot be bought or coerced in an ordinary way does not mean that they do not exist as real factors in an individual's preference system, nor does it mean that their production cannot be analyzed by economists.

[3] One could divide each of these cases into many other sub-cases. For example, case four could itself be broken into separate cases for each type of altruism whose existence may give Taney pleasure. Some types of altruism whose existence gives Taney pleasure may be more amenable to societal determination than others. As we shall see later, differences as to which kinds of altruism please Taney may be crucial to whether a society can affect social welfare by trying to affect the level of altruism.

[4] Titmuss, as Arrow points out, does not make the case that this is the blood donor's dilemma in a society that buys blood. It may, nevertheless, be that this problem is part of what Titmuss has in mind.

[5] My treatment of this category of goods derived from a very helpful discussion with my colleagues Bruce A. Ackerman of the University of Pennsylvania Law School and Alvin K. Klevorick of the Yale University Department of Economics.

There is also likely to be a set of characteristics which may not be bought or coerced and whose presence gives pain. Hatred may be hateful even if its effects are controlled through coercion or bribes.

The need to recognize their existence in individual preference systems is essential, for unless they are recognized, what may seem to be an optimal allocation of resources will in no sense be optimal (quite apart from traditional problems of distribution). In this sense, they are analogous to that whole family of external costs and benefits (of which they are in fact a sub-set) which I have elsewhere called moralisms.[6] Like the pain which Lecher's viewing of pornography causes Prude, or the pleasure which Saint's resisting of temptation gives Clerical, the pleasure Taney gets from the existence of altruism must be considered in evaluating a society's allocation of resources. Like them also, it is instead generally ignored by economists.

Nor can ignoring those goods which cannot be bought or coerced in ordinary ways be justified on the ground that nothing can be done about them. For it is far from true that their production cannot be influenced. In the first place, though they cannot be bought in an ordinary way, it may well be that indirect bribes, like tax deductions, can increase the production of some of these attitudes in a way that does not fully destroy the pleasure their existence gives. Similarly, though the pleasure given by the existence of some of these attitudes is destroyed by any form of coercion, the pleasure given by other attitudes may be destroyed only by legal and not by moral coercion. Finally, education, a peculiar form of moral coercion, may lead to greater production of most of these attitudes without destroying the pleasure their presence gives, even if other forms of moral coercion would. In other words, as we expand our horizon to para-bribes and para-coercions, we may well find that optimization of at least some of these attitudes is not impossible.[7] The precision economists like may well be lost, but that, of course, is quite another matter.

Obviously, a comment like this is no place to get deeply into the problems and advantages of para-bribes, and para-coercion. Nor is it the place to examine fully the relationship between moralisms in general and that sub-set of moralisms which cannot be bought or coerced in ordinary ways. All one can do here is to suggest that the problem of altruism and its optimization is part of two broader problems which economists—or at least lawyers with some economic training—must face: the problem of non-physical external costs and benefits, and the problem of the

---

[6] See Calabresi and Melamed, "Property Rules, Liability Rules and Inalienability: One View of the Cathedral," 85 *Harvard Law Review* 1089 (1972).

[7] The point is not that *all* attitudes whose presence gives Taney pleasure are amenable to para-bribes or para-coercion without destroying Taney's pleasure. Some may not be, and as to these there is little worth doing. Others instead may be subject to societal control in ways which do not fully destroy Taney's pleasure, provided the appropriate control device is found. Case four may not, in short, be as stark as my use of McKean's example might lead one to think.

production of goods whose desirability depends, in part at least, on the fact that their production is neither induced by direct market bribes or coerced. So viewed, an analysis of altruism, like this conference, must be no more than a challenging first step.

Comment

Thomas Nagel

While the most conspicuous departures from self-interest in economic transactions are no doubt caused by folly rather than by altruism, some form of consideration for the welfare of others certainly plays a significant role in economic life. I shall discuss three kinds of cases: (1) The contribution of support to an institution or practice from which the contributor benefits, even though his benefit is not contingent on his contribution; (2) the attempt to pursue and avoid certain causal relations between one's own welfare and that of others; (3) the inclusion of altruistic motives within the scope of a service offered for sale. I shall close (4) with some remarks about the generality of altruism and the factors that restrict its operation.

(1) When a person donates money to his old college, or gives blood, or gets at the end of the line to buy subway tokens, or cleans up a campsite after he has used it, he may explain such behavior by saying that he has benefited or may in the future benefit from similar behavior by others. This has the look of a straight exchange, but it is not: he benefits from like actions by others, but neither those actions nor the benefit are contingent on what he himself is doing now. And if you point out that his likelihood of receiving blood in the future if he should need it is not significantly increased by his giving today, that will rightly be dismissed as irrelevant. He is not under the illusion that he is engaged in a *trade*.

What is the correct account of the motive for such behavior? It is not simple self-interest, nor simple altruism either, for the explanation does refer to benefits received. The person is making a contribution to a practice or institution in the knowledge that it benefits him and is dependent for survival on contributions from people like him. He is not willing to be a free rider because it would be unfair.

Now while the sense of fairness may be in a moral category by itself, having to do with the betrayal of mutual understanding in cooperative arrangements,[1] I believe it is also partly explained as a special case of general altruism. When someone benefits from a practice to which others contribute, he is aware not only of his benefit but of its relation to their prior actions, and to the general prevalence of the practice. He is in a particularly good position to realize how their failure to behave in this way would have affected him, and to be grateful for their participation in the practice. When he finds himself in a position to make a similar contribution, he can understand in terms of his own case how a failure to contribute would affect others, and can apply to himself the resentment or gratitude he would feel if the tables were turned.

This capacity to put oneself in another person's shoes is behind most altruistic behavior. It is because they encourage that capacity and assist the imaginative process that practices of the kind mentioned give rise to such behavior. They give the false appearance of an exchange of services, but really they work by making vivid to each participant what it is like for the others who depend on him. If he is able to refer to his direct experience of dependence on them when the situations are reversed, he will have no difficulty in following the argument: "How would you like it if someone did that to you?" This question, which underlies much of ethics, is not a threat or a suggestion for an exchange, but an appeal to the imagination. It is intended to evoke the judgment that one person's interests can in themselves provide reasons for another to act.[2] It succeeds because in your own case, when you need blood or arrive at a garbage-strewn campsite, you become quickly aware of your view about these matters. And the interchangeability of roles in certain situations facilitates the generalization of the judgment to cover your own behavior. If you yourself have actually benefited or hope to benefit from cooperative behavior of a similar kind by others, it is particularly difficult to resist the force of the generalization.

---

[1] See John Rawls, *A Theory of Justice* (Cambridge: Harvard University Press, 1971), p. 112: "The main idea is that when a number of persons engage in a mutually advantageous cooperative venture according to rules, and thus restrict their liberty in ways necessary to yield advantages for all, those who have submitted to these restrictions have a right to a similar acquiescence on the part of those who have benefited from their submission."

[2] See T. Nagel, *The Possibility of Altruism* (Oxford: Oxford University Press, 1970), Chap. IX, Sec. 2.

(2) Another factor leading to consideration of the interests of others, pointed out by Kenneth Arrow, is the desire to be the *cause* of benefits to others, as opposed to the mere desire *that* they benefit. This is evinced in an act like giving blood, but it belongs to a wider set of phenomena which have great importance. People care about their causal relations to the benefit and harm of others in various ways: Most of them, other things equal, want to benefit others and avoid harming them. They also do not want to benefit from the misery of others, or be harmed as a result of the benefit of others. Naturally they also want to be benefited by others and not harmed, but they are not indifferent among the ways this can happen: they prefer not to benefit from the misery or disadvantage of others (and when they do so benefit, they will tend to disguise the fact from themselves), nor do they want to be harmed for the benefit of others. On the whole, they would rather be injured by a natural mishap than by another person sacrificing them for his advantage.

In short, among the things that matter to a person must be counted not only his own welfare, plus other people's welfare, but also certain causal relations between his own welfare and that of others. A person conceives of himself as hanging in a network of relationships, rather than as an individual atom. And the preference for this conception lends strength to certain kinds of cooperative arrangements from which all participants can derive benefit. In other arrangements, where advantages to some are obtained at the expense of disadvantages to others, the production of those disadvantages must be counted as a cost to the exploiter as well as to the exploited.

This has a systematic bearing on the operation of social institutions of all kinds, and adds to their stability. First, if people are reluctant to become free riders or to cheat their fellow participants, they will tend to abide by the practices of institutions that are generally beneficial, even if deviation would result in a personal gain. This supports stability directly. Secondly, if participants in a practice know that other participants are so motivated, they have less reason to withhold cooperation and trust out of fear that they will be taken advantage of. This removes the second source of instability: apprehension. Finally, even if stability could be gained in other ways, by instituting a sufficiently powerful, public, and omniscient policing authority to punish all deviations from cooperative practices (the analogue of Hobbes's sovereign), the cost would be severe, if it has to be extended to every practice whose stability now relies on the widespread existence of cooperative motives. Therefore the existence of such motives contributes to the efficiency of social and economic practices as well.[3]

---

[3] These points are made more thoroughly by Rawls, *op. cit.*, pp. 497-98. He expresses caution about their application to economics, however; see *ibid.*, p. 492.

(3) One source of doubt that altruism can play a significant role in economic life might be the view that there is a contradiction in the idea of paying someone to be altruistic. Even if this were so, there would still be a role for altruistic motives, but in fact the contradiction disappears upon inspection: altruistic motives can be present as an essential element even in the most fundamental economic exchanges.

Basically, it is an error to assume that what we pay for is always something within the control of the seller. If it *is* entirely in his control, and if he makes it available to us in exchange for money, his motive is gain and not altruism. But in fact, though a person may control the *availability* of something he produces or does in exchange for money, this does not mean that he controls the thing itself. A fashion model, for example, is hired for her beauty, and she controls its availability in order to earn a living. Beyond a certain point, however, she cannot control her beauty, so it would be a mistake to say that she is beautiful for money.

Likewise, we have only limited control over our own motives; yet just as some people may be hired for their pleasant appearance, others may be hired for their benevolent disposition and concern for others. When one hires a doctor, a nurse, or a baby-sitter, one pays them not only to perform certain tasks and exercise certain skills which they can make available or withhold at will: one also pays them to act for certain motives which they cannot control at will. One wants a baby-sitter who likes the children and cares about them, and who will treat them properly *not* just because she has been paid to do so. So one pays her to spend an evening with them, and the sense in which she is being paid to be altruistic or benevolent is not that she chooses to be, in exchange for a fee, but that one would not hire her if she were the sort who wouldn't treat children kindly except for money. In that sense altruism or benevolence can be paid for. It seems likely that some motive broader than strict self-interest is part of what is being paid for when someone is hired to perform almost any service or task—not only those tasks which consist primarily of taking care of people.

(4) Concern for the welfare of others enters into economic life in various ways, often as a vital factor in the efficiency of arrangements from which all the participants benefit. It is important for this reason among others to understand the conditions which evoke such concern, and to see how they can be more widely met.

Roland McKean notes that considerateness is more prevalent in small communities, and this may be partly due to the greater likelihood of direct retaliation for inconsiderateness which they provide. However, another factor may be the heightened reality people have for us if they lead lives like ours and are engaged in similar enterprises. It is easier to put ourselves in their place, and their good and harm become vivid to us. If everyone is at some level susceptible to a general altruism once he properly contemplates the needs of others from their point of view, then it becomes very important to enhance the vividness of their experiences for him, and to facilitate the imaginative shift which will allow him to realize what he would feel and judge in their place. This will help to mobilize the general altruistic capacity, and attach to it particular objects.

Institutions and practices that foster interchangeability of positions, needs, and predicaments should therefore lead to increased cooperation and benevolence, and the greater the population that such institutions connect, the broader will be the application of the benevolence that they foster. We tend to counteract the inconvenience of our altruism by blotting out the reality of other people, when given the chance. The best way to get people to behave as if they were all in the same boat would be to construct a boat large enough to hold them all, but small enough so they could tell they were all in it. What it would be to realize such an ideal in modern social and economic arrangements is not at all clear.

Part 2

The Samaritan's Dilemma[*]

James M. Buchanan

This paper is an essay in prescriptive diagnosis. It represents my attempt to show that many different "social problems" can be analyzed as separate symptoms of the same disease. The diagnosis, as such, may be accepted without agreeing that the disease amounts to much or that, indeed, it is disease at all. Prescription for improvement or cure is suggested only if the disease is acknowledged to be serious. Even if the diagnosis and prescription be accepted, however, prospects for "better social health" may not be bright because, as the analysis demonstrates, the source of difficulty may lie in modern man's own utility function. We may simply be too compassionate for our own well-being or for that of an orderly and productive free society.

I.

Consider a very simple two-by-two payoff matrix confronting two players, A and B. Player A chooses between rows; Player B chooses between columns. The payoffs are utility indicators, and these are arranged in ordinal sequence; there is no need to introduce cardinal utility at this point. As indicated in Figure 1, for Player A the second row dominates the first, in the strict game-theory sense. In a simple game setting, he will choose Row 2 regardless of what Player B

*A preliminary version of this paper was presented in seminars at Harvard, Kentucky, UCLA, West Virginia, and Western Michigan Universities in the spring of 1971, and an early revised version was presented in the Seminar on the Mathematical Theory of Collective Decisions, Hilton Head, South Carolina, in August 1971. The final version was prepared for presentation at the Conference on Altruism and Economic Theory held at Russell Sage Foundation.

does or is predicted to do. Furthermore, and this is important for the main points of this paper, Player A will select Row 2 even if he fails to recognize that he is in a game at all. Row 2 is simply his pragmatic or independent-behavior response to the choice situation that he confronts, whether or not A recognizes that B exists as a choice-making entity who opposes him in a game-like situation.

Note, however, that Player B does not find himself in a comparable position to A. The way that B chooses does depend on A's action, observed or predicted. If A should choose Row 1, B will choose Column 1. But if A chooses Row 2, Player B will always select Column 2. If B knows A's payoff matrix, he will predict that A will choose Row 2. Hence, the "solution" of this simple game would seem to be Cell IV of the matrix. If we look carefully at this outcome, however, we see that Player A is worse off than he would be in Cell III. His payoff is maximized in Cell III, but he cannot, in and of himself, accomplish a shift into Cell III. Nonetheless, since Player B's choices depend strictly on those of A, the latter should be in the driver's seat in one way or the other. Player A surely could, by some appropriate changes in behavior or strategy, insure an outcome in Cell III. To secure this, however, A must first recognize that he is in a game with B. That is to say, he must realize that his own choice behavior does, in fact, influence the choice behavior of B. Secondly, Player A must begin to behave "strategically"; that is, he must make his own choices on the basis of predictions about the effects of these on B's behavior. If A knows precisely what B's utility payoffs are, he can insure that an outcome in Cell III is realized. He can do so by playing the game in terms of the false payoffs that would be indicated by switching his own utility indicators as between Cells II and IV.

		B: 1	B: 2
A	1	I 2, 2	II 1, 1
A	2	III 4, 3	IV 3, 4

Figure 1.

This strategy may be quite difficult for A, however, when we allow for the problems of communication and credibility between the players. Player A cannot simply announce to B what his strategy is and then expect Player B to believe him. We are interested here only in a sequential game, and A's strategy is revealed only through his behavior on particular plays of the game itself. In order to convince B that he is playing strategically, A must actually act as if the false payoffs are real. Only in this way can he establish credibility.

But this raises difficulties for A precisely because of the dominance features of his true payoff matrix. If strategic behavior dictates that he actually act as if the false rather than the true payoffs exist, Player A must suffer utility loss. He must, in order to make the strategy viable, choose Row 1 rather than Row 2 when Player B is observed or predicted to select Column 2. This will "hurt" A. Admittedly, the utility losses may be short-term only, and there may be offsetting long-term utility gains in a sequential game. But once the tradeoff between short-term utility and long-term utility is acknowledged to be present, we must also acknowledge that A's subjective discount rate will determine his behavior. If this rate is sufficiently high, A may choose to behave nonstrategically, even in the full recognition of the game situation that he confronts.

I shall return to this when I introduce examples, but, before this, let us consider a second game, which involves merely the transposition of the payoff numbers for Player A as between Cells I and III. This is illustrated in Figure 2. In this setting, dominance no longer characterizes A's choice; his behavior initially becomes dependent on that of B, either observed or predicted. Here we shall expect to secure either a Cell I or a Cell IV outcome, depending strictly on who gets there first, so to speak. For purposes that will, I hope, become clear later, let us assume that a continuing sequential solution in Cell I is in being. Player A faces no dilemma of the sort discussed earlier. He need not introduce strategic behavior.

Suppose, however, that Player B becomes cognizant of A's utility payoff matrix and that B begins to behave strategically. Suppose that B, independently, shifts to a Column 2 strategy, in the knowledge that A will quickly adopt a Row 2 course of action. B will, of course, suffer in the process, but let us suppose that he willingly takes the short-term utility losses that are required here. Clearly, A will have been placed in a position less desirable than the initial one by B's strategic behavior. Player A will be forced into the Cell IV outcome. In this event, B can be said to have exploited A successfully.

If we look at this situation from A's vantage point, the required strategic offsets to B's behavior are the same as those indicated for the first game discussed. To prevent being exploited by B, Player A must refuse to be influenced by B's shift to Column 2. Once again, A must act as if his utility payoffs as between Cells II and IV are reversed. Once again, however, A may find this difficult to carry out because he must suffer utility losses in the

		B	
		1	2
A	1	I 4, 2	II 1, 1
	2	III 2, 3	IV 3, 4

Figure 2.

process. B's introduction of strategic behavior in this game places A in an acute position of suffering unless he acquiesces in a shift into Cell IV.

II.

I have quite deliberately presented these two very simple two-player interactions without identification or example, although the title of the paper may have already tipped my hand. I have left off labeling the players because I want to forestall, to the maximum extent that is possible, the instant emotional identification that my examples seem to arouse. But I cannot go beyond this point without examples, so I shall now attach specific labels. I shall call the first situation the *active samaritan's dilemma*, and the second situation the *passive samaritan's dilemma*. Let me emphasize, however, that I am attempting to develop a hypothesis that is generalizable to much of the behavior that we observe in the modern world. The samaritan example is used for descriptive clarity, in part because I could think of no better one. You may have suggestions here. The hypothesis does apply to certain aspects of the current policy discussion of welfare reform, but this is only one among many applications, and by no means the most important one.

Stated in the most general terms possible, the hypothesis is that modern man has become incapable of making the choices that are required to prevent his exploitation by predators of his own species, whether the predation be conscious of unconscious. The weakness here may be imbedded in man's utility function. The term "dilemma" seems appropriate because the problem may not be one that reflects irrational behavior on any of the standard interpretations. Origins of the dilemma are, in part, economic, and these are found in the increasing affluence of choice-makers. Analysis here lends substance to the cliché that modern man has "gone soft." His income-wealth position, along with his preference order, allows him to secure options that were previously unavailable. What we may call "strategic courage" may be a markedly inferior economic good, and what we may call " pragmatic compassion" may be markedly superior.

If my general hypothesis is accepted, the direction of reform and improvements lies first in an explicit recognition of the dilemma by those who are caught up in it. Before "play" can even begin, the players must recognize that a game exists. Once this sort of recognition is passed, the players involved must, individually and collectively, accept the possible necessity of acting *strategically* rather than pragmatically. The very meaning of a game implies that the behavior of one player can control, to some extent, the behavior of his opponent. Optimal behavior for one player is dependent on the predicted reciprocal or response behavior on the part of the others in the game. One objective of strategy is precisely that of influencing the behavior of others in such a way as to produce the preferred outcome oı solution. The implied strategy may and normally will violate norms for simple utility maximization in an assumed nongame or state of nature setting.

In the first game discussed, which I have now called the active samaritan's dilemma, strategic behavior may be dictated for the samaritan even if the opposing player does not, himself, recognize the existence of the game, as such. That is to say, the player who is in the role of the potential samaritan may find it desirable to behave strategically even if his opponent, whom I have labeled the potential parasite, behaves pragmatically. In the second game, however, strategic behavior on the part of the potential samaritan may be dictated only when a specific gaming situation is forced upon him by his opponent.

In a very broad sense, the argument suggests the appropriateness of adopting rules for personal choice behavior as opposed to retaining individual flexibility of action. The ethic that is closely related to, if not exactly derivable from, the samaritan's dilemma is one of individual responsibility. Initially, the dilemma is discussed in an individualistic choice setting, but there are important social and group implications that emerge from widespread adherence to the behavioral norms. More significantly, the analysis lends itself readily to extension to situations where separate individual choices are clearly interdependent.

III.

To facilitate specific discussion, let me identify Player A as a "Potential Samaritan" and Player B as a "Potential Parasite." Furthermore, let us suppose that the potential samaritan faces two possible courses of action. He may do nothing vis-à-vis the potential parasite; that is, he may behave noncharitably (Row 1). Alternatively, the potential samaritan may behave charitably, and, for purposes of discussion here, let us suppose that this involves the transfer of $30 per month to the potential parasite (Row 2). To the other person in the interaction, there are also two courses of action open. He may work (Column 1), in which case we may assume he earns an income, say, one-fourth as large as that earned by the more capable samaritan (or more talented or more lucky). Or, the potential parasite may refuse work (Column 2).

As indicated earlier in the discussion of the nonidentified game, an outcome in Cell IV might be predicted to emerge as the continuing solution of the sequential game unless the samaritan recognizes the strategic prospects open to him and begins to behave accordingly. But this may be difficult for him. Vague threats or promises to cut off his charity in the absence of work on the part of the recipient parasite will remain empty unless there is demonstrated willingness to carry out such threats. But to carry these out, the samaritan will, in actuality, suffer disutility which may be severe. He may find himself seriously injured by the necessity of watching the parasite starve himself while refusing work. Furthermore, even if the parasite works, the samaritan suffers by his own inability to provide charity. The samaritan's task becomes more difficult to the extent that the parasite also recognizes the game situation and himself responds strategically. If the samaritan's strategic plan is to be at all effective, which requires first of all that credibility be established, he must accept the prospect of personal injury.

A family example may be helpful. A mother may find it too painful to spank a misbehaving child ("This hurts me more than it does you"). Yet spanking may be necessary to instill in the child the fear of punishment that will inhibit future misbehavior. If the temporal interdependence of choice is fully recognized, adjustments in behavior may, of course, be noted. A samaritan's payoff matrix that incorporates present values may not look like that shown in Figure 1. Unfortunately, however, the samaritan's dilemma cannot be resolved fully by appeal to a temporal extension of the rationality postulate. Failure of the samaritan's telescopic faculty may explain much of what we seem to observe, and a correction in this faculty may be important. But such a correction, in itself, cannot remove the dilemma in all cases. Even when she fully discounts the effects of her current action on future choice settings, the mother may still find it too painful to spank the misbehaving child. Behavior that will influence the potential parasite to act in preferred ways must involve short-term utility losses to the samaritan. And if his subjective discount rate is high, present-value payoffs may still indicate that the charitable or acquiescent course of action is the dominating one.

Is there any objective sense in which we may say that the samaritan's discount rate is "too high"? This rate is purely subjective and it is derived solely from the person's intertemporal utility function. It seems improper to label any rate as "too high" without resort to some externally based "social welfare function."

We might, for example, say that a person's portfolio adjustment reflects irrationality if he is observed to be borrowing at, say, 10 percent, while simultaneously lending at 5 percent, transaction costs neglected. Rational behavior implies that marginal rates of return on all alternatives be equalized. It is not clear, however, just how a discount rate appropriate for portfolio adjustment might be brought into equality with that which is implicit in a person's intertemporal behavioral tradeoffs, nor is it self-evident that a rationality postulate implies such equalization. Will the mother vary the severity of child discipline as the real rate of return of investment varies? If she does not, the hypothesis of equalization is refuted. This would, in turn, allow for the possibility that observed behavior of persons in samaritan-like settings reflects discount rates greatly in excess of those to which these same persons adjust their portfolios. Unfortunately, there seems to be no direct means to corroborate or to refute this proposition.

When the illusory nature of the short-term utility losses dictated by strategic behavior is fully recognized, the rationality of applying almost any positive discount rate may be questioned. For the samaritan, utility losses are directly related to the potential parasite's disbelief in his strategic plan. To the extent that the parasite believes that the samaritan has, in fact, adopted a strategic behavioral plan and that he will, in fact, abide by this plan once adopted, there need be *no* utility loss to the samaritan at all. The situation is one where the samaritan must convince the potential parasite of his willingness to suffer utility loss in order to insure that the expected value of this loss be effectively minimized.

An understanding of the dilemma confronted by those whom I have called "active samaritans" points directly toward means through which credibility can be increased and/or utility loss reduced. In the setting described, there should be genuine advantages to be gained by the samaritan from locking himself into a strategic behavior pattern in advance of any observed response on the part of his cohort. A Schelling-type advance commitment may be central to the more sophisticated rationality that is dictated here.[1] This may be accomplished in several ways. The samaritan can, in the first place, delegate the power of decision in particular choice situations to an agent, one who is instructed to act in

[1] *Cf.* Thomas C. Schelling, *The Strategy of Conflict* (Cambridge: Harvard University Press, 1960). Also, see his later paper, "Game Theory and the Study of Ethical Systems," *Journal of Conflict Resolution*, XII (March 1968), pp. 34-44. This paper raises somewhat indirectly the central issues discussed here. See in particular p. 40.

accordance with the strategic norms that are selected in advance. The agency device serves two purposes simultaneously. The potential parasite is more likely to believe that the agent will behave in accordance with instructions. Secondly, by delegating the action to the agent, the samaritan need not subject himself to the anguish of situational response which may account for a large share of the anticipated utility loss.

We may return to our family example. The mother may delegate child-spanking to the nanny, with definite and clear instructions for spanking upon specific instances of misbehavior. This delegation increases the child's awareness of the consequences of misbehavior. At the same time, it removes from the mother the actual suffering which personal infliction of punishment might involve. The nonspanking, misbehaving option (Cell IV) is effectively eliminated from the mother's choice set as well as the child's.

In general terms, the analysis points toward the choice of utility-maximizing rules for personal behavior as opposed to the retention of single-period or single-situation choice options. Having once adopted a rule, the samaritan *should not* be responsive to the particulars of situations that might arise. He should not act pragmatically and on a case-by-case basis. The argument specifically confutes the rationality of situational ethics in samaritan-like settings.

Practical examples are readily available. Standards for determining welfare eligibility, either for governmental or private programs, should not be left to the discretion of social workers who get personally involved with potential recipients. This institutional arrangement would force social workers into an acutely painful form of the dilemma discussed. University administrators should not enter into direct dialogues with "concerned" students and faculty members. By so doing, the administrators invite difficulties which might be avoided by detached adherence to preselected rules.

IV.

Much of the analysis can be extended directly to the problem confronted by "passive samaritans," the second game discussed. In the case with the active samaritan, pragmatic or nonstrategic behavior by both parties produces results that are not desired by the samaritan. He must first recognize the game that he plays and then behave strategically. In contrast with this, the passive samaritan finds himself in an optimally preferred position so long as *both* players continue to behave nonstrategically. In the illustrative matrix of Figure 2, the only change from Figure 1 is the transposition of the samaritan's utility payoff indicators between Cell I and Cell III.

So long as the potential parasite fails to recognize the game setting, he will view Column 1 as his only alternative. The outcome in Cell I will be stable over a sequence of choices. The dilemma of the passive samaritan emerges only when the potential parasite wakes up to his strategic prospects while the samaritan is left sleeping at the switch. If the parasite begins to adopt a Column 2 course of action, the samaritan who responds pragmatically will modify his own behavior to avoid the threatened utility loss of Cell II. As a result, the outcome will settle in Cell IV. Once in this situation, the passive samaritan's position becomes fully analogous to that confronting the active samaritan previously discussed. He must recognize that he is in the game, and he must consider behaving strategically rather than reactively. The analysis points similarly toward the advance selection of rules for behavior, rules that are chosen independently and in advance of particular choice situations.

Real world examples of this model are perhaps even more familiar than the first one, both in international relations and in domestic affairs. Ecuador and Peru seize tuna boats on the presumption that the United States will not itself respond strategically. North Korea captures the *Pueblo.* Terrorists kidnap diplomats in South American countries. Militant students throw Molotov cocktails and burn buildings. Prisoners go on hunger strikes.

V.

In a strict sense the analysis to this point has been limited to interactions between two players with an anticipated sequence of choices. However, as the several examples possibly suggest, the problem discussed has much wider applicability. To the extent that comparable choice settings are faced by different players and to the extent that behavior is interdependent, the implications can be readily extended.

Consider, first, a setting where a samaritan is confronted with only one choice vis-à-vis a single opponent. Simple utility maximization will be indicated only if a comparable choice with some other opponent is not anticipated, or, if such is anticipated, there are no behavioral interdependencies. On the other hand, if the samaritan expects to confront a whole set of possible parasites, one at a time, and if he predicts that his own choice behavior in confronting any one will influence the behavior of others, the motivation for considering the prospects for strategic behavior is as strong or stronger than in the simpler sequential choices with a single opponent. Most instructors are familiar with instances in which modification of the grade of a single complaining student offers the short-run utility-maximizing course of action. Experienced instructors will recognize, however, that this behavior will increase the number of student complaints generally, and that long-run utility maximization may require rigid adherence to some sort of no-grade-change rule.

So long as the interdependence anticipated is that among the treatment of different cohorts of the single persons in a samaritan-like setting, we may remain within an individualistic decision model. More relevant implications emerge, however, when interdependencies among the behavior patterns of different samaritans are recognized as pervasive. Each samaritan may find himself confronted with the necessity of making a once-and-for-all choice concerning his treatment of a single potential parasite. The uniqueness of this choice insures that there are no direct future-period consequences; simple utility-maximizing behavior dictates that the samaritan take the soft option. If other persons are expected to confront similar choices with respect to other potential parasites, and if the treatment afforded in one setting modifies the expectations of payoff from similar ones, the dilemma becomes a "public" or "social" one rather than "private." In this case, self-interest on the part of an individual samaritan might never imply strategic behavior of the sort discussed. The rules describing such behavior become fully analogous to "public goods" in that the person producing them secures only a small portion (zero in the limit) of the benefits. His action confers external economies on remaining samaritans in the community, on all those who might anticipate being placed in comparable situations.

Airplane hijacking provides a single dramatic example. A single captain is unexpectedly confronted with a choice, and simple utility maximization dictates accession to the demands of the hijacker. Nonetheless, the benefits to the whole community of airline captains (and other members of the community) from a no-surrender course of action may far exceed the more concentrated possible losses. Strategic courage exercised by a single captain or crew member may generate spillover benefits to all others who might face hijacking threats. This will occur if the predictions of potential hijackers are modified and if their behavior is adjusted accordingly. This direction of effect can be denied only if all elements of rationality are assumed absent in potential hijackers' choices.

VI.

Avoidance of the samaritan's dilemma in its "public" form can be secured by voluntary adherence to individual rules of conduct or by explicit cooperative action to impose such rules. Voluntary acceptance of what we may call "responsible" standards requires that acting parties behave in ways different from those indicated by direct and apparent self-interest. Some pressure toward following such rules will exist if persons fully recognize the interdependence among behavior patterns, that is, if they acknowledge the generalized game setting in which they find themselves. An individual ethic of responsibility is akin to the Kantian generalization principle, although here it is necessarily limited to the group of potential samaritans in the community.

Individual adherence to such an ethic has in no way disappeared from the modern scene. Its widely observed appearance may, however, be explained as an anachronistic carryover from earlier periods rather than as a reflection of voluntarily chosen current commitment. At least two influences have been at work to undermine motivations for responsible behavior in the sense defined here. An individual's motivation for behaving so as to influence the behavior of others in the direction of generating preferred outcomes for the all-inclusive community varies inversely with the size of the group.[2] The expected influence of any one person's behavior on that of others diminishes sharply as numbers are increased. Beyond some critical size limit, the individual who finds himself in a samaritan-like setting must rationally treat the behavior of others, parasites and samaritans alike, as beyond his power of influence. When this point is reached, the pattern of behavior in others is accepted as a parameter for his own choice; others' actions become a part of the "state of nature" that the individual confronts. The game setting disappears in his subjective calculus, and there are no rationally derived reasons for behaving with the strategic courage that the community may require.

The effective size of community has become larger over time, and this size factor has been reinforced by a complementary influence. Western societies have been increasingly "democratized" in the sense that a larger and larger proportion of the potential membership has been effectively enfranchised in the formation of the social environment. The power of an "establishment," a possibly small and well-defined group of "leaders" to set patterns of behavior that might then serve as norms for others has been reduced, often dramatically. A familiar descriptive cliché classifies the modern age as one without heroes. Without heroes to emulate, each man "does his own thing."

VII.

The quasi-revolutionary shift in modern behavioral standards that widespread adherence to the responsibility ethic would represent does not seem likely to occur. Indeed all signs point in the opposing direction, and we shall probably witness a continuing erosion in strategic courage at all levels of decision.[3] There may be no escape from the generalized samaritan's dilemma, in its public form, except through the collective adoption and enforcement of rules that will govern individual situational responses. As they are applied, such rules must be coercive, and they must act to limit individual freedom of action. This need not, however, imply that individuals may not freely agree to their adoption

---

[2] See James M. Buchanan, "Ethical Rules, Expected Values, and Large Numbers," *Ethics*, LXXVI (October 1965), pp. 1-13. See also Mancur Olson, *The Logic of Collective Action* (Cambridge: Harvard University Press, 1965).

[3] Implicit in this whole analysis is my own attitude that "improvement" lies in reversing the direction of change, in escaping, wholly or partially, from the samaritan's dilemma. This value judgment may, of course, be rejected. Even if the analysis is fully accepted, and the vulnerability to exploitation acknowledged, the benefits from behavior that reflects increased "compassion" generally may be judged larger than the costs that would be involved in any attempt to encourage more discrimination in personal choices.

at some prechoice, or constitutional stage of deliberation. Indeed, if the public form of the dilemma is a genuine one, it will be in the potential interest of most members of the community to adopt some such rules.[4] The implied limitations on individual freedom of response which such rules must embody are no different, conceptually, from those limitations that are embodied in the necessity to pay taxes for the financing of jointly consumed public goods and services.

If the collectivity acts to impose uniform behavioral rules on all potential samaritans, and if these rules are observed to be enforced, the response patterns of potential parasites will be modified. As a result, the whole community of potential samaritans enjoys the benefits. Examples may be found in university administration or in airplane hijacking. Separate university administrators in, say, a statewide or nationwide system may welcome the imposition of uniform rules for dealing with militant students, rules which effectively bind their own choice-making under pressure. Similarly, separate airline companies may welcome the imposition of governmental regulations regarding countermeasures against potential hijackers, despite the fact that no company would find it profitable to introduce such measures independently.

It should be evident both from the analysis and from the examples that the samaritan's dilemma as it appears often involves a mixture of its several forms. There may be an expected sequence of choices with the same potential parasite such that the samaritan is placed in a dilemma of the sort discussed in Section I. At the same time, however, the samaritan may expect to confront a series of decisions with respect to different potential parasites. Furthermore, he may also recognize that some effects of his own behavior will impose potential costs or benefits on other potential samaritans. Once again, the university provides a good example. Administrative officials, faced with a single disruptive group, know that they must make decisions over a sequence of events. To the extent that they expect to be confronted by the same group, they are, in the personal or private version of the dilemma, discussed in Section I. They may recognize, however, that their own behavior with respect to the single group will also affect the behavior of other groups which they may confront in subsequent periods. Finally, who can doubt but that the choice behavior of administrators on one campus exerts significant effects on disruptive activity on other campuses?

Because the dilemma appears mixed in several forms there are interdependencies in corrective adjustments. The adoption of individual rules for behavior aimed at removing the personal dilemma does much toward resolving the group or social dilemma that may exist simultaneously. Strategic utility maximization may reduce the necessity of reliance on an explicit ethic of responsibility.

---

[4] For a general discussion of the distinction between the constitutional stage and the operational stage of choice-making, see James M. Buchanan and Gordon Tullock, *The Calculus of Consent* (Ann Arbor: University of Michigan Press, 1962).

Conversely, general acceptance of this ethic makes personal calculations of optimal strategies less necessary, and resort to collective action less important. On the other hand, collective selection and enforcement of uniform codes of conduct reduces the pressure on the individual to select either an economically or an ethically optimal course of action. The dilemma is most pervasive in a situation where individuals do not maximize utility in the strategic sense, where they do not adhere to an ethic of responsibility, and where no collective action is taken toward laying down jointly preferred codes of conduct. Perhaps this describes modern society all too well.

VIII.

Increasing economic affluence is only one among many explanations for the pervasive importance of the phenomenon that I have called the samaritan's dilemma in twentieth century Western society. As incomes have increased, and as the stock of wealth has grown, men have increasingly found themselves able to take the "soft options."[5] Mothers can afford candy to bribe misbehaving children. Welfare rolls can be increased dramatically without national bankruptcy.

The economic explanation may, however, be dwarfed in significance by other historical developments. The influence of organized religion in earlier periods was exerted in the direction of inhibiting personal behavior that was aimed solely at gratification of instant desires, whether these be charitable or selfish. There is content in the "Puritan ethic," and when this is interpreted favorably, it resembles the ethic of responsibility suggested above. As it was institutionally represented, Christian "love" was "love of God" which was effectively translated into a set of precepts for personal behavior.

It is difficult to be optimistic about the prospects for escaping the samaritan's dilemma. There are few if any signs of a return to the behavioral standards of a half-century past. If anything, short-term utility maximization seems on the ascendancy, and even for the individual, long-term utility maximization seems less characteristic of behavior now than in periods that are

---

[5] In earlier and impoverished epochs, survival may have depended on man's willingness and ability to make strategic choices, and evolutionary selectivity may have instilled behavioral characteristics in man that remain irrational in modern environments. As these characteristics disappear from observed behavior patterns, the necessity for conscious recognition of the dilemma increases.

Benjamin Klein has suggested that the sheer animal instinct for protecting property, which has been emphasized by Robert Ardrey and others, may serve an important "social" purpose in inhibiting courses of action that seem to be preferred in a short-term or nonstrategic context.

In more general terms, Schelling discusses at some length the role of instincts in imposing constraints on behavior. *Cf.* "Game Theory and the Study of Ethical Systems," *op. cit.*, pp. 36-39.

past.[6] Individuals who find themselves in positions comparable to that of the samaritans in the models of this paper seem unwilling to behave strategically or to adopt rules of conduct that will achieve the differing outcomes through time.

There is little to be observed in the behavior of collective units to counter the individualistic patterns of selecting the soft options. There might be grounds for guarded optimism if we should observe collectivities laying down rules for personal behavior in those situations where individual norms have not appeared. What we see is just the opposite. Collectivities, in their separate arms and instruments, are expanding the soft options. They seem everywhere to be loosening up on prescribed rules for behavior and, in this way, they encourage similar reactions on the part of individuals. When the conventional wisdom of government is exemplified in the slogan "kindness for the criminals," we can hardly expect individuals to become enforcers. The correspondence between the individual and collective responses might be predicted. Governments do little more than reflect the desires of their citizens, and the taking of soft options on the part of individuals should be expected to be accompanied by an easing up on legal restrictions on individual behavior.

The phenomenon analyzed here takes on its most frightening aspects in its most general biological setting. A species that increasingly behaves, individually and collectively, so as to encourage more and more of its own members to live parasitically off and/or deliberately exploit its producers faces self-destruction at some point in time. Unless an equilibrium is established which imposes self-selected limits on samaritan-like behavior, the rush toward species destruction may accelerate rather than diminish. The limit that is defined by existing utility functions may lie beyond that which is required for maintaining viable social order. By some leap of biological faith, we may believe that behavior will be constrained to insure species survival. I can conceive of no such leap of faith which might allow us to predict that our innate behavior patterns must preserve a social-civil order that is at all similar to that which we have historically experienced.

I conclude with a paradox. If you find yourself in basic agreement with me, my hypothesis is at least partially falsified. Agreement would signal that you are fully aware of the dilemma that I have discussed, and your awareness could be taken as reflective of general awareness in the academic community.

On the other hand, and I suspect this is the case, if you find yourself in basic disagreement with me, my hypothesis is at least partially corroborated. Disagreement would signal your failure to recognize the dilemma, along with

[6] Interestingly in this connection, it is precisely short-term utility maximization, as opposed to long-term utility maximization, that E. C. Banfield singles out to be characteristic of the lower classes. In this context, and if my predictions are correct, what we are witnessing is a transition into lower class habits on a massive and pervasive scale. *Cf.* E. C. Banfield, *The Unheavenly City* (Boston: Little Brown, 1970).

your implied willingness to submit to further exploitation than we yet have witnessed.

*The Indeterminacy of Game-Equilibrium Growth in the Absence of an Ethic**

Edmund S. Phelps

A recent paper by Robert Pollack and myself[1] essays the optimal saving problem when, by reason of (limited) selfishness on the part of each generation, future generations will not consume and save the capital they inherit in the proportions that the current generation would like them to do. This situation poses for each generation a "second best" problem or "sub-optimization" problem—neither term is wholly appropriate—whose solution depends upon the assumptions made by each generation about future saving behavior.

If each generation expects future generations to behave as it would behave in their situations, then there may result a kind of game-equilibrium growth path which is self-warranting: Every generation acts in such a way as to validate earlier assumptions as to how it will act and, given these assumptions, no generation acting alone can increase its estimated overall utility—despite the fact that cooperative action among the generations, were it enforceable, could produce an improvement in every generation's utility.

That paper postulated a discrete-time production process in which the

*This paper is a revision of a discussion paper dated May 1968 and presented at the Econometric Society Congress in September 1970. This version corrects the admissible range of the asymptotic capital-labor ratio and it elaborates the potential role of an ethic in rescuing the determinacy of the growth path.

In the minds of some, my dynamic-programming analysis makes excessive demands on intuition. I am grateful therefore to Dr. Pauwels for recasting the argument in terms of differential game analysis. See his Mathematical Note which follows this chapter.

[1] E. S. Phelps and R. A. Pollak, "On Second-Best National Saving and Game-Equilibrium Growth," *Review of Economic Studies* 35 (April 1968).

output-capital ratio is constant and labor is inessential and unproductive. The population is constant in size and is completely replaced each period.

The present contribution postulates an exponentially growing population and continuous-time production under possibly variable proportions and constant returns to scale along the lines of the one-good Solow-Swan neoclassical growth model.[2] Every generation is born directly into the labor force and dies with its boots on. There is no overlap—no births intervene during a generation's tenure. I shall study only the limiting case in which every generation's tenure shrinks to zero. In any finite length of time, then, infinitely many generations hold sway in a continuum, one after the other, each for an infinitely short time. It is hoped that there is heuristic value in such a model.

I. BOUNDED SUSTAINABLE CONSUMPTION PER CAPITA AND UNBOUNDED RATE OF UTILITY

The production-and-growth equations are

$$\dot{L}/L = \gamma = \text{constant} > 0 \tag{1}$$

$$f(k) = F(k, 1) = F(K, L)/L, \qquad k = K/L \tag{2}$$

with the following specifications in the first model:

$$f(0) \geqslant 0, \ f'(k) > 0, \ f''(k) < 0, \ f'(0) > \gamma, \ f'(\infty) = 0 \tag{2a}$$

$$\dot{k} = f(k) - \gamma k - c = g(k) - c, \tag{3}$$

with

$$g(0) \geqslant 0, \ g'(0) > 0, \ g''(k) < 0, \ g'(\hat{k}) = 0, \ 0 < \hat{k} < \infty. \tag{3a}$$

Here K and L denote capital and labor (or population), respectively, k the capital-labor ratio and c the rate of consumption per head (or per unit of labor). The lower quadrant of Figure 1 graphs the g function. Note that g is bounded and, further, a unique global maximum occurs at the Golden Rule capital intensity, $\hat{k}$.[3]

Now to the matter of saving behavior. The objective is to find and characterize some "policy function" or "consumption function," $c(k)$, that is

---

[2] R. M. Solow, "A Contribution to the Theory of Economic Growth," *Quarterly Journal of Economics* 70 (February 1956), and T. W. Swan, "Economic Growth and Capital Accumulation," *Economic Record* 32 (November 1956).

[3] For an exposition of the Golden Rule concept, see for example E. S. Phelps, *Golden Rules of Economic Growth* (New York: Norton, 1966), Chapter 1.

consistent with utility maximization by the generations and possesses the game-equilibrium property.

Imagine first some generation, born at time b, with lifetime Δ. Let it consider the contemporaneous per capita consumptions of the survivors and newborn during the interval Δ to be equivalent in worth to its own per capita consumption. Consumption standards are equalized among people at any given moment of time. Let the generation have complete control of national saving until $b+\Delta$ at which it bequeaths $k(b+\Delta)$ per capita. The latter will have a utility for the generation of $V_b(k(b+\Delta))$. Let $u(c(t))$ denote the instantaneous "rate of utility," untainted by time preference, produced by consumption at time t, $b \leqslant t \leqslant b+\Delta$. The generation's "lifetime utility," $U_b(\Delta)$, is

$$U_b\,(\Delta) = V_b(k(b+\Delta)) + \int_b^{b+\Delta} u(c(t))dt \tag{4}$$

where it will be specified in this first model that

$$u'(c) > 0, \quad u''(c) < 0, \quad u(\infty) = \infty, \quad u(0) = -\infty. \tag{4a}$$

See Figure 1 for a picture of the u function.

For any provisional size of per capita bequest, x, the generation must, for a utility maximum,

$$\text{maximize} \qquad \int_b^{b+\Delta} u(c(t)dt$$

$$\begin{aligned} \text{subject to} \qquad & k(b) = k_b > 0 \\ & k(b+\Delta) = \mathrm{x} \geqslant 0 \\ & \dot{k} = g(k) - c \end{aligned} \tag{5}$$

The solution is of the form

$$c(t) = h(t; k_b, \mathrm{x}), \qquad b \leqslant t \leqslant b+\Delta \tag{6}$$

The utility-maximizing bequest must thus satisfy

$$\frac{\partial U_b\,(\Delta)}{\partial k(b+\Delta)} = V_b'\,[k(b+\Delta)] + \int_b^{b+\Delta} u'\left\{h\,[t; k_b, k(b+\Delta]\right\} \frac{\partial h}{\partial k(b+\Delta)} \cdot dt \tag{7}$$

Letting $\bar{c}$ denote the average per capita consumption rate over the interval Δ, we can, for small Δ, approximate the latter integral by

$$\Delta u'\ (\bar{c}) \frac{\partial \bar{c}}{\partial k(b+\Delta)} \tag{8}$$

which, using the further approximation,

$$k(b + \Delta) = k_b + \Delta\,[g(k_b) - \bar{c}]$$

can then be written

$$\frac{\Delta u'(\bar{c})}{\partial[k_b + \Delta(g(k_b) - \bar{c})]\,/\,\partial\bar{c}} = -\,u'\,(\bar{c})\,\frac{\Delta}{\Delta} = -\,u'\,(\bar{c})\,. \tag{9}$$

Hence utility maximization equates the marginal utility of average consumption to the marginal utility of the bequest.

In the limit, as $\Delta \to 0$ and overlapping vanishes, utility maximization by any generation requires consuming so as to equate the marginal utility of consumption to the marginal utility of the bequest,

$$u'(c(b)) \;=\; V_b'(k_b), \tag{10}$$

the latter being completely predetermined in the limiting case.

The marginal utility for the present generation of the capital it bequeaths depends upon the value the present generation assigns to future consumptions and the disposition of capital for consumption by future generations.

Let each generation make the assumption that all generations infinitely far into the future will consume according to some unknown, to-be-calculated, stationary and continuous consumption function, $c(k)$; such a function derives from *their* utility maximization and their making the like assumption. Further, let it be assumed by all that $c(k)$ makes $k(t)$ approach some constant, $\tilde{k} > 0$, independent of initial k_0. This means that $c(k)$ intersects $g(k)$ from below at one and only one point, as illustrated in the lower quadrant of Figure 1. This convergence of $k(t)$ to $\tilde{k}$ might, for example, arise from a constant saving-income ratio, equivalently $c(k) = \alpha f(k)$, $0 < \alpha < 1$.

Formally, then,

$$\begin{aligned} & c(k) \begin{bmatrix} \leq \\ = \\ > \end{bmatrix} g(k) \text{ according as } k \begin{bmatrix} \leq \\ = \\ > \end{bmatrix} \tilde{k}, \qquad 0 < \tilde{k} = \text{constant}, \\ & \tilde{c} = c(\tilde{k}) \;=\; g(\tilde{k}) \;>\; 0, \\ & c'(\tilde{k}) \;\geqslant\; g'\,(\tilde{k}). \end{aligned} \tag{11}$$

I postulate that every generation exhibits symmetrical or identical preferences for its own consumption vis-à-vis the consumption of generations subsequent to it. Specifically, each generation's preferences with respect to the *per capita* consumptions of generations *following it* are describable by application of the "overtaking principle" and an identical Ramsey-like utility functional lacking "pure time preference" or "myopia."[4] The overtaking principle states that one path is better than another if its functional at some point in time exceeds the functional corresponding to the other and does so continuously thereafter. This principle can be implemented by use of a functional whose integrand is the excess of the utility rate over that steady instantaneous rate of utility to which the utility rate is asymptotic if $k(t)$ is asymptotic to $\tilde{k}$, namely $u(g(\tilde{k}))$ or $u(\tilde{c})$.

But there is this departure from the Ramsey model with population growth: Though generations are "alike," they disagree about the best growth path—each one tending to like best the path that gives *it* higher consumption. Each generation is selfish to the extent that, for equal per capita consumption rates, it assigns itself a marginal utility that is $1/\delta$ times the marginal utility it assigns to any future generation's per capita consumption, $\delta < 1$. Each generation tilts the marginal rate of substitution in its favor by a constant amount, yet refuses to discriminate among future generations on considerations of their relative proximities *per se.* (Making per capita consumption the desideratum already fails to attach weight to the fact that swapping a given amount of capital from sparsely to densely populated generations will increase the mean living standards in the two generations combined if only $f'(k) > 0$.)

The lifetime utility of our Δ-lived generation born at b can therefore be written

$$U_b(\Delta) = \int_b^{b+\Delta} [u(c(t)) - u(\tilde{c})]\,dt + V_b(k(b+\Delta)) \tag{12}$$

where, with $\delta < 1$,

$$\begin{aligned} V_b(k(b+\Delta)) &= \delta \int_{b+\Delta}^{\infty} [u(c(t)) - u(\tilde{c})]\,dt \\ &= \delta \int_{b+\Delta}^{\infty} [u(c(k(t))) - u(\tilde{c})]\,dt, \end{aligned}$$

The marginal utility of bequeathed capital, $V_b'(k(b+\Delta))$, resides in the implication that additional capital will advance the time schedule with which $k(t)$ approaches the unknown asymptote and hence the time schedule of the advance of $u(c(t))$ toward $u(\tilde{c})$. In formal terms, noting that the function $c(k)$ makes k a derived function of time,

$$\frac{dV_b\,(k(b+\Delta))}{dk(b+\Delta)} = \frac{dV_b\,(k(b+\Delta))}{d(b+\Delta)} \Bigg/ \frac{dk(b+\Delta)}{d(b+\Delta)} \tag{13}$$

[4] For a simple exposition of Ramsey, with and without population growth, and of the overtaking principle, see E.S. Phelps, *op. cit.*, Ch. 5. See also F.P. Ramsey, "A Mathematical Theory of Saving," *Economic Journal* 38 (December 1928).

where the denominator is the rate at which capital is accumulating by virtue of the $c(k)$ policy of the immediately following generations. Upon calculating the derivative in the numerator we obtain

$$V_b'(k(b+\Delta)) = -\frac{\delta[u(c(k(b+\Delta))) - u(\tilde{c})]}{\dot{k}(b+\Delta)} \tag{14}$$

The trick here is that used by Keynes to show Ramsey how his no-discount formula for the optimal saving rate could be obtained without the calculus. Suppose "tomorrow's" generation would save one unit if it inherits the amount today's generation contemplates bequeathing to it. Then if today's generation adds one unit to its bequest, tomorrow's generation will be in the position that the next day's would otherwise have been in. Since it will then save precisely as the next day's would otherwise have, the next day's generation will similarly find itself as its successor would have. *Und so weiter*. Consequently, the utility shortfall that would otherwise have occurred tomorrow, $\delta[u(\tilde{c}) - u(c)]$, is forever eliminated and the rest of the future is unchanged. If there were positive time preference, the advancement of the consumption schedule would have additional effects upon the utility of bequeathed capital.

In the limit, as $\Delta \to 0$, the marginal utility of consumption is equated to the limiting marginal utility of bequeathed capital:

$$u'(c(b)) = -\frac{\delta[u(c(k(b))) - u(\tilde{c})]}{\dot{k}(b)} \tag{15}$$

But note that since $k(t)$ must be continuous and $c(k)$ is assumed by every generation to be continuous, our generation's calculated per capita consumption rate, $c(b)$, must equal $c(k(b))$, the per capita consumption rate immediately in the future or else our generation will realize it has assumed the wrong value of $c(k(b))$. For the next moment's generation, having essentially the same per capita capital and symmetrical preferences, will calculate essentially the same per capita consumption rate. This means that the present generation must assume a value of $c(k(b))$ which causes it to calculate an "optimal" consumption rate equal to it. Of course, there is a corresponding requirement on other generations. The game-equilibrium consumption rate at any time t, $c(t)$, therefore satisfies

$$u'(c(t)) = -\frac{\delta[u(c(t)) - u(\tilde{c})]}{g(k(t)) - c(t)} \tag{16}$$

This differs from the Ramsey-Keynes relation with respect to δ, which is unitary in Ramsey's model, and with respect to $\tilde{c}$ (about which more will be said).

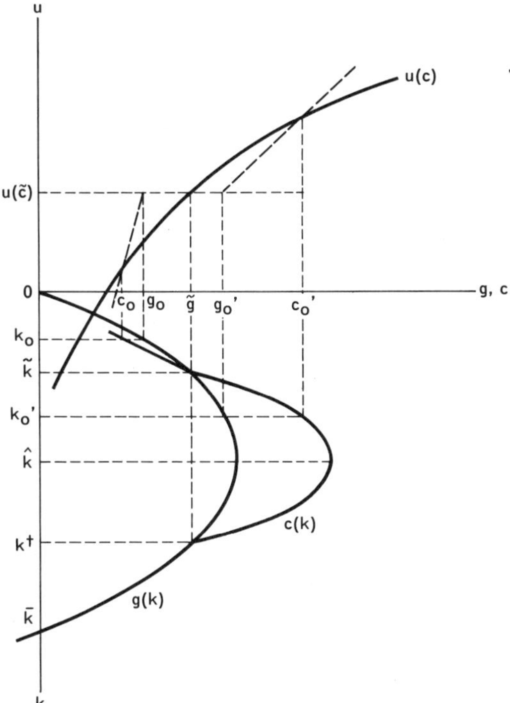

Figure 1. Unbounded Instantaneous Utility Rate and Bounded Sustainable Consumption Per Head.

Figure 1 shows a geometric method, due to Ramsey, of calculating $c(t)$ and displaying its dependence upon $k(t)$. Consider the initial per capita endowment k_0. The corresponding $g_0 = g(k_0)$ is smaller than $g(\tilde{k})$, the asymptotic consumption rate. To find the corresponding game-equilibrium consumption rate, c_0, we construct a straight line—the lefthand sloping dashed line in Figure 1—from the point $(\tilde{u}, g_0)$ which intersects $u(c)$ with a slope $1/\delta$ times the slope (which is marginal utility) of the $u(c)$ function at that point. There must exist just one such point if $u'(0)$ is infinite. Its abscissa, c_0, must be less than g_0, whence k will be increasing.

With alternative endowment k_0', the corresponding $g_0' = g(k_0')$ exceeds $g(\tilde{k})$. A symmetrical construction of a line cutting through $u(c)$ with a slope $1/\delta$ times the slope of u determines a corresponding c_0' that is greater than k_0' so that k will be decreasing.

The geometry of Figure 1 assures us that, when $k(0) < \tilde{k}$, game-equilibrium c is monotone increasing in $g(k)$, therefore also in k. But when $k(0) > \tilde{k}$, our geometrical sense warns us that straight lines emanating from the u curve and bearing the right multiple, δ, to the slopes of the curve at their origin could *intersect* one another *below* $u(c)$ on the $u(\tilde{c})$ horizontal. Hence, for $g_0 > g(\tilde{k})$, $c(k)$ need not be monotone and there may exist no single-valued function $c(k)$. This is borne out by calculating from (16) the derivative

$$c'(k) = \frac{u'(c)\ g'(k)}{u'(c)\,(1-\delta) - u''(c)\,[g - c]} \tag{17}$$

The denominator may vanish and change signs any number of times as k is increased over the range in which $g - c > 0$. So a continuous function $c(k)$ apparently need not exist over the whole domain of k.

As k is increased beyond the Golden Rule value, $\hat{k}$, every g value encountered in the climb to $\hat{k}$ is encountered again. Since c depends only on $g(k)$, not upon k itself, $c(k)$ must, in a sense, "double back." In particular, another intersection of the $c(k)$ curve with the $g(k)$ curve must occur at some $k^{\dagger}$ where $g(k^{\dagger}) = g(\tilde{k})$. For $k > k^{\dagger}$, if not for smaller k, any such $c(k)$ function is nonsense, since present saving sufficient to make $\dot{k} = g - c > 0$ there only *reduces* future per capita consumption, plunging society into a headlong rush toward self-destructive altruism at consumptionless $\bar{k}$. At $k < k^{\dagger}$, however, some "gross" per capita saving in the ordinary sense of $f(k) - c > 0$ is not obviously senseless as it will ultimately retard the slip-back of k and the *average* future per capita consumption rate, even if it depresses or slows the rise of per capita consumption for a while.

Assume however that a well-behaved $c(k)$ function exists over some relevant domain. Is there just one such function or many? The question involves the determinateness of the asymptote $\tilde{k}$.

First of all, it is worth establishing that any admissible asymptote $\tilde{k}$ cannot be larger than the Golden Rule $\hat{k}$. Despite the absence of positive pure time preference, no game-equilibrium growth path will drive capital intensity beyond the Golden Rule level.

We know that any "stable" asymptote $\tilde{k}$ must have the property of equality between the marginal utilities of consumption and bequeathed capital as in (10).

We can calculate $V'(\tilde{k})$ directly from the following linearization argument. An extra bequest Δk_0 received at the beginning of "day zero" will produce a vanishing sequence of capital-bequest deviations around $\tilde{k}$ in subsequent "days." A linear approximation of this sequence is the following:[5]

[5] The linear approximation is inadequate in the singular case where the functions $c(k)$ and $g(k)$ are tangent at $\tilde{k}$, as equations (19) and (20) clearly reveal.

$$\Delta k_1 = \Delta k_0 [1 - c'(\bar{k})] \frac{1 + f'(\bar{k})}{1 + \gamma} \tag{18}$$

$$\Delta k_2 = \Delta k_1 [1 - c'(\bar{k})] \frac{1 + f'(\bar{k})}{1 + \gamma}$$

$$= \Delta k_0 \left\{ [1 - c'(\bar{k})] \left[\frac{1 + f'(\bar{k})}{1 + \gamma}\right] \right\}^2$$

$$\vdots$$

$$\Delta k_n = \Delta k_0 \cdot \left\{ [1 - c'(\bar{k})] \left[\frac{1 + f'(\bar{k})}{1 + \gamma}\right] \right\}^n$$

For sufficiently short "days," we make the further approximation

$$[1 - c'(\bar{k})] \frac{1 + f'(\bar{k})}{1 + \gamma} = 1 + f'(\bar{k}) - \gamma - c'(\bar{k}) \tag{19}$$

$$= 1 + g'(\bar{k}) - c'(\bar{k})$$

The sum of the per capita bequest deviations thus exhibits a "multiplier" effect:

$$\sum_{t=0}^{\infty} \Delta k_t = \Delta k_0 \left(\frac{1}{c'(\bar{k}) - g'(\bar{k})}\right) \tag{20}$$

Therefore the sum of the increments in utility from the consumption increments induced by the geometrically declining bequest increments is approximately

$$\delta \sum_{t=0}^{\infty} \Delta u_t = \frac{u'(\bar{c})c'(\bar{k})}{c'(\bar{k}) - g'(\bar{k})} \Delta k_0 \tag{21}$$

Since the departures from $\bar{c}$ and $\bar{k}$ are small for small Δk_0, in the limit, as Δk_0 shrinks to zero and as we move to continuous time, the following result holds exactly:

$$V'(\bar{k}) = \delta \frac{u'(\bar{c})c'(\bar{k})}{c'(\bar{k}) - g'(\bar{k})} \tag{22}$$

Equality of our two marginal utilities therefore entails

$$u'(\bar{c}) = \delta \frac{u'(\bar{c})c'(\bar{k})}{c'(\bar{k}) - g'(\bar{k})} \tag{23}$$

Note that in the Ramsey model, where $\delta = 1$, $g'(\tilde{k})$ is implied to be zero, whence $\tilde{k} = \hat{k}$.

Now $c'(\tilde{k}) - g'(\tilde{k}) \geqslant 0$ for stability. And $u'(c) > 0$ for all c. Therefore $c'(\tilde{k}) \geqslant 0$. At any *stationary* equilibrium capital intensity, consumption is nondecreasing in capital. From (23) we have

$$c'(\tilde{k}) = \frac{g'(\tilde{k})}{1-\delta} \tag{24}$$

It follows that $g'(\tilde{k})$ must also be non-negative, like $c'(\tilde{k})$. Hence $\tilde{k}$, whatever its value or values, must be no larger than the Golden Rule $\hat{k}$ at which $g'(\hat{k}) = 0$.

Note that (24) is consistent with the more general expression for $c'(k)$ in (17) since $g - c = 0$ on any stationary path. One might, one would think, have used (17) directly to obtain (24). However the existence of two independent routes is reassuring; and my derivation of (17) requires that $\dot{k}$ be non-zero.

When $\dot{k} \neq 0$, differentiation of (16) with respect to time yields a kind of Euler equation that is of some interest:

$$\dot{k}\frac{u''(c)c}{u'(c)}\frac{\dot{c}}{c} = -\frac{d\dot{k}}{dt} - \delta\frac{dc}{dt} \tag{25a}$$

$$\dot{k}\left\{\frac{\frac{d}{dt}u'(c)}{u'(c)}\right\} = -[f'(k) - \gamma - \frac{dc}{dk}]\dot{k} - \delta\frac{dc}{dt} \tag{25b}$$

$$-\frac{\frac{d}{dt}u'(c)}{u'(c)} = f'(k) - \gamma - (1-\delta)\frac{dc}{dk} \tag{25c}$$

so that marginal utility of consumption may "level off" *before* $f'(k)$ is driven down to γ, unlike the Ramsey case where $\delta = 1$.

The puzzle is that $\tilde{k}$ cannot apparently be made determinate. I am not raising any question of whether any given "solution," a $c(k)$ function, produces just one "stable" $\tilde{k}$.[6] The question is whether there is just one such $c(k)$ function or many.

[6] In fact, the uniqueness of admissible $\tilde{k}$ points at which any continuous $c(k)$ function crosses from below the $g(k)$ function appears to be deducible. Suppose that in addition to one "stable" $\tilde{k}$ there exists at least one other intersection point. Then at least one of these must be an unstable value, $k\dagger$, at which $c(k\dagger) = g(k\dagger)$ and $c'(k\dagger) < g'(k\dagger)$. Equation (17) indicates that, for $c(k)$ continuously differentiable, the limit as $k \to k\dagger$ of $c'(k)$ is $g'(k\dagger)/(1-\delta)$ since $g = c$ in the limit. Therefore $g'(k\dagger) > 0$ is impossible; any unstable intersection point must lie on the falling part of the $g(k)$ function. Consequently, it is impossible that there should exist a pair of stable $\tilde{k}$ values—each one necessarily on the rising part of the $g(k)$ curve—for they would have to bracket a nonexistent unstable $k\dagger$ on the rising part of the $g(k)$ curve.

There seems to be no obstacle to finding *another* $c(k)$ function that is anchored to a different $\tilde{k}$ in the lower quadrant of Figure 1 such that the upper quadrant's constructions and given u function will generate it and thus validate it. The algebra appears to show that *any* assumed $\tilde{k}$, $0 < \tilde{k} \leqslant \hat{k}$, will generate a $c(k)$ function that will intersect the g curve at $\tilde{k}$ with a slope, by virtue of (17), that equals the required slope given by (24). Choose any value of capital intensity smaller than the Golden Rule level, say k°. If $\tilde{c}$ is assigned the value $g(k^{\circ})$, then (17) makes $c(k) = g(k)$ and $dc/dg = 1/(1 - \delta)$ in the limit as $k \rightarrow k^{\circ}$. Hence any value of $k < \hat{k}$ can constitute the $\tilde{k}$ anchor for a $c(k)$ function calculable from u and g.[7]

To obtain a $c(k)$ function at all, therefore, it appears necessary in the present model that each generation assign to its successors the same expectation of $\tilde{k}$ that it expects itself. But such an assignment is apparently arbitrary within limits and there is no reason why any arbitrary expectation should be shared.

"Variable proportions" itself has nothing to do with this conclusion. Even if $g'(k)$ were a positive constant up to $\hat{k}$, more than one $c(k)$ anchored on different $\tilde{k}$ cannot apparently be ruled out. In this case we know simply that $c'(\tilde{k})$ is the same number for every admissible $\tilde{k}$.

If this conclusion of indeterminacy is correct, how does the Phelps-Pollak paper obtain determinateness? In that model, $g(k)$ is unbounded. Utility satiation was postulated in the only case where zero time preference was admissible. This satiation could not be realized in any steady state with finite k; the satiety rate of utility was approached asymptotically. This is a known quantity (in the model) and it played the role of $u(\tilde{c})$ in the new model just discussed. Knowledge of the asymptotic $u(t)$ permits $c(k)$ to be uniquely determined. But how is asymptotic utility saturation deduced? I now examine a continuous-time model more like the Phelps-Pollak model in order that this question of the determinacy of game-equilibrium growth paths can be more broadly understood and the results here can be reconciled with the Phelps-Pollak conclusions.

II. UNBOUNDED SUSTAINABLE CONSUMPTION PER CAPITA AND BOUNDED RATE OF UTILITY

We now modify (3a), specifying that $f'(k)$ is bounded above γ, so that g is monotone increasing and unbounded:

$$g(0) \geqslant 0, \quad g'(k) > 0, \quad g''(k) \leqslant 0, \quad g(\infty) = \infty. \tag{3a}$$

See Figure 2.

[7] As for the admissibility of $\hat{k}$, this is possible with $c'(\hat{k}) = g'(\hat{k}) = 0$. Applying L'Hôpital's rule and (17) we have $dc/dg = c''(k)/g''(k) = 1/(1 - \delta)$.

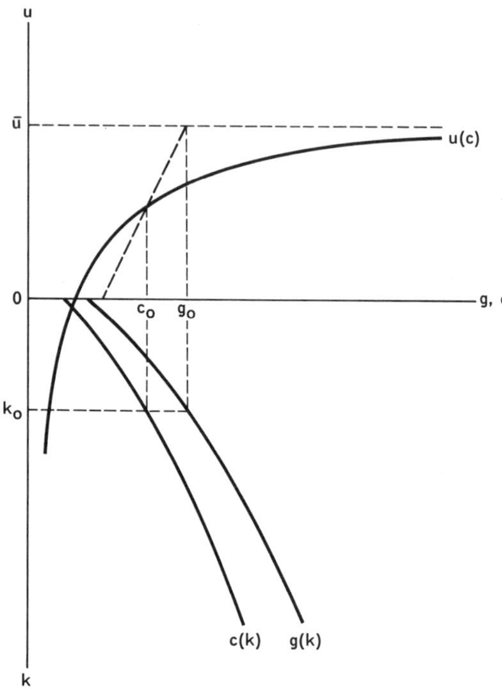

Figure 2. Bounded Instantaneous Utility Rate and Unbounded Sustainable Consumption Per Head.

The instantaneous rate of utility is now bounded, the upper bound, $\bar{u}$, being reached only in the limit as c goes to infinity. This is also illustrated in Figure 2.

$$u(0) = -\infty, \quad u'(c) > 0, \quad u''(c) < 0, \quad u(\infty) = \bar{u} < \infty. \tag{4a'}$$

(This specification entails that the marginal utility of per capita consumption be at least asymptotically elastic with respect to per capita comsumption.)

First, let us postulate that each generation takes it for granted that all future generations will find their optimal game strategy to call for increasing $k(t)$ at a non-vanishing rate. Then the asymptotic rate of utility is the satiety rate, $\bar{u}$. Using the overtaking principle, they will introduce the "subtractor," $\bar{u}$, to compare the respective total utilities of per capita consumption streams that drive c to infinity. A generation living for an instant at time b will calculate the marginal utility of bequeathed capital to be

$$
\begin{aligned}
V_b'(k(b)) &= \delta \frac{\partial}{\partial k(b)} \int_b^\infty [u(c(k(t))) - \bar{u}]\; dt \\
&= \frac{-\delta\,[u(c(k(b))) - \bar{u}]}{\dot{k}(b)}
\end{aligned}
\tag{26}
$$

On this postulate, the postulates of utility maximization and of a continuous $c(k)$ function, we find that the relation

$$
u'(c(t)) = \frac{-\delta\,[u(c(t)) - \bar{u}]}{g(k(t)) - c(t)}
\tag{27}
$$

must hold along the game-equilibrium path. In fact, (27) determines a unique $c(t)$ path and unique $c(k)$ function, with k, $c(k)$ and $g(k)$ all monotonically going to infinity. This solution is illustrated in Figure 2.

The Phelps-Pollak paper utilized the particular class of utility-rate functions of the form

$$
u(c) = \bar{u} - c^{\eta+1}, \qquad \eta < -1
\tag{28}
$$

where

$$
\eta = \frac{u''(c)c}{u'(c)}
$$

is the (negative) elasticity of the marginal utility function, $u'(c)$. Substitution of this function for $u(c)$ in (27) yields

$$
\begin{aligned}
\frac{\dot{k}}{g(k)} &= \frac{\delta}{-\eta - (1 - \delta)} \\
\frac{c(k)}{g(k)} &= \frac{-(\eta + 1)}{-(\eta + 1) + \delta}
\end{aligned}
\tag{29}
$$

In the Ramsey case where $\delta = 1$ —he actually constructed an example using (28) with the further assumptions that $\gamma = 0$ and $f' = r = \text{const.} > 0$ —there is per capita growth by virtue of the essential restriction $\eta < -1$. With $\delta < 1$, growth of capital per head is slower. In either case, there is constancy of a kind of "saving ratio" though the ordinary saving-income ratio will be constant only if $f(k)$ is proportional to $g(k)$.

One can liken the Phelps-Pollak model to the present one if labor is made inessential and constant over time and if $g(k)$ is made proportional to k. Hence the solution of that model made consumption proportional to capital or to "income." It was postulated there that each generation expects future generations to adopt a *common* "saving ratio." Each generation therefore asked: What common future saving ratio would cause it to wish to choose the same saving ratio? The answering saving ratio, shown to be unique, was the game-equilibrium solution in that paper.

The assumption that future generations will follow a linear-homogeneous comsumption policy has some merit, for if future people were assumed so to behave then every present generation would find its optimal consumption function likewise to be linear homogeneous when the utility rate takes the homogeneous form in (28). This was one way of imagining that the present generation could break the Gordian knot of indeterminacy among game-equilibrium paths. The assumption earlier in this section that each generation expects future generations to accumulate capital per head without bound is another way. While the assumed equality of future saving ratios is a commendably natural assumption—and not demonstrably false with the utility function in (28)—it is not logically necessary. Neither is the weaker and equally natural assumption of unbounded capital growth.

It will be indicated now that the expectation of inhomogeneous future consumption behavior can induce actual inhomogeneous consumption policies along a game-equilibrium path.

Let every generation expect that $c(k) = g(k)$ at just one k with $c'(k) > g'(k)$. Then we are back to the problem of Part I of this paper. If such a $\tilde{k}$ is to be utility maximizing for the present generation to maintain when $k_0 = \tilde{k}$, it need satisfy only

$$g'(\tilde{k}) = (1 - \delta)c'(\tilde{k}) \tag{30}$$

The utility-maximization condition governing $c(k)$ states that

$$u'(c) = -\delta \frac{[u(c) - u(\tilde{c})]}{g(k) - c}, \qquad \tilde{c} = g(\tilde{k}) \tag{31}$$

whence

$$c'(k) = \frac{u'(c)g'(k)}{u'(c)(1 - \delta) - u''(c)(g - c)} \tag{32}$$

and

$$\lim_{k \to \tilde{k}} c'(k) = \frac{g'(\tilde{k})}{1 - \delta} \tag{33}$$

These conditions cannot invalidate any assumed $\tilde{k}$. To illustrate this, the reader can simply introduce a construction like that of Figure 1 onto the u and g functions of Figure 2.

III. CONCLUSIONS

If sustainable consumption per head is unbounded, the common assumption that consumption per head will grow without bound offers a natural means to anchor a game-theoretic consumption function. But the common assumption that consumption per head will instead converge to some finite value also admits the calculation of a game-equilibrium path. If steady-state consumption per head is bounded in the manner of the Golden Rule model, one has to know the capital intensity level towards which the economy is commonly assumed to converge. In both types of models, the asymptotic capital intensity remains a parameter, undetermined by the model, at best arbitrary only within limits. It does not appear that economics alone can completely determine the game-equilibrium path. What, then, can (if anything can)?

I suggest that, in otherwise indeterminate situations like this, there may develop an "ethic" that specifies some obligations that each generation is expected to meet. By telling each generation what to expect of other generations, morals may make determinate the altruistic behavior of each generation.

Public morals may be grounded in some underlying ethical axioms that express what the society considers just in relationships between persons and between generations. I shall give an example of that. But it is also possible that the role of morals may be filled more primitively by a myth that recounts the evil consequences to a society that would depart from some traditional pattern of behavior. The myth of the disaster that befalls the society that indulges in deficit spending is an example within the present context of economic growth. The deficit taboo encourages each generation to believe that the capital bequest its balanced budget would produce will not be dissipated to some unknown degree at some future time. In this case, intergenerational capital accumulation could be viewed not as the economist's game equilibrium but rather as the sociologist's ritual equilibrium.

In some intertemporal choice problems, however, ethics might operate instead of a taboo. In the problem of national capital accumulation modelled here, it is conceivable that the society's ethics (together with its technology and utility functions) would permit each generation to deduce the asymptotic capital intensity and thus serve to anchor the game-equilibrium path. Under the Paretian ethic—where any change that is preferred by at least one person is counted a social gain if it is not opposed by the others—each generation would presumably anticipate the economy's approach to the Golden Rule state because each prefers that equilibrium path to the other ones. Then the game-equilibrium growth path, shaped by the partially selfish preferences of each passing generation, would indeed approach the Golden Rule state.

Appendix

These notes are intended to provide a more rigorous basis, or at any rate a fancier one, for the results obtained in the text and also to extend those results to the case of exponential "myopia." The pertinent scripture, freely adapted here, are the imperishable pp. 263–64 of R. E. Bellman's *Dynamic Programming* (Princeton, 1957).

Let us define

$$f(b, m, \Delta) = \underset{c[b,\, b+\Delta]}{\text{Max}} \left\{ \int_b^{b+\Delta} e^{-\rho t} [u(c(t)) - \delta u(\bar{c})] dt + V(b + \Delta, k(b + \Delta)) \right\} \tag{A.1}$$

subject to

$$k(b) = m \tag{A.2}$$

and

$$\dot{k}(t) = G(k(t), c(t)) = g(k(t)) - c(t) \tag{A.3}$$

where

$$V(b + \Delta, k(b + \Delta)) = \delta \int_{b+\Delta}^{\infty} e^{-\rho t} [u(c(k(t))) - u(\bar{c})] dt \tag{A.4}$$

$$= \delta e^{-\rho(b+\Delta)} \int_0^{\infty} e^{-\rho s} [u(c(k(b + \Delta + s))) - u(\bar{c})] ds$$

We are interested in the limit as $\Delta \to 0$. The subtractor, $\delta u\ (\bar{c})$, is gratuitous if $\rho > 0$ but implements the overtaking principle if $\rho = 0$.

Letting c denote the average consumption rate around time b, we have, for small Δ,

$$f(b, m, \Delta) \cong \underset{c}{\text{Max}} \{[u(c) - \delta u(\bar{c})] e^{-\rho b} \Delta + V(b, m) + V_b(b, m)\Delta + V_m(b, m) G(m, c)\Delta\} \quad (A.5)$$

or, since $V(b, m)$ is independent of c, given b and m,

$$f(b, m, \Delta) - V(b, m) = \underset{c}{\text{Max}} [u(c) - \delta u(\bar{c})] e^{-\rho b} \Delta + V_b(b, m)\Delta + V_m(b, m) G(m, c)\Delta\} \quad (A.6)$$

From (A.4) it is clear that $f(b, m, \Delta) - V(b, m)$ is not a variable but depends only upon b, m and Δ through the unknown function $c(m)$. We can write, by virtue of (A.1) and (A.4) the relation, for small Δ,

$$f(b, m, \Delta) - V(b, m) \cong u(c(m))(1 - \delta) e^{-\rho b} \Delta \quad (A.7)$$

Upon substituting (A.7) into (A.6), dividing both sides by Δ and letting $\Delta \to 0$, we obtain the equation

$$u(c(m)(1 - \delta) e^{-\rho b} = \underset{c}{\text{Max}} \{[u(c) - \delta u(\bar{c})] e^{-\rho b} + V_b(b, m) + V_m(b, m) G(m, c)\} \quad (A.8)$$

Note that, by (A.4),

$$V(b, m) = e^{-\rho b} V(0, m) \quad (A.9)$$

$$V_m(b, m) = e^{-\rho b} V_m(0, m) \quad (A.10)$$

$$V_b(b, m) = -\rho V(b, m), \text{ each for every } m. \quad (A.11)$$

Maximization of the righthand side of (A.8) with respect to c thus entails, at the maximum,

$$u'(c) e^{-\rho b} + V_m(b, m) G_c(m, c) = u'(c) - V_m(0, k) = 0 \quad (A.12)$$

The second order condition for a maximum, given m and V_m, is

$$u''(c) \leqslant 0 \quad (A.13)$$

At any time h, therefore, the currently game-optimal consumption rate, c, must satisfy

$$u(c)(1 - \delta) = u(c) - \delta u(\tilde{c}) + V_h(0, m) + V_m(0, m)G(m, c) \qquad (A.14)$$

or, using (A.11) and (A.12),

$$\frac{\rho V(0, m) - \delta[u(c) - u(\tilde{c})]}{G(m, c)} = u'(c) \qquad (A.15)$$

Implicit differentiation of (A.15) yields

$$\frac{dc}{dm} = \frac{\rho V_m(0, m) - u'(c)g'(m)}{-(1 - \delta)u'(c) + u''(c)[g(m) - c]} \qquad (A.16)$$

$$= \frac{u'(c)[g'(m) - \rho]}{(1 - \delta)u'(c) - u''(c)(g - c)} \qquad \text{by (A.12)}$$

This differs from (17) and (32) of the text only in that the excess, $g'(m)$, of the social rate of return over the Golden Rule rate of return is replaced by the excess of the rate of return over the so-called Golden Utility rate of return whose value is $\gamma + \rho$. It follows that, when $\rho > 0$, the Golden Utility capital intensity, rather than the Golden Rule capital intensity, places the upper bound upon the set of admissible values of $\tilde{k}$.

*A Mathematical Note**

Wilfried M. A. Pauwels

The purpose of this note is twofold. First, we want to propose an alternative and simpler derivation of the results obtained [above] by E.S. Phelps. Secondly, we want to apply these results to a continuous version of the earlier model on game-equilibrium growth examined by E. S. Phelps and R. A. Pollak.[1]

In section I we examine the general properties of the game-equilibrium consumption function using the Hamilton-Jacobi partial differential equation. In section II we apply these results to a model which uses the same production function and utility function as Phelps and Pollak. Finally, in section III, we derive the same results as in section II via the calculation of the "second-best" optimum as proposed by Phelps and Pollak.

I. THE GAME-EQUILIBRIUM CONSUMPTION FUNCTION

Using the same notation as in Phelps, we can formulate the present generation's problem as follows: Find a consumption function $c(t)$, $t_0 \leqslant t \leqslant t_1$, so as to maximize

$$J[k_o,t_o;c] = V[k(t_1)] + \int_{t_o}^{t_1} [U[c(t)] - \tilde{U}]\, e^{-\rho t} dt \tag{1}$$

*The author is indebted to E. S. Phelps with whom he had the opportunity to discuss this note.

[1] E. S. Phelps and R. A. Pollak, "On Second-Best National Saving and Game-Equilibrium Growth," *Review of Economic Studies* 35 (April, 1968).

subject to

$$\dot{k}(t) = g(k) - c(t) \; ; \; k(t_o) = k_o > 0 \tag{2}$$

It is assumed that the present generation lives from t_0 till t_1, at which time it bequeaths $k(t_1)$ of capital per capita to the next generation. The utility to the present generation of this bequest is represented by $V[k(t_1)]$. $\tilde{U}$ can be interpreted, either as $\tilde{U} = U(\tilde{c})$, where $\tilde{c} = c(\tilde{k}) = g(\tilde{k})$ (see section I of Phelps), or as $\tilde{U} = \bar{U}$ (see section II of Phelps).

Let

$$\hat{J}[k(t),t] = V[k(t_1)] + \int_t^{t_1} [U[\hat{c}(s)] - \tilde{U}] e^{-\rho s} ds \tag{3}$$

where $\hat{c}(t)$, $t_0 \leqslant t \leqslant t_1$, is the optimal consumption policy of the present generation.

$\hat{J}[k(t),t]$ must then satisfy the following Hamilton-Jacobi partial differential equation[2]:

$$\frac{\partial \hat{J}[k(t),t]}{\partial t} + \underset{c(t)}{\text{maximum}} \left\{ \frac{\partial \hat{J}[k(t),t]}{\partial k(t)} [g(k) - c(t)] + U[c(t)] e^{-\rho t} - \tilde{U} e^{-\rho t} \right\} = 0 \tag{4}$$

subject to

$$\hat{J}[k(t_1),t_1] = V[k(t_1)] \tag{5}$$

Maximization of the expression in brackets in (4) gives

$$U'[c(t)] e^{-\rho t} = \frac{\partial \hat{J}[k(t),t]}{\partial k(t)} \tag{6}$$

From (5), we then obtain for the terminal time $t = t_1$

$$U'[c(t_1)] e^{-\rho t_1} = \frac{\partial \hat{J}[k(t_1)]}{\partial k(t_1)} \tag{7}$$

[2] See, e.g., E. B. Lee and L. Markus, *Foundations of Optimal Control Theory* (New York: John Wiley & Sons, Inc., 1968), pp. 340–60.

Let us now specify $V\,[k(t_1)]$ as

$$V[k(t_1)] = \delta \int_{t_1}^{\infty} [U[c(k(t))] - \tilde{U}]\, e^{-\rho t} dt \tag{8}$$

Then

$$\frac{\partial V[k(t_1)]}{\partial k(t_1)} = \delta \int_{t_1}^{\infty} \frac{d[U[c(k(t))] - \tilde{U}]}{dk(t_1)} e^{-\rho t} dt$$

$$= \frac{\delta}{\dot{k}(t_1)} \int_{t_1}^{\infty} e^{-\rho t} d[U[c(k(t))] - \tilde{U}]$$

$$= \frac{\rho V[k(t_1)] - \delta\,[U[c(k(t_1))] - \tilde{U}]\, e^{-\rho t_1}}{\dot{k}(t_1)} \tag{9}$$

assuming the convergence condition

$$\lim_{t\to\infty} e^{-\rho t}[U[c(k(t))] - \tilde{U}] = 0 \tag{10}$$

holds.
Using (7), we then obtain

$$U'[c(t_1)] = \frac{\rho e^{\rho t_1} V[k(t_1)] - \delta\,[U[c(k(t_1))] - \tilde{U}]}{\dot{k}(t_1)} \tag{11}$$

Let us now make the assumption that the lifetime of each generation, $t_1 - t_0$, tends to zero so that at each moment of time there is a generation that disappears. The implication of this assumption is that (7), and hence (11), must hold for all t, $t_0 \leqslant t \leqslant \infty$. We can then write

$$U'[c(t)]\, e^{-\rho t} = \frac{\partial V[k(t)]}{\partial k(t)} \tag{12}$$

and

$$U'[c(t)] = \frac{\rho e^{\rho t} V[k(t)] - \delta\,[U[c(k(t))] - \tilde{U}]}{\dot{k}(t)} \tag{13}$$

By the game-equilibrium property, we also require $c(t) = c(k(t))$, so that, from (13) and (2), we obtain

$$U'[c(k(t))] = \frac{\rho e^{\rho t} V[k(t)] - \delta[U[c(k(t))] - \tilde{U}]}{g(k(t)) - c(k(t))} \tag{14}$$

This is the basic condition characterizing the game-equilibrium consumption function.

Taking the derivative of (14) with respect to $k(t)$, and making use of (12), we obtain

$$\frac{dc(k(t))}{dk(t)} = \frac{U'[c(k(t))]\,[g'(k(t)) - \rho]}{U'[c(k(t))]\,(1 - \delta) - U''[c(k(t))]\,[g(k(t)) - c(k(t))]} \tag{15}$$

which characterizes the slope of the consumption function.

If we interpret $\tilde{U}$ as $\tilde{U} = U(\tilde{c})$, where $\tilde{c} = c(\tilde{k}) = g(\tilde{k})$, we can gain some insight about the asymptote $\tilde{k}$ by evaluating (14) at $k = \tilde{k}$:

$$\lim_{k \to \tilde{k}} U'[c(k(t))] =$$

$$= \lim_{k \to \tilde{k}} \frac{\rho e^{\rho t} V[k(t)] - \delta[U[c(k(t))] - \tilde{U}]}{g(k(t)) - c(k(t))}$$

$$= \lim_{k \to \tilde{k}} \frac{\rho U'[c(k(t))] - \delta U'[c(k(t))]\,c'(k(t))}{g'(k(t)) - c'(k(t))}$$

(using L'Hôpital's rule, and (12)).
From this we obtain

$$U'(\tilde{c}) = \frac{[\rho - \delta c'(\tilde{k})]\,U'(\tilde{c})}{g'(\tilde{k}) - c'(\tilde{k})}$$

or,

$$c'(\tilde{k}) = \frac{g'(\tilde{k}) - \rho}{1 - \delta} = \frac{f'(\tilde{k}) - (\gamma + \rho)}{1 - \delta} \tag{16}$$

II. GAME-EQUILIBRIUM GROWTH IN A SIMPLE MODEL

We will now apply the above results to a continuous version of the model examined in Phelps and Pollak. This model postulates a production process in which the output-capital ratio is equal to $\lambda - 1 =$ constant > 0, and in which labor is inessential and unproductive. Also, the population is constant in size.

The production function can then be written as

$$Y(t) = (\lambda - 1) K(t) = C(t) + \dot{K}(t) \tag{17}$$

($Y(t)$ is the rate of output at time t).
The saving ratio, $\sigma(t)$, can then be defined as

$$\sigma(t) = \frac{Y(t) - C(t)}{Y(t)} \tag{18}$$

(17) can then be written as

$$\dot{K}(t) = \sigma(t)(\lambda - 1)K(t) \; ; \; K(t_o) = K_o \tag{19}$$

The instantaneous rate of utility $U[C(t)]$ is given by

$$U[C(t)] = \frac{1}{1 - \epsilon} [C(t)]^{1-\epsilon} \; ; \; \begin{matrix} \epsilon > 0 \\ \epsilon \neq 1 \end{matrix} \tag{20}$$

while, in (1), $\tilde{U}$ is put equal to zero.

Using (17), (18) and (20) in (15), we obtain

$$\frac{dC}{dY} = \frac{dC}{(\lambda - 1)dK} = \frac{\lambda - 1 - \rho}{\left[(1-\delta) + \epsilon\left[\frac{\sigma(t)}{1-\sigma(t)}\right]\right] (\lambda - 1)} = 1 - \sigma(t)$$

from which we can calculate the game-equilibrium saving ratio $\hat{\sigma}(t)$

$$\hat{\sigma}(t) = \frac{\delta}{\epsilon + (\delta - 1)} - \frac{\rho}{(\lambda - 1)\,[\epsilon + (\delta - 1)]} \tag{21}$$

It follows that the game-equilibrium saving ratio is constant: $\hat{\sigma}(t) = \hat{\sigma}$.

Using the solution of (19) for $\sigma(t) = \hat{\sigma}$, the convergence condition (10) can be written as

$$\lim_{t \to \infty} e^{-\rho t} \frac{1}{1 - \epsilon} \left[(1-\hat{\sigma})(\lambda - 1)K_o e^{\hat{\sigma}(\lambda - 1)t}\right]^{1-\epsilon} = 0$$

or,

$$\hat{\sigma}(1-\epsilon)(\lambda - 1) - \rho < 0 \tag{22}$$

III. CALCULATION OF THE GAME-EQUILIBRIUM SAVING RATIO VIA THE "SECOND-BEST" OPTIMUM

It is possible to derive the game-equilibrium saving ratio (21) via the calculation of the second-best saving ratio. In Phelps and Pollak such a derivation is given for a discrete version of the model. The second-best saving ratio is defined as the saving ratio which is optimal for the present generation, given that the saving ratios of all future generations are known constants and are equal to $\bar{\sigma}$.

For the purpose of the present section, we formulate the present generation's problem as follows (compare with (1)-(2) in section I): Find a consumption function $C(t)$, $t_0 \leqslant t \leqslant t_1$, so as to maximize

$$J[K_o,t_o;C] = \int_{t_o}^{\infty} \left\{U^p[C(t)] + \delta U^f[C(t)]\right\} e^{-\rho t} dt \tag{23}$$

subject to (19). The functions U^p and U^f are defined as

$$\begin{aligned} U^p[C(t)] &= U[C(t)] && \text{for } t_o \leqslant t \leqslant t_1 \\ &= 0 && \text{for } t_1 \leqslant t \leqslant \infty \\ U^f[C(t)] &= 0 && \text{for } t_o \leqslant t \leqslant t_1 \\ &= U[C(t)] && \text{for } t_1 \leqslant t \leqslant \infty \end{aligned}$$

where $U[C(t)]$ is given by (20).

For $t_1 \leqslant t \leqslant \infty$, the Hamilton-Jacobi partial differential equation is given by

$$\frac{\partial \hat{J}[K(t),t]}{\partial t} + \frac{\partial \hat{J}[K(t),t]}{\partial K(t)} \bar{\sigma}(\lambda-1)K(t) + \frac{\delta e^{-\rho t}}{1-\epsilon}(1-\bar{\sigma})^{1-\epsilon}(\lambda-1)^{1-\epsilon}[K(t)]^{1-\epsilon} = 0 \tag{24}$$

subject to

$$\hat{J}[K^{(\infty)},\infty] = 0 \tag{25}$$

Provided the convergence condition (22) holds, (24)-(25) has a unique solution given by

$$\hat{J}[K(t),t] = \frac{e^{-\rho t}\delta(1-\bar{\sigma})^{1-\epsilon}(\lambda-1)^{1-\epsilon}}{(1-\epsilon)[(\epsilon-1)(\lambda-1)\bar{\sigma} + \rho]}[K(t)]^{1-\epsilon} \tag{26}$$

For $t_0 \leqslant t \leqslant t_1$, the Hamilton-Jacobi partial differential equation is given by

$$\frac{\partial \hat{J}[K(t),t]}{\partial t} + \underset{\sigma(t)}{\text{maximum}} \left\{ \frac{\partial \hat{J}[K(t),t]}{\partial K(t)} \sigma(t)(\lambda-1)K(t) + \right. \tag{27}$$

$$\left. \frac{e^{-\rho t}}{1-\epsilon} [1-\sigma(t)]^{1-\epsilon}(\lambda-1)^{1-\epsilon}[K(t)]^{1-\epsilon} \right\} = 0$$

The boundary condition for this differential equation is given by the value of (26) at $t = t_1$.

Maximization of the expression in brackets in (27) gives us

$$\sigma^*(t) = 1 - \frac{e^{-(\rho/\epsilon)t}}{(\lambda-1)K(t)} \left[\frac{\partial \hat{J}[K(t),t]}{\partial K(t)}\right]^{-(1/\epsilon)} \tag{28}$$

If $t_1 - t_0$ tends to zero, the solution of (27) is uniquely given by

$$\hat{J}[K(t),t] = \frac{(1-\epsilon)^{-1} e^{-\rho t} \delta (1-\bar{\sigma})^{1-\epsilon} (\lambda-1)^{1-\epsilon}}{(\epsilon-1)(\lambda-1)\bar{\sigma} + \epsilon} [K(t)]^{1-\epsilon} \tag{29}$$

Using (29) in (28), we obtain

$$\sigma^*(t) = 1 - \left[\frac{\bar{\sigma}(\epsilon-1)(\lambda-1) + \rho}{\delta(1-\bar{\sigma})^{1-\epsilon}(\lambda-1)}\right]^{1/\epsilon} \tag{30}$$

which expresses the second-best saving ratio $\sigma^*(t)$ as a function of the given saving ratio $\bar{\sigma}$. The game-equilibrium saving ratio $\hat{\sigma}$ is then characterized by the property

$$\hat{\sigma} = 1 - \left[\frac{\hat{\sigma}(\epsilon-1)(\lambda-1) + \rho}{\delta(1-\hat{\sigma})^{1-\epsilon}(\lambda-1)}\right]^{1/\epsilon}$$

which gives us

$$\hat{\sigma} = \frac{\delta}{\epsilon + (\delta-1)} - \frac{\rho}{(\lambda-1)[\epsilon + (\delta-1)]}$$

which coincides with our result (21).

*Charity: Altruism or Cooperative Egoism?**

Peter Hammond

If a Covenant be made, wherein neither of the parties performe presently, but trust one another; in the condition of meer Nature, (which is a condition of Warre of every man against every man,) upon any reasonable suspition, it is Voyd: But if there be a common Power set over them both, with right and force sufficient to compell performance; it is not Voyd. For he that performeth first, has no assurance the other will performe after; because the bonds of words are too weak to bridle mens ambition, avarice, anger, and other Passions, without the feare of some coerceive Power; which in the condition of meer Nature, where all men are equall, and judges of the justnesse of their own fears cannot possibly be supposed. And therefore he which performeth first, does but betray himselfe to his enemy; contrary to the Right (he can never abandon) of defending his life, and means of living. [Hobbes's "Leviathan," chapter XIV]

INTRODUCTION

It is evident that altruism *can* be invoked to explain any charitable behavior we may observe. But it is not quite obvious that altruism *must* be invoked to explain *all* charitable behavior. May not a person be charitable because he

*I am especially conscious of and grateful for the influence upon this paper of discussions with and comments by Kenneth Arrow, Christopher Bliss, Avinash Dixit, James Mirrlees, Edmund Phelps and Amartya Sen. But none of these is responsible for the contents.

believes that his present charity increases the likelihood that charity will also occur in the future, when the person may himself be in need? If so, charity is compatible with complete egoism, together with certain beliefs about the future.

The beliefs that an egoist needs to have, in order for charity to be rational, can be of two somewhat different kinds. He may believe that, even though he is not altruistic, charitable behavior may encourage altruism in the future, when he may be in need. He may, for example, believe that, if his children see him being charitable, they are more likely to grow up to be altruistic. Of course, he may encourage this by exhortation as well, but such words usually need the backing of deeds.

Alternatively, the egoist may believe that he is involved in a dynamic game. In this game, intertemporal cooperation is possible, and takes the form of charitable behavior.

The first alternative—in which future tastes are influenced—is no more than a temporary departure from altruistic charity. The egoist is only charitable because he hopes that this will bring about altruistic charity if he needs it. This explanation of charity is not very convincing. Moreover, it is hard to say very much more about it. Accordingly, I shall not discuss it further.

The second alternative—in which charity is an outcome of a game—is much more interesting.[1] It is also closely related to the theory of social contracts. Charitable behavior could be regarded as complying with a social contract. The egoist is worried that, if he breaks the contract, then many others may also decide to break the contract later on, with the result that the egoist's needs are not adequately met if he should ever require help in the future.

It is evident that charity is only likely to be an outcome of a dynamic game. In a static game, the rich are in no real danger of becoming poor. They may bribe the poor in order to gain their cooperation, but bribes are fairly easily distinguished from charitable gifts, it would seem. It is only when the return on a charitable gift is uncertain or fairly remote in time that we are likely to regard it as charity rather than a bribe.

It should also be observed that games in normal form miss the whole point. A cooperative solution—e.g., a core solution—may well involve egoists making transfers in different periods. An egoist will be prepared to exchange income in periods when he is rich for income when he is poor. But these are clearly not charitable transfers; they are merely transactions in a simple financial market—or intertemporal exchange economy. But this is not the main objection to the normal form I have in mind. Rather, the problem is that which Hobbes discusses. If the egoist makes a charitable transfer now, what guarantee has he that charitable transfers take place later? After all, by the time the rich egoist is poor, there is a new game. Why should other egoists take account of past generosity?

---

[1] It is also, I believe, a generalization of the first alternative.

The answer to this seems obvious. Egoist A can only expect egoist B to be charitable later, if egoist B also expects egoist C (or A) to be charitable later still. And even then, if egoist B is charitable because he expects C to be charitable later, what relevance does the charity of A have to B's decision? At first, it seems, the answer must be none. In which case there was no reason for A to be charitable in the first place. But I believe this reasoning to be false—even for completely rational egoists. Indeed, I hope to demonstrate that egoists *can* rationally be charitable, under certain conditions.

Nevertheless, it should be clear that the normal form of the game is not the appropriate one for considering charity. Intertemporal agreements, which one looks for in the normal form, may be broken in practice. Only the extensive form of the game allows us to deal with this.

There seems to be, at present, two approaches to games in extensive, as opposed to normal, form. The first approach considers "supergames"—i.e. repeated plays of a static game.[2] This is a restricted type of dynamic game. In fact, it is not directly applicable to the charity problem, because that involves plays of games in which at least one player is rich in some periods, and poor in others—i.e., it is not the *same* game being repeated in different periods.[3] A second approach looks at slightly more general games, but considers only noncooperative equilibria.[4] This, too, misses the point of the charity game. For the noncooperative solution which is proposed, B takes no account of whether A was charitable before, when B is deciding whether to be charitable. As we saw above, this gives no incentive for A to be charitable.

For this reason, I have found it necessary to experiment with a new type of solution for dynamic games. It does, however, bear a certain resemblance to both of the above approaches.

The rest of the paper consists of an extended discussion of two particular dynamic games—the "Poverty Game" and the "Pension Game"—together with suggestions for treating more general games of this kind.

THE "POVERTY GAME"

There are two players, P_1 and P_2. Time is discrete. In each odd-numbered period, P_1 is endowed with one chocolate, and P_2 has nothing.[5] In each

[2] See Luce and Raiffa (1957) (section 5.5.), Aumann (1959 and 1967), Friedman (1971).

[3] This is a little too sweeping. In some cases it may be possible to fit a charity problem into a supergame framework. See the "poverty game" below.

[4] The precise definition of noncooperative equilibrium is left until section II of this chapter. It has been common to identify it with Nash equilibrium. Here, I shall use noncooperative equilibrium in a somewhat different sense, as in Phelps and Pollak (1968) and Phelps (this volume). I am grateful to Menahem Yaari for drawing my attention to the distinction.

[5] "Chocolates" are suggested by Shell (1971).

even-numbered period, P_2 is endowed with one chocolate, and P_1 has nothing. The game lasts for T periods, where T is even.[6] Chocolate cannot be stored, but it can be costlessly and instantaneously transferred between the players. Each player has the same utility function:

$$U(c_1, \ldots, c_T) = \Sigma_{t=1}^{T} \; u(c_t)$$

where c_t is the amount of chocolate he eats in period t. Here, u is strictly concave, strictly increasing, differentiable, and $u'(c)$ tends to infinity as c tends to zero.

In the absence of transfers, the players alternate between extreme hunger and comfortable over-eating. If transfers take place because of agreement, then we are not inclined to call them "charitable." But, any agreement can be broken, and so transfers might be regarded as charitable. In any case, we can ask whether they will take place.

Consider P_2 (who is the last to receive chocolate) in period T. He has a chocolate, but P_1 does not. There is no future. Why, then, would P_2 share his chocolate? Even if he promised P_1 a share, there is no incentive for him to keep his promise. So we may presume that an egoist would keep all his chocolate.[7] Now consider P_1 in period $T-1$. P_1 knows that P_2 is an egoist, and so, that P_2 will not give any chocolate in period T whatever P_1 does in period $T-1$. So he also has nothing to gain, and his chocolate to lose, if he shares his chocolate with P_2.

Once again, if P_1 is an egoist, we may presume that he does not share his chocolate with P_2, even if he promised to do so. The same argument applies to P_2 in period $T-2$, and then to P_1 in period $T-3$, to P_2 in period $T-4$,..., and so on, right back to P_1 in period 1. Therefore, if P_1 and P_2 are both egoists, we may presume that chocolate transfers never take place. This is the noncooperative equilibrium to the poverty game (as is easily checked). It is also disastrously inefficient, in the Pareto sense.

Of course, this argument is not new. It is precisely that of Luce and Raiffa (*Games and Decisions*, pp. 97–102), who took exception to the conclusion. It is, of course, also a generalization of Hobbes. But, old as the argument is, there is no satisfactory suggestion for getting around it, if the horizon really is finite and known.[8]

If, however, the horizon is infinite, the game is totally different. There is no last period to start the argument going. Then it is possible to look for a cooperative equilibrium. Indeed, it is almost too easy to find one; a continuum of equilibria giving efficient outcomes will now be found.

---

[6] This makes the analysis a little easier without really affecting anything.

[7] We assume that P_2 is deaf to the rumblings of discontent from P_1 and P_1's stomach, and that P_2 would beat P_1 in any chocolate fight.

Two streams of chocolate consumption—one for each player—are Pareto efficient if and only if each player's consumption is constant for all time, and no chocolate is discarded. To see the need for constancy, suppose that P_1 consumes c_s in period s and c_t in period t, where $s \neq t$. P_2 consumes $1-c_s$ and $1-c_t$ in these two periods. A Pareto improving move occurs if P_1 consumes $\frac{1}{2}(c_s + c_t)$ in both the periods s and t, and P_2 consumes the rest in both periods.

Let $\bar{x}$ denote P_1's constant level of consumption, on some Pareto efficient path. Then $1-\bar{x}$ is P_2's constant level of consumption. Let x_t denote the chocolate transfer in period t from the player who is rich that period to the player who has nothing that period. To maintain the levels of consumption, we have:

$$x_t = \begin{cases} 1-\bar{x} & (t \text{ odd}) \\ \bar{x} & (t \text{ even}) \end{cases}$$

It is easy to show that any such Pareto efficient sequence of transfers can be sustained by noncooperative equilibrium strategies. Indeed, consider the following pair of strategies, which are reminiscent of the supergame strategies studied by Aumann (1959 and 1967) and also Friedman (1971).

For t odd, P_1's strategy is:

$$x_t = \begin{cases} \bar{x} & (\text{if } x_k \geqslant 1 - \bar{x} \text{ for all odd } k \text{ such that } k < t) \\ 0 & (\text{otherwise}). \end{cases}$$

For t even, P_2's strategy is:

$$x_t = \begin{cases} 1 - \bar{x} & (\text{if } x_k \geqslant \bar{x} \text{ for all even } k \text{ such that } k < t, \text{ or if } t = 1) \\ 0 & (\text{otherwise}) \end{cases}$$

Each player cooperates as long as the other does—but as soon as one player breaks the agreement, it collapses completely. There is consequently a tremendous incentive to keep to the agreement. Of course, the proposed strategies are in strong equilibrium (see Aumann, 1967).

---

[8] As Christopher Bliss has pointed out to me, the argument is uncomfortably close to that in the "Unexpected Examination" Paradox—see, for example, Nerlich (1961). In fact, P_1 can make the following statement to P_2:

> For some t, provided that in each previous period when you had chocolate you shared it with me, I shall share my chocolate with you on the first t occasions when I have chocolate. Immediately after you stop sharing chocolate, I shall stop. After t occasions, I shall stop sharing anyway. You will not succeed in anticipating the period in which I stop sharing chocolate—if I am the first to stop sharing.

This is just like the Unexpected Examination. P_2 cannot disprove this statement. Does he share his chocolate, in the hope that P_1's chocolate sharing will continue?

Consider what form cooperation takes in this game. Somehow, a value of $\bar{x}$ is hit upon, through bargaining, threats, etc. Maybe $\bar{x} = ½$ is agreed upon because it is generally seen to be fair. Then, each player cooperates in the sense that he holds the right beliefs, and acts upon them. It is rational for P_1 to choose his equilibrium strategy if and only if he believes that P_2 will choose his equilibrium strategy, and vice versa. If each player believes that the other will be uncooperative, no transfers occur.

THE "PENSION GAME" – GENERAL DISCUSSION

This game is based on an exchange economy first discussed by Samuelson (1958) and, more recently, by Shell (1971). There are an infinite number of players, P_t (t=0,1,2,...).

In period t (t=1,2,3,...) P_t is endowed with one chocolate, and no other player has any endowment. Each player (including P_0) has utility function:

$$U_t \equiv u(c_t^t) + u(c_{t+1}^t)$$

where c_k^t is P_t's consumption of chocolate in period k. The function u, and the physical properties of chocolate, are exactly the same as in the poverty game.

This model has a fairly obvious interpretation. P_t lives in period t, when he is young and earns a chocolate—and in period t+1, when he is old and earns no chocolate, but wants chocolate to eat. In period t+1, P_t relies on a chocolate pension, which only P_{t+1} can provide for him.

If the game stops in period T, the solution is as miserable as in the poverty game with a finite horizon. Every old man goes without chocolate. What happens if the game never stops?

It seems that we run straight into Phelps's indeterminacy problem.[9] P_t's action is determined by his beliefs about P_{t+1}'s reaction. There is an infinite chain of successive expectations, and there is no way of breaking it, or getting to the end. Let us assume, for simplicity, that each player P_t considers only two possible actions—giving P_{t-1} half a chocolate, or giving P_{t-1} nothing. Then, the typical link of the chain can be described as follows. Should P_t believe that he will receive a pension from P_{t+1} *if and only if* he pays P_{t-1} a pension, P_t will surely pay a pension. Should, however, P_t believe that P_{t+1} will pay P_t a pension, whatever P_t does (because of P_{t+1}'s expectations about P_{t+2}'s reactions), then P_t has no incentive to pay a pension. Similarly, if P_t believes that P_{t+1} will not pay P_t a pension, whatever P_t does (because of P_{t+1}'s

[9] See Phelps (this volume).

expectations about P_{t+2}'s expectations concerning P_{t+3}'s reactions to P_{t+2}'s decision), then P_t again has no incentive to pay a pension.

Clearly, then, in order to determine P_t's beliefs, we need to determine P_{t+1}'s strategy. Suppose first that the game is a stationary game—i.e. one in which each player's problem at each moment of time looks precisely the same. Then we expect any equilibrium to be stationary. In other words, P_t and P_{t+1} will have effectively identical strategies. Then, we can look for some kind of fixed point s^* in strategy space. The fixed point has the property that, if P_t expects P_{t+1} to adopt s^*, then it is optimal for P_t to adopt s^*. But the multiplicity of these fixed points is *precisely* the Phelps problem.[10]

Even in a nonstationary game, we can define equilibrium strategy sequences. A strategy sequence $s = (s_1, s_2, ...)$ is a list of strategies, one for each player. The sequence s^* is a noncooperative equilibrium if and only if, for all t, s_t^* is P_t's optimal strategy, given that he expects the players who follow him—P_k $(k>t)$—to adopt the strategies s_k^* $(k>t)$. Of course, there are just as likely to be multiple equilibria in this case as in the stationary case.

It seems that this problem comes about because there are not enough restrictions on an equilibrium. The only restriction put on an equilibrium has been that of consistency—if s^* is an equilibrium, then, *given that each player expects* s^*, there should be no incentive for any player to depart from s^*. But, even if s^* *is* an equilibrium in this sense, why should each player expect s^*, if other equilibria are possible? In particular, if $\hat{s}$ is also a solution, and each player is better off with $\hat{s}$ than with s^*, why should s^* be expected? There is every incentive for each player to expect $\hat{s}$ rather than s^*.

In the pension game, for example, there is obviously, in one sense, an "equilibrium" in which pensions are never paid. But, if, as will be seen later, there is also an equilibrium in which pensions *are* paid, and then every player is better off, surely it is rational to pay pensions.

EQUILIBRIA IN THE PENSION GAME

Let x_t denote the amount of chocolate which P_t donates to P_{t-1} (at time t, of course). Let h_t denote the historical sequence of pensions preceding time t—i.e. $h_t = (\ldots, x_{t-2}, x_{t-1})$. Then we expect an equilibrium strategy to be a function of the form:

$$x_t^* = f(h_t).$$

[10] It is interesting that the problem does not arise in Phelps and Pollak (1968). But I believe that this is because they only considered constant saving ratio policies, which were quite independent of the past. In fact, if more general policies are considered—in particular, ones which do depend on the past—then many more solutions are possible, I believe.

Let us assume for the moment that the game had a definite starting date, which we may as well take to be one.[11] Then, for $h_t = (x_1, \ldots, x_{t-1})$, define

$$k^*(h_t) = \begin{cases} 0 \text{ (if } x_k < \tfrac{1}{2} \ (k = 1, 2, \ldots, t-1) \\ \max \{k \mid x_k \geqslant \tfrac{1}{2}\} \text{ (otherwise).} \end{cases}$$

$k^*(h_t)$ was the last date on which a fair pension was paid—or else is zero if a fair pension was never paid.

Define $n(h_t) = t\text{-}k^*(h_t)-1$—the number of periods in which unfair pensions have been paid, since a fair pension was last paid.

Now consider the strategy:

$$f(h_t) = \begin{cases} 0 \text{ (if } n(h_t) \text{ is odd)} \\ \tfrac{1}{2} \text{ (if } n(h_t) \text{ is even) (including 0)} \end{cases}$$

This demands an explanation. Suppose $x_{t-1} \geqslant \tfrac{1}{2}$. Then the strategy tells P_t to pay P_{t-1} a fair pension. P_{t-1} has been fair—so P_t is fair to P_{t-1}. Then, moreover, every succeeding player gives and receives a fair pension. Suppose $x_{t-2} \geqslant \tfrac{1}{2}$, $x_{t-1} < \tfrac{1}{2}$. Then P_{t-1} has been "unfair" to P_{t-2}, and so P_{t-1} is to be punished. Suppose $x_{t-3} \geqslant \tfrac{1}{2}$, $x_{t-2} < \tfrac{1}{2}$, $x_{t-1} = 0$. Then P_{t-2} has been unfair to P_{t-3}, and P_{t-1} has punished him. Now P_{t-1} is not to be punished—rather, he is to be rewarded for punishing P_{t-2}'s unfairness. We can go on like this, working out what happens for various histories h_t. But the idea is that, if $n(h_t)$ is odd, then P_{t-1} has been unfair to P_{t-2}, either because $x_{t-2} \geqslant \tfrac{1}{2}$, or because P_{t-2} punished P_{t-3}, who had been unfair to P_{t-4}, either because $x_{t-4} \geqslant \tfrac{1}{2}$, or because P_{t-4} punished $P_{t-5}, \ldots$ On the other hand, if $n(h_t)$ is even (including 0), then either $x_{t-1} \geqslant \tfrac{1}{2}$, or P_{t-1} punished P_{t-2}, who had been unfair to P_{t-3}—either because $x_{t-3} \geqslant \tfrac{1}{2}$, or because P_{t-3} punished $P_{t-4}, \ldots$

Notice that, if $n(h_t)$ is odd, P_t has nothing to gain by choosing $x_t > 0$—provided that all later players follow the strategy f—because he secures a pension of ½ by choosing $x_t = 0$. Conversely, if $n(h_t)$ is even (or zero), P_t has nothing to gain by choosing $x_t \neq \tfrac{1}{2}$; if $x_t > \tfrac{1}{2}$, he secures no larger pension than ½, and if $x_t < \tfrac{1}{2}$, then he is severely punished by P_{t+1}. Thus, we have proved:

Lemma 1: *The strategy sequence* $x_t^* = f(h_t)$ $(t=1,2, \ldots)$ *is a noncooperative equilibrium for the pension game.*

[11] To maintain stationarity, we had better assume that at time 1 there was a player P_0 who never experienced youth.

In other words, if all players after P_t adopt f (the players before P_t do not affect him), then P_t can do no better than he does by adopting f. So f is a noncooperative equilibrium in the pension game. Moreover, the outcome of adopting f, after history h_t, is

$$(0,½,½,½, \ldots) \quad (\text{if } n(h_t) \text{ is odd})$$

$$(½,½,½,½, \ldots) \quad (\text{if } n(h_t) \text{ is even}).$$

This outcome—at least after period t—is clearly all that can be desired. It is both Pareto efficient and perfectly egalitarian. But starving the old is another "equilibrium" outcome. Is there no way of persuading rational men that they *must* choose f, without appealing to ethical arguments?

Let f' denote the strategy of starving the old. It is clear that f dominates f', in the sense that everybody (except perhaps P_{t-1}, who is at worst indifferent) prefers the outcome of f, given h_t, to the outcome of f'. This alone seems enough to ensure that f' will never be chosen—in fact, we should not regard it as an "equilibrium" at all.

Since few would quibble at the desirability of f for the pension game, it seems proper to enquire precisely what properties f has which make it an "equilibrium."

There are an embarrassingly large number of different types of "equilibrium" in cooperative games. But all of them require, by definition, some form of agreement between the members of a coalition. The orthodox view of coalitions is that they are bodies of agents who make binding agreements.[12] These agreements specify a coordinated strategy for the coalition as a whole—and so, a strategy for each member of the coalition. The agreements are reached because a coordinated strategy is better for each member of the coalition than the alternative uncoordinated strategy.

But there is no mention of how agreements are to be enforced. It seems that cooperative game theory is either a theory of honorable agents, or else, implicit in any agreement is the possibility of drastically punishing any member of a coalition who fails to keep his word. It seems clear therefore that such a theory is not applicable to the pension game. The agents are not necessarily honorable, and the possibilities of punishment are completely explicit. Does this imply that cooperation is impossible?

I have already suggested that, in the poverty game, cooperation takes the form of holding appropriate beliefs about the other player's strategy.[13] This kind of cooperation is perfectly possible in the pension game as well. P_t can be

[12] This "orthodox view" is stated, for example, in Von Neumann and Morgenstern (1953), section 21.2, and in Luce and Raiffa (1957), chapter 6.

[13] Von Neumann and Morgenstern's "understanding" seems an appropriate term here.

cooperative by believing that P_{t+1} will choose the strategy f (because P_{t+1} believes that P_{t+2} will choose f, because P_{t+2} believes that P_{t+3} will choose f, because . . . .); then P_t will choose f. On the other hand, P_t can be uncooperative by believing that P_{t+1} will choose f' (because P_{t+1} believes that P_{t+2} will choose f', because P_{t+2} believes that P_{t+3} will choose f', because . . . .); then P_t will choose f'.

I shall assume that all players are willing to cooperate by holding appropriate beliefs. This is, of course, an additional demand on the rationality of "rational egoists," and one that is at least as much open to dispute as the other demands.[14] But it seems no stronger than the traditional assumption of cooperative game theory, that egoists join coalitions and keep agreements.

It remains to decide what are "appropriate beliefs." This will be attempted by defining "dynamic equilibrium." It is easier to treat a generalized form of pension game first. So the solution of the pension game will be left until section 7.

GAMES WITH SEQUENTIAL PLAYERS

Consider a game Γ in which no player has more than one move. There may be a finite or an infinite number of players.

The assumption that each player has no more than one move is less restrictive than it first seems. If a player i has more than one move, he can be regarded as a number of players, or "egos," each of whom has the same preferences, and has no more than one move. By regarding a player with more than one move in this way, we may overlook possibilities for cooperation between the "egos" of a single player. But I hope to be able to show, in later work, that even this is not a major problem.

We shall also assume perfect information and no uncertainty. At each moment of time t, there will have been a sequence of moves up to time t; t and this sequence together determine

(i) The set of feasible move sequences which include the game.
(ii) The player who is to move at time t.
(iii) The preferences of the player who is to move at time t.

The time and earlier move sequence can be summarized in a history vector h—the dimension of h may depend upon t. Given h, let the feasible set of concluding move sequences be $X(h)$, and let the preferences of the player who is to move be described by the weak preference relation $R(h)$ and the strict preference relation $P(h)$. It will be assumed that $R(h)$ is transitive, as well as reflexive and connected.

---

[14] The additional demand lies at the heart of Schelling's discussion of coordination and tacit bargaining. See Schelling (1960).

Suppose that, given the history h, the player to move makes a move m. This results in a new history vector h' which depends only on h and m. Write $h' = \psi(m, h)$. ψ is the *history updating function.*

Now, a game Γ which is completely described by the sets $X(h)$, the preorders $R(h)$, and the history updating function ψ, will be called a *game with sequential players.* Examples are the pension game, and the game studied in Phelps and Pollak (1968). The game in Phelps (this volume) is a similar type of game in continuous time—such games will not be considered here, although much of the analysis is probably applicable to them. Note also that a finite game with sequential players is a particular type of the extensive games studied by Kuhn.

For each history h, there is a subgame $\Gamma(h)$ involving move sequences which conclude Γ. We expect the solution to Γ, and to each of its subgames, to involve *strategy sequences* $s(.)$ specifying the move which is to be made after history h, for each possible h. Associated with each strategy sequence is a *history generating function* ϕ. Given the strategy sequence $s(.)$, $\phi(s, h)$ specifies the history which results when s is followed for a single period. In fact, given the history updating function ψ, ϕ must satisfy

$$\phi(s, h) = \psi(s(h), h)$$

for all possible $s(.)$ and h. It is convenient to have an expression for the history which results from following $s(.)$ for k periods, starting from h. This will be written as $\phi^k(s, h)$.

By convention, $\phi^0(s, h) = (\text{all } s(.), h)$

and $\phi^1(s, h) = \phi(s, h)$ (..,,)

Of course:- $\phi^2(s, h) = \phi(s, \phi(s, h))$

$\phi^3(s, h) = \phi(s, \phi(s, \phi(s, h)))$, etc.

There is also an *outcome function* $x(s, .)$ associated with each $s(.)$. The outcome function specifies the entire move sequence which results from following $s(.)$ for ever, starting with h. In fact, $x(s, h)$ can be regarded as $\phi^\infty(s, h)$ (or as $\phi^T(s, h)$, if the outcome has only a finite number of moves before the end of the game).

It is convenient to have notations for the set of feasible strategy sequences, and the set of feasible histories. So define

$$S(h) = \{ s(.) \mid x(s,h) \in X(h) \}$$

the set of feasible strategy sequences, given history h. Define

$$H(h) = \{ h' \mid \exists k \geqslant 0 \text{ and } s \in S(h) \text{ s.t. } h' = \phi^k(s,h) \}$$

the set of histories—including h itself—which can follow h. Define

$$\tilde{H}(h) = \{ h' \mid \exists\ k > 0 \text{ and } s \in S(h)\ s.t.\ h' = \phi^k(s,h) \}$$

the set of histories—not including h itself—which can follow h.

DYNAMIC EQUILIBRIA

This paper has already moved far from its real subject, and a full discussion of dynamic equilibrium would take us even further astray.

Nevertheless, in connection with the poverty game, it was suggested that the noncooperative equilibrium is an appropriate type of solution for a finite horizon. The definition of "dynamic equilibrium" which follows is therefore designed to reduce to the noncooperative equilibrium when the horizon is finite. When the horizon is infinite, cooperative beliefs are embodied in the definition.

With this in mind, consider what a dynamic equilibrium must look like. For each subgame $\Gamma(h)$, dynamic equilibria will be strategy sequences in $S(h)$. If s^* is an equilibrium, for each $h' \epsilon H(h)$, the player at h' must be willing to make his prescribed move $s^*(h')$, given his expectations about the strategies of his successors. Moreover, as there is perfect information and no uncertainty, these expectations must be fulfilled, in an equilibrium.

These considerations give us two properties of dynamic equilibria immediately. The first is that, if $s^* \epsilon E(h)$, then the player at h must be expecting his successors to follow s^*. Such expectations only make sense if s^* is an equilibrium from his successors' points of view as well. So, if $s^* \epsilon E(h)$, then, for all $h' \epsilon H(h)$, $s^* \epsilon E(h')$. Secondly, $s^*(h)$ must be the optimal reaction of the player at h, if he expects his successors to follow s^*. As this is true for all h, it follows that any dynamic equilibrium is also a noncooperative equilibrium.

These two considerations alone are sufficient to determine the dynamic equilibrium for a finite game with sequential players. It is any noncooperative equilibrium. But, in infinite games, as Phelps has clearly shown, indeterminacy is a major problem.

The definition of dynamic equilibrium will make use of a "dynamic dominance" relation $D(h)$ defined on the set $S(h)$ of strategy sequences as follows:

$s_1 D(h) s_2$ if and only if

(i) $x(s_1,h)P(h)x(s_2,h)$, and $s_1(h) \neq s_2(h)$

(ii) For all $h' \epsilon \tilde{H}(h)$, either (a) $x(s_1,h')P(h')x(s_2,h')$
or (b) $s_1(h') = s_2(h')$
(or both).

Notice that $D(h)$ is an asymmetric relation–i.e. if $s_1\, D(h)\, s_2$, then not $s_2\, D(h)\, s_1$. Also:

Lemma 2: If $s_1\, D(h)\, s_2$, $h' \epsilon \tilde{H}(h)$, and $s_1(h') \neq s_2(h')$ then $s_1\, D(h')\, s_2$.

Proof: Immediate.

The relationship of $D(h)$ to noncooperative equilibria is shown in the following two theorems.

Theorem 1: Suppose that s^* is a strategy sequence for which there is no h and no $s \epsilon S(h)$ such that $s\, D(h)\, s^*$. Then s^* is a noncooperative equilibrium.

Proof: Suppose s^* is not a noncooperative equilibrium. Then there exists an h_0 and an $\hat{s} \epsilon S(h_0)$ such that $x(\hat{s}^*, \phi(\hat{s}, h_0))\, P(h_0)\, x(s^*, h_0)$ and $s^*(h_0) \neq \hat{s}(h_0)$.

$$\text{Define } s(h) = \begin{cases} \hat{s}(h) & (h = h_0) \\ s^*(h) & (\text{otherwise}) \end{cases} .$$

Then it is easy to check that $s\, D(h_0)\, s^*$.

Theorem 2: Suppose that there is a finite upper bound, N, on the possible number of moves in the game. Then, if there exists h and $s \epsilon S(h)$ such that $s\, D(h)\, s^*$, s^* cannot be a noncooperative equilibrium.

Proof: The proof will be by induction on $N(h)$, the maximum possible number of moves in the subgame $\Gamma(h)$.

If $N(h) = 1$, then $s\, D(h)\, s^*$ implies $x(s,h)\, P(h)\, x(s^*, h)$. Since the player at h has the last move, or no move at all, it is obvious that s^* is not a noncooperative equilibrium.

Suppose that the result is true whenever h satisfies $N(h) \leqslant n$. Consider any h such that $N(h) = n+1$. Suppose that, although $s\, D(h)\, s^*$, s^* is a noncooperative equilibrium strategy sequence for the subgame $\Gamma(h)$. Then, for all $h' \epsilon \tilde{H}(h)$, s^* is a noncooperative equilibrium for the subgame $\Gamma(h')$. But $N(h') \leqslant n$, so, by the induction hypothesis, $s\, D(h')\, s^*$ is impossible. Together with $s\, D(h)\, s^*$, this implies that, for all $h' \epsilon \tilde{H}(h)$, $s(h') = s^*(h')$. But $x(s, h)\, P(h)\, x(s^*, h)$. Therefore $s(h) \neq s^*(h)$, and so s^* is not a noncooperative equilibrium for the subgame $\Gamma(h)$. Therefore the result is true for $N(h) \leqslant n+1$. This is what remained to be proved.

So, for any *finite* game with sequential players–i.e. one in which the possible number of moves has a finite upper bound–a strategy sequence s^* is a noncooperative equilibrium if and only if there is no h and no $s \epsilon S(h)$ such that $s\,D(h)\,s^*$. But this has not been shown for an infinite game. Indeed, it is false. It is not hard to see that, for the pension game, the strategy f dominates the strategy f' of always starving the old. In fact, for all histories h, $x(f, h)\,P(h)\,x(f', h)$. But f' is a noncooperative equilibrium.

This suggests that the dominance relation may give what is required for cooperative expectations.

Say that s^* is a *dynamic equilibrium* for the subgame $\Gamma(h)$ if and only if there exists no $h' \epsilon H(h)$ and no $s \epsilon S(h)$ such that $s\,D(h')\,s^*$. Write $E(h)$ for the set of dynamic equilibria for $\Gamma(h)$.

Is this definition plausible?

Suppose that the player to move at h is trying to convince himself that s^* is not an equilibrium strategy. He must show that, for some $h' \epsilon H(h)$, $s^* \notin E(h')$. He might argue that $s^* \notin E(h')$ because there is some $h'' \epsilon H(h')$ such that $s^* \notin E(h'')$, but this is just delaying the finding of a proper reason. Really, the player at h must have in mind an alternative strategy sequence $s \epsilon S(h)$. Ideally, this should be an equilibrium, but such a restriction leads to an infinite regress. So let us see what happens if s is not required to be an equilibrium.

Suppose that the player at h can find an $s \epsilon S(h)$ such that $s\,D(h)\,s^*$. Then $x(s, h)\,P(h)\,x(s^*, h)$, and so he would prefer to regard s rather than s^* as an equilibrium. As $s(h) \neq s^*(h)$, the player at h is tempted to follow s rather than s^*. He can safely yield to this temptation, it seems, unless a later player will be subject to the reverse temptation—to follow s^* instead of s. But if $s\,D(h)\,s^*$, no later player will be subject to this reverse temptation.

In fact, no later player will be subject to this reverse temptation if (in addition to $s(h) \neq s^*(h)$, $x(s, h)\,P(h)\,x(s^*, h)$), for all $k > 0$, either

(a) $x(s, \phi^k(s, h))\,P(\phi^k(s, h))\,x(s^*, \phi^k(s, h))$ or

(b) $s(\phi^k(s, h)) = s^*(\phi^k(s, h))$

(or both)

so the condition $s\,D(h)\,s^*$ may appear too strong. However, the extra strength is illusory:

Lemma 3: *Suppose that there exists* $s \epsilon S(h)$ *such that*

(i) $s(h) \neq s^*(h)$ $x(s, h)\,P(h)\,x(s^*, h)$

(ii) For all $k > 0$, *either* *(a)* $x(s, \phi^k(s, h))\,P(\phi^k(s, h))\,x(s^*, \phi^k(s, h))$

or *(b)* $s(\phi^k(s, h)) = s^*(\phi^k(s, h))$

(or both)

Then there exists $\hat{s} \epsilon S(h)$ such that $\hat{s}\ D(h)\ s^*$.

Proof: Define $\hat{s}(h') = \begin{cases} s(h') & (\text{if } h' = \phi^k(s, h), \text{ for some } k \geqslant 0) \\ s^*(h') & (\text{otherwise}). \end{cases}$

Now, if $\hat{s}(h') \neq s^*(h')$, $x(s, h')\ P(h')\ x(s^*, h')$. Then it is easy to confirm that $\hat{s}\ D(h)\ s^*$.

For $s^* \epsilon E(h)$, it is necessary and sufficient that no player in the subgame $\Gamma(h)$ be tempted to change his strategy. So, the argument above supports the definition of dynamic equilibrium.

Finally, what are "appropriate beliefs"? They are simply that each player believes that his successors will not follow dominated strategies. Since it is certainly against the relevant players' interests to follow a dominated strategy, such beliefs seem sensible.

DYNAMIC EQUILIBRIA IN THE PENSION GAME

For the pension game, Lemma 1 shows that the strategy f is a noncooperative equilibrium. Here, it will be shown that f is a dynamic equilibrium.

Lemma 4: In the pension game, there is no history h_t and no strategy g such that $g\ D(h_t)\ f$.

Proof:

(1) Suppose $g\ D(h_t)\ f$.

Write $g_k = g(\phi^{k-1}(g, h_t))$

$f_k = f(\phi^{k-1}(g, h_t)) \quad (k = 1,2,3, \ldots)$

If history is $\phi^{k-1}(g, h_t)$, and g is followed, the player at h_t has consumption $(1-g_k, g_{k+1})$ But if f is followed, he has $(1-f_k, ½)$.

Then $u(1-g_1) + u(g_2) > u(1-f_1) + u(½)$, and $g_1 \neq f_1$.

Also, $u(1-g_k) + u(g_{k+1}) > u(1-f_k) + u(½)$, or $g_k = f_k \quad (k = 2,3,4, \ldots)$

(2) Suppose that, for some k, $g_k > ½$ and $f_k = ½$.

Then, for $u(1-g_k) + u(g_{k+1}) > 2u(½)$ to be true, we must have $g_{k+1} > g_k$, because $½u(1-g_k) + ½u(g_{k+1}) \leqslant u(½(1-g_k) + ½g_{k+1})$. In particular $g_{k+1} > ½$ and also $f_{k+1} = ½$. Therefore, by induction, for all $m \geqslant k$,

$$g_{m+1} > g_m > ½ \text{ and } f_m = ½.$$

Since the sequence g_m is clearly bounded above by 1, it has a limit $\hat{g}$. As u is continuous, we must have $u(1-\hat{g}) + u(\hat{g}) \geqslant 2u(½)$. But, because $\hat{g} > ½$ and u is strictly concave, this is impossible.

It follows that, if $g\ D(h_t)\ f$, there can be no k such that $g_k > ½$ and $f_k = ½$.

(3) Suppose that $n(h_t)$ is odd. Then $f_1 = 0$.

To get $u(1-g_1) + u(g_2) > u(1) + u(½)$, we clearly need $g_1 < ½$ and $g_2 > ½$. But, since $g_1 < ½$, $n(\phi(g, h_t))$ is even, and so $f_2 = ½$. So $g_2 > ½$ and $f_2 = ½$. By (2), it follows that $g\ D(h_t)\ f$ is false.

(4) Suppose that $n(h_t)$ is even. Then $f_1 = ½$.

(a) Suppose that $g_1 \geqslant ½$. Then we need $g_2 > ½$. But $f_2 = ½$. So, by (2), $g\ D(h_t)\ f$ is false.

(b) Suppose that $g_1 < ½$. Then $f_2 = 0$. Also, for $u(1-g_1) + u(g_2) > 2u(½)$, we need $g_2 > 0$. So $f_2 \neq g_2$. We therefore need $g\ D(\phi(g, h_t))\ f$. Since $n(\phi(g, h_t))$ is odd, this is impossible, by (3).

CONCLUSION

It seems that this paper has strayed far from a theory of charitable behavior. In addition, it is dangerous to draw conclusions from an analysis of very special cases. But it does seem that the initial hypothesis—that some charitable behavior could arise even in a world of total egoists, provided these egoists have appropriate expectations—has been confirmed for a special case. How generally this explanation might work is not yet known. Moreover, it obviously ignores the most important questions which charitable behavior raises. Do we really believe that charity is to be explained by cooperative egoism?

But, if it is shown that some kinds of behavior, usually regarded as altruistic, can in fact arise from egoism, the implications are in any case more normative than positive. In particular, it is a weapon to be used in arguments about certain issues of public policy. For example, the wealthy may object to paying taxes which are required to finance state benefits. But they may object less if they know that the level of benefits in the future, when they may need them, is related to the level today.

REFERENCES

Aumann, R. J., "Acceptable Points in General Cooperative *n*-person Games," *Contributions to the Theory of Games IV* (Princeton: Princeton University Press, 1959), pp. 287–324.

Aumann, R. J., "A Survey of Cooperative Games Without Side Payments," M. Shubik (ed.), *Essays in Mathematical Economics in Honor of Oskar Morgenstern* (Princeton: Princeton University Press, 1967), pp. 3–27.

Friedman, J. W., "A Non-Cooperative Equilibrium for Supergames," *Review of Economic Studies* 38 (1), Jan. 1971, pp. 1–12.

Kuhn, H. W., "Extensive Games and the Problem of Information," *Contributions to the Theory of Games II* (Princeton: Princeton University Press, 1953), pp. 193–216.

Luce, R. D., and Raiffa, H., *Games and Decisions* (New York: John Wiley & Sons, Inc. 1957).

Nerlich, G. C., "Unexpected Examinations and Unprovable Statements," *Mind* 70, Oct. 1961, pp. 503–13.

Phelps, E. S., "The Indeterminacy of Game-Equilibrium Growth in the Absence of an Ethic" (this volume).

Phelps, E. S., and Pollak, R. A., "On Second-Best National Saving and Game-Equilibrium Growth," *Review of Economic Studies* 35 (2), April 1968, pp. 185–200.

Samuelson, P. A., "An Exact Consumption Loan Model of Interest with or without the Social Contrivance of Money," *Journal of Political Economy* 66 (6), Dec. 1958, pp. 467–82.

Schelling, T. C., *The Strategy of Conflict* (Cambridge: Harvard University Press, 1960).

Shell, K., "Notes on the Economics of Infinity," *Journal of Political Economy* 79 (5), Sept./Oct. 1971, pp. 1002–11.

Von Neumann, J., and Morgenstern, O., *Theory of Games and Economic Behavior*, third edition, (Princeton: Princeton University Press, 1953).

Comment

Edward F. McClennen

James Buchanan has treated us to a most interesting and provocative analysis of what he regards as a crucial problem facing modern, affluent society. Like himself, I find the game matrices on which he bases much of his analysis to be both interesting and suggestive. But I find myself somewhat in disagreement with him about the merits, from the point of view of a calculus of rational choice, of player *A* attempting a "strategic" as opposed to a "pragmatic" approach to the sequential version of the *first* matrix. There is a problem of parity of reasoning here, which might lead one to the (I assume) unwanted conclusion that player *B* should also play "strategically," in which case the joint prescription would call for a deadlock on the outcome (1,1). Perhaps, however, the asymmetrical feature of the game, viz., that player *A* has a strongly dominating strategy, is designed to take care of this problem. But no such asymmetry obtains in the case of his second matrix, and I find his analysis here much less convincing. Parity of reasoning leads in this case directly into a "prisoner's dilemma" situation. My own sense is that the "reasonableness" of his prescriptions hinges to a much greater extent than he admits upon the moral force of the terms "samaritan" and "predator (parasite)" which he introduces subsequently in his paper.

Since the matrices are themselves silent on the question of the moral credentials of the players, we can, for example, imagine that player *A*, in the first matrix, is a tyrant whose past successes have brought him so much affluence that he is now in danger of going "soft," while player *B* is some group of his subjects, who have awakened to this possibility and are contemplating putting pressure on him to force him to ease their burden. If, as Buchanan suggests, his prescriptions really flow from the (neutral) game matrix itself, they are dispensable in this case also, although we may choke a bit more at this medicine when we cast ourselves into the role of advisors to sagging tyrants rather than decent folks. And, following through the logic of his argument, we could then come to the conclusion that not only has modern, affluent man become incapable of making the choices that are required to prevent his exploitation by predators of his own species, he has also become less able to make the choices which are required if he is to be an effective predator upon members of his own species.

Contrary to what the economists here might expect from a moral philosopher, I do not want to exploit this point. I happen to share Buchanan's passion for looking at things from the point of view of a calculus of rational choice, and I have had to defend myself all too often from those who are eager to point up the moral ambiguities of such an approach to inflict this sort of criticism on my colleague. I mention the problem of ambiguity, i.e., different ways of conceiving the relation between the two players in the first game, because it prepares the way for what I hope you will agree with me is a more substantial criticism, viz., that there is considerably more that can and needs to be said about the very (putatively) decent (potential) samaritans and (putatively) exploitive parasites upon which he has chosen to focus his analysis. I suggest that the first matrix is ambiguous in a much more startling way than my example of the tyrant-gone-soft would suggest. If we listen to what some of the more articulate spokesmen of Buchanan's parasitical types have to say, we find, not (as we might expect) that they conceive of themselves as exploited (as opposed to exploiting) persons in the *role of player B*; rather, we find that they conceive of themselves as exploited persons in the *role of player A.* In short, many of them would accept Buchanan's interpretation of the situation in terms of matrix in Figure 1, and also accept his prescription: their only quarrel with him would be over the question of which position in the game they occupy. Let me try to illustrate what I have in mind with an (abstract) concrete example, viz., that of a confrontation between university officials and dissident students. Figure 3 represents what I take to be the way in which the university officials would interpret such a situation. Buchanan's prescription of "strategic courage" requires of the university officials that they make it clear to the dissident students that acts in violation of university rules will be dealt with in strict accordance with the rules (and that they be prepared to carry out such a threat, unpleasant as it may be to them personally), while still

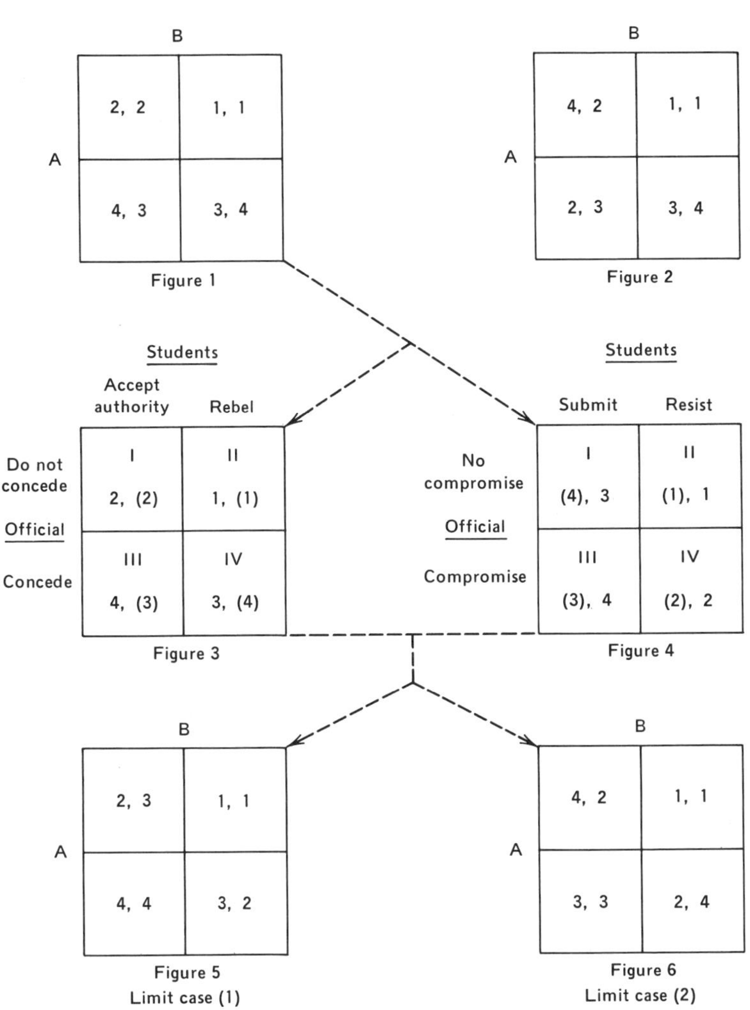

making it clear to the dissidents that they are prepared to seriously consider all reasonable changes in rules, etc. That is, the strategy is to convince the students that they have in the last analysis only an option between the outcomes (1,1) and (4,3). This is the "difficult" course for the university officials to take, since on this interpretation of the decision problem, the officials are "potential samaritans" and a concession approach seems called for regardless of what the students do. If the students are aware of this, however, they are in a position to take advantage of the situation and exploit the "potential samaritans." Numerous hypotheses can and have been adduced in support of the notion that in such situations students are likely to prefer cell IV to cell III: Tullock's theory of the entertainment value of revolution, the tendency of people in general to feel a certain elation and satisfaction at having "beaten down" the other side, the expectation (or hope) that by taking a "hard line" against the university officials, the students may be able to wring even more concessions, etc.

Suppose now, however, we cross the battle-lines and ask the dissident students to give their account of the situation. If we cut through their own rhetoric, I suggest that Figure 4 gives a plausible interpretation of the situation seen from the side of the dissident students. This matrix, you will note, is simply the matrix in Figure 3, with columns and rows exchanged. Judging the situation from this perspective, "strategic courage" requires of the dissident students that they make it clear to the university officials that an unyielding position on the part of the latter will be met with demonstrations, sit-ins, etc., which will only be called off when the officials agree to negotiate. That is, the strategy is to convince the officials that they have in the last analysis only an option between the outcomes (1,1) and (3,4). This is the "difficult" course for students to take, so they will argue, because personal costs to them can be very high if a deadlock occurs (e.g., closing of the school can result in loss of credit for courses incompleted, they run the risk of being denied degrees or expelled, participating younger faculty members risk loss of tenure or denial of promotion, etc.); and even if confrontation does result in concessions being made, they will have had to expend much time and energy, without advancing their own careers in any way. But if university officials are aware of this, they can exploit the situation to maintain the status quo. Moreover, students will earnestly argue that the university officials really prefer cell I to cell III: that institutional roles foster a spirit of authoritarianism and rigidity, that the officials have a vested interest in maintaining the status quo, etc. The student movement no less than the establishment has had to face the continuing crisis brought on by the disposition of its membership to opt for "soft" as opposed to "strategically courageous" approaches; and student leaders no less than members of the establishment have felt compelled to urge adoption of the ethics of personal responsibility and commitment to "rules."

This parallelism presents a real problem, for we no longer have simply two quite different applications of the first matrix, but conflicting applications to one and the same situation. We could, of course, simply note that one or the other assignment of ordinal values must be correct, and proceed to apply Buchanan's prescription to whichever group was revealed to have a correct perception of the preferences involved. But I am sure that no one in this room supposes that this sort of question can be settled out of hand. It is sometimes said that the typical "man in the street," faced perhaps with intellectual and emotional budgetary constraints, has devised an efficient solution to this problem: he simply shoots from the hip with whatever ideological gun he possesses. Fortunately, none of us here are subject to such constraints, and I should like to offer, therefore, a somewhat more complicated way of looking at and possibly resolving this problem.

I suggest that it is plausible to suppose that neither side has a monopoly of insight into the correct ordering of preferences. This in turn immediately suggests that there are two limit cases which it will be useful to consider.

(1) If, as many philosophers and economists are inclined to argue, we must suppose that each man is likely to be the best judge of what his own preferences are, then the disparity in viewpoints expressed in the matrices of Figures 3 and 4 could be explained in terms of a failure on the part of each side to correctly perceive the preference orderings of the other side. In the limit case, this would imply that Figure 5 gives the true preferences for such a confrontation situation. (Figure 5 is derived by taking all the values not enclosed in parentheses in Figures 3 and 4.) It can be seen by inspection of this matrix that if both sides (continuing to view the situation in terms of their own interpretation of the preferences) adopt Buchanan's prescription, the result will be a locking into the mutually disadvantageous outcome of (1,1). Such an outcome would be both tragic and ironic. It would be tragic, because were both sides to perceive the actual game they were playing, they would see that "strategically," or "pragmatically," or just plain "rationally," the best choice for each leads to the outcome (4,4), for it strongly dominates all other outcomes. It would be ironic, because *either single or joint* adoption of Buchanan's prescription turns out to be self-defeating: it prevents reaching and locking into precisely that outcome it was designed to guarantee.

(2) Alternatively, one could consider the possibility that while both sides have a more or less correct perception of the preference orderings of the other side, they misconceive (or perhaps are self-deceived about) their own preferences. In the limit case, this would imply that Figure 6 gives the true preferences. (Figure 6 is derived by taking all the values in parentheses in Figures 3 and 4.) Once again, if both sides adopt the prescription of "strategic courage" the outcome is a locking into the mutually disadvantageous (1,1). What, if anything, constitutes the rational solution to such a

game is a more controversial matter, but perhaps Buchanan would agree with me that we are involved in this case with a bargaining situation upon which it is reasonable to impose a condition of Pareto optimality for solutions.

The whole matter becomes much more complicated once we consider the possibility that the truth lies somewhere in between these two limit cases, i.e., that each side is given to a certain amount of misconception about the preferences of others, and a certain amount of misperception (or self-deception) about its own preferences. A significantly broad range of such intermediate cases are, however, cases of bargaining games in which joint adoption of the policy of "strategic courage" leads to non-Pareto optimal outcomes.

Let me briefly sketch now some of the conclusions I would draw from the above analysis. In those cases in which it can be shown that the matrix in Figure 1 accurately captures the preferences of the parties, and where, in addition, there is some reasonably objective way to establish that it is the person or group in position *A* who is subject to exploitation, I find Buchanan's analysis and prescriptions convincing and important. With him, I hold the ethics of personal responsibility and commitment to practices (rules)—as opposed to "situational ethics"—in high esteem. And I am inclined to agree with him that such an ethics can be given a rational defense, although the lines along which I would argue this point diverge somewhat from his. I shall come back to this matter in a moment. However, I am strongly convinced that many of the situations which he discusses are situations in which the sort of double, conflicting application of the matrix occurs, and are thus situations in which his prescription is not defensible. Consequently, I find unconvincing his thesis that there has been a disturbing increase in the taking of "soft" (and by long-term standards, irrational) options. I find it just as plausible, and indeed I must confess, more plausible, to suppose that this increase is at least in part a function of people coming to have a more accurate perception of the preferences of all parties involved, and consequently having greater insight into the possibilities of mutual gain through cooperation. In this respect part of what he finds disturbing I find encouraging.

But I am not overly sanguine about this trend. I would tender the hypothesis that what afflicts modern affluent society is what has always afflicted societies: the failure, not so much to resist exploitation by other men, as to exploit fully the possibilities for mutual gains through cooperation. And the irony is that the ethics of personal responsibility and commitment to practices, when espoused by men who misperceive the values of others, and misperceive their own values, may contribute in no small measure to this failure.

For a society of persons with a clear and well-developed conception of justice—I use the term here in the sense that it has been eloquently and carefully expounded by John Rawls—an ethics of personal responsibility and commitment to practices is indispensable to the avoidance of mutually disadvantageous situations. It is along these lines, by appeal in this sense to considerations of Pareto efficiency, that I would argue the case for the rationality of such an ethics; for it appears to be the most efficient way to resolve the whole manifold of "prisoner's dilemma" problems which continually confront any society of mutually self-interested persons.

But the articulation and implementation of such a conception of justice is also indispensable. To the extent that the members of a society fail at this task, to that extent there will be those for whom the society represents not a true community, but a relationship among men founded on force; and all members of such a society are likely to share in the disadvantages of the ensuing conflict and antagonism. And it is precisely with regard to this matter that I find myself less sanguine, for the capacity of men to partially misjudge the values of their fellow men, and to misjudge or even deceive themselves about their own values, appears to stand as a formidable barrier to the development and implementation of such a conception of justice. I mean to suggest here that such misperception appears to be no mere intellectual error which we can optimistically expect to be corrected through the enlightenment of education, for it appears to be the psyche's own (and from a limited point of view, efficient) way of resolving the conflict between its desire to get as much as possible of the things which men value, and its desire to justify itself to itself and to others. So long as a person can convince himself that he really would be content with much less than the most, but that he must continually deal with people around him who are disposed to always take as much as they can get, and to be exploiters in this sense, the conflict is resolved. Such a consciousness, moreover, ends up exploiting and thereby stunting that very sense of justice which needs the fullest of development, for it is a commonplace that those who are modest in their demands, but who are exploited by others, have been done an injustice which must be resisted and set right. But a society of men who have so rationalized their positions in this manner are doomed to act over and over in ways which work to their mutual disadvantage; and an ethics of personal responsibility and commitment to practices, when it serves such a false sense of justice, can only perpetuate such a "prisoner's dilemma," not resolve it.

Comment

Karl Shell

The static general equilibrium model has left us with a fundamental proposition in welfare economics: If "external effects" are absent from consumption and production, then a competitive equilibrium allocation is also a Pareto optimal allocation. Much of social policy may be thought of as an attempt to cope with or exploit these externalities. Phelps's paper on game-equilibrium growth focuses on a *dynamic* economy with consumption externalities. Individuals are neither perfectly selfish nor perfectly altruistic. The utility function of a generation depends upon its own consumption and upon the consumption of each of the future generations.

Since Phelps's generations are not "hard atoms" (they are not perfectly selfish), equilibrium growth may not be Pareto optimal. Even if the generations are hard atoms—as in Hammond's paper—the equilibrium allocation may not be Pareto optimal. The fundamental theorem of welfare economics fails to apply because of two basic differences between the dynamic models and the essentially static Arrow-Debreu model. (1) In continuous-time models with infinite futurity, the set of agents (or generations) can be identified with the open half-time-line (running from today or time zero into the indefinite future). In discrete-time models with infinite futurity, the set of agents can be identified with the nonnegative integers. There are a finite number of agents in the basic Arrow-Debreu model. (2) In the Arrow-Debreu model, trades can be thought of as taking place in a single Walrasian market which includes all individuals under consideration. In the dynamic model, however, some generations do not meet and hence cannot trade or make agreements. As Hammond's Pension Game illustrates, there is even a special problem for overlapping generations. While they can participate in some exchange, there may be limited ability to enforce agreement.

I would like to illustrate the importance of these two qualities of the models—the infinity of traders and the nonsimultaneity of generations—in the context of a simple economy based on Paul Samuelson's famous consumption-loan model. Individuals live for two periods. There is no population growth. The representative of the tth generation has a simple utility function of the form $u^t(c_t^t, c_{t+1}^t) = c_t^t + c_{t+1}^t$, where c_s^t is consumption of generation t in period s. The hard atoms of generation t care only for their own consumptions during the periods in which they are alive, namely periods t and $t+1$. Assume no production or storage possibilities and assume that each representative individual is endowed with one consumption unit for each of the two periods of his life.

Individual \ Period	1	2	3	4	5	·
0	1	0	0	0	0	·
1	1	1	0	0	0	·
2	0	1	1	0	0	·
3	0	0	1	1	0	·
4	0	0	0	1	1	·
·					·	·
·						·

Figure 1. Endowment Matrix

Notice that if the interest rate is zero (i.e. $p_s = p_t$ for $s = 1, 2, \ldots$ and $t = 1, 2, \ldots$, where p_t is the price of consumption in the tth period), then autarchy (no trade) is a competitive equilibrium. An allocation which is superior to this equilibrium allocation can be found. For example, require man one to give man zero a unit of consumption good in period one. Man zero is better off. Compensate man one by requiring man two to give man one a unit of consumption good in period two, and so forth, making the *ur*-father better off and no one worse off.

Individual	Period 1	2	3	4	5	·
0	2	0	0	0	0	·
1	0	2	0	0	0	·
2	0	0	2	0	0	·
3	0	0	0	2	0	·
·					·	
·						·

Figure 2. Pareto Superior Allocation

While the most natural interpretation of the consumption-loan model is in the dynamic setting, we could consider a *Gedankenexperiment* in which all traders meet in a single market. Nonetheless, we have exhibited a competitive equilibrium which is not Pareto optimal. The fundamental theorem of welfare economics does not hold because of infinity—infinity of traders and infinity of dated commodities.

What is the "cure" for this inefficient competitive economy? Let the *ur*-father (man zero) invent money, declaring it to be worth one unit of consumption in any period. Man zero trades money for consumption in period one. Consumption is passed backward while the money "hot potato" is passed forward. Consumption is Pareto optimal; the money economy duplicates the allocation shown in Figure 2.

In a truly dynamic world as opposed to a game in normal form, some future generation may refuse to catch the "hot potato." In doing so, the preceding generation is harmed and its expectations have been disappointed. After refusing the money of its parents, a generation might print its own currency (monetary reform!), thus aggrandizing themselves at the expense of their parents. This then is the Hobbes-Phelps-Hammond problem which depends on the true dynamic nature of society—not merely on the finiteness or infiniteness of horizons. Such economies may benefit from the acceptance of an ethic or taboo: for example, "Thou shalt not repudiate thy father's legal tender." In the Hobbes-Phelps-Hammond world, ethics and taboos may (by constraining the actions of hard or somewhat hard atoms) serve to improve intertemporal allocation.

In Phelps's model, generations do not overlap. Each generation bequeaths capital to the succeeding generation, fully aware that the saving-consumption decisions of future generations are outside its control. In the particular model he presents, growth is determinate only after specification of the "transversality" (or infinite end-point) condition, $\tilde{k}$. Since game-equilibrium does not provide $\tilde{k}$, Phelps looks for an ethic, myth, or taboo to "close the model." It is my opinion that many of our most interesting and important social arrangements either reflect the fact or are made possible by the fact that there is no date known with perfect certainty for the end of the world or for the breakdown of human society. I applaud Phelps's turning to philosophy and our sister social sciences for an understanding of social arrangements that exploit the "free-endpoint" property of infinite horizons. Such arrangements may appear to be mythical or even magical in the eyes of the classically trained economist, but this is only because the intuition of classical economics is almost entirely formed from the study of finite-horizon models.

Of course, not all indeterminacy is because of the infinite-time horizon. It should be noted that if the Phelps model is somewhat generalized, indeterminacy can be a problem even in a finite-horizon, period model. Let the utility of generation t be $u_t(c_t, u_{t+1}, u_{t+2}, \ldots u_T)$, t=1,2, . . . ,T, and c_t be the consumption of generation t. Given the anticipated actions of subsequent generations, the tth generation's choice problem can be rewritten as that of maximizing $\phi_t(c_t, k_{t+1})$, where k_{t+1} is capital bequeathed to generation t+1 and $\phi_t(\cdot)$ is a "derived utility function," subject to inheritance of capital k_t. In Phelps's special separable-utility-function case, derived utility $\phi_t(\cdot)$ satisfies the Weak Axion of Revealed Preference (in $c_t - k_{t+1}$ space). That is, the indifference curve defined by $\phi_t(c_t, k_{t+1}) = \beta$ (a constant) is strictly convex to the origin.

In both the general and particular cases, the last generation (T) consumes all the resources it inherits. In the Phelps case, generation T–1 knowing the behavior of generation T adopts a unique consumption-bequeath strategy, and so on back to the first generation. Thus, for the *finite* case with Phelps-like utility functions, full development is uniquely determined. In the more general finite-period case, however, there may be a generation, t^*, that is indifferent between two points on the frontier of its feasible consumption-bequeath set. It may also be the case that the welfare of generation t^*-1 is not independent of which of these two points is chosen by generation t^*. Within the calculus of Phelps's paper, no criterion of choice is given for generation t^*-1. Should generation t^*-1 assign probabilities to its children's choices—then maximize expected utility? Perhaps an ethic would be helpful: if indifferent between two points, choose the point your parents would have preferred. (But, of course, this would not necessarily be the point your grandparents would have preferred you to choose.)

We have seen that even though the finite-time model has a natural transversality (or end-point) condition, a generalized version of that model may not be determinate. Something is needed to "close" the model. We may call this something "constitution," "ethic," "myth," "taboo," or whatever, but as social scientists and social philosophers we will want to study in detail what stands behind the word. In such a study, we should not lose sight of the rich pattern of generational overlap in the real world. I conjecture that the "richness" of generational overlap substantially contributes to the viability of arrangements—such as constitutions, generation-skipping wills, trusteeships, etc.—that permit those alive today to influence future resource allocation.

Edward McClennen has commented at length on the Buchanan paper; therefore, my remarks should be brief. Buchanan presents examples of repeated games with threats or potential threats. In these games, the degrees of "strategic courage" (or, more tamely, the rates of time preference) of the players can be important to the outcome of the game.

Turning to the particular game of Figure 1, it might be useful to analyze the game from the viewpoint of each player. (Somehow, after having dubbed Player *A* the "potential samaritan," the author begins to empathize with him.) Cells III and IV are the Pareto optimal outcomes. A long-run conflict-free solution might "average out" to $(4-x, 3+x)$ where $x \in [0,1]$ would depend on the players' relative strategic courage and their relative capabilities for inflicting punishment in case of conflict. If $(3\frac{1}{2}, 3\frac{1}{2})$ were "the solution" (i.e., $x = \frac{1}{2}$), it could be "approximated" in repeated play if *A* plays row 2 each time and *B* alternates between column 1 and column 2. *A* might threaten *B*: If you ever play column 2 twice in succession, I will then choose row 1 for the succeeding twenty plays.

Analysis of the game described in Figure 2 is a bit more complicated and I have promised to be brief. As before, I see no special reason to empathize with *A* rather than *B*. Indeed, now that neither player has a single-play dominant strategy, it is hard to see why *A* is any more the "potential samaritan" than *B*. Buchanan's observations on the current social setting are often keen and can be profitably understood without full acceptance of his analysis and interpretation of the Figure 1 and Figure 2 games.

In closing, I offer a technical comment on the question about the effect of a change in the interest rate on parents' decisions about child-rearing. Even if we think of spanking as an investment good, it does not necessarily follow that spanking should be increased when the rate of return on alternative investment falls. This direct relationship between the rate of interest and the rate of permissiveness is probably deducible from a model with perfect markets for buying, selling, renting and renting out children. Without these markets it would seem that this relationship need not necessarily hold.

Part 3

Private Philanthropy and Public Finance

William Vickrey

FORMS OF FISCAL SUPPORT FOR PHILANTHROPY

Fiscal support for private philanthropy can take a number of forms. These include the making of outright grants to private philanthropic agencies, assignment of parts or all of certain revenues, exemption of philanthropic institutions from various taxes on property used or on transactions involved in their activities, exemption from taxes on investments, the proceeds of which are devoted to philanthropic activities, exemption from estate, gift or inheritance tax of amounts contributed to such philanthropies, and the granting of credits or deductions for charitable contributions under individual and corporation income taxes. These measures have varying impacts on philanthropic activity and have been justified in various ways; the pattern of such subventions has also varied widely from time to time and from country to country. The results have often been unanticipated and at times perverse.

INCOME TAX DEDUCTION, INDIVIDUAL

One of the most important of the concessions made to philanthropy is the deduction allowed for charitable contributions in the personal income taxes of the United States, including most state income taxes, and in some other countries. The deduction allowed under the U.S. federal income tax law was first introduced beginning with the income year 1917, concurrently with an increase in the top bracket rates from 15 percent for 1916 to 67 percent for 1917 as a war finance measure. The amount of the deduction was then limited to 15 percent of net income, somewhat more than the traditional "tithe," but the scope of the provision has been gradually expanded over the years, both by legislative enactment and by interpretation.

The first explicit enlargement came in 1924 with the addition of the so-called nun's clause, whereby taxpayers meeting fairly stringent conditions of giving substantially all of their income to philanthropic agencies during the past five years would be allowed to deduct their contributions without limit. This was intended as quasi-personal legislation designed to deal with the special case of a nun who had in fact taken vows of poverty and created a situation where tax was due but there was no income available net after contributions with which to pay it.

COMPOUNDING OF THE DEDUCTION

The principal enlargements, however, have arisen more or less without explicit legislative enactment through interpretations of the provisions relating to the taxation of capital gains and the inventiveness of taxpayers and their counsel in taking advantage of these provisions. The main element in this process has been the interpretation of the gift of securities or other property as a gift of the current market value of the property given, in itself a reasonable enough interpretation, but in combination with a failure to recognize any realization of capital gain on the transaction, this amounted to a substantial double allowance where the property given had appreciated substantially in value in the hands of the taxpayer. Thus the gift of an asset having a "basis" (e.g., cost) for tax purposes of a fraction b of its current market value A would not only result in a reduction in capital gains tax of $A(1-b)g$, g being the effective rate on capital gains, but in addition a reduction in tax by reason of the deduction of the contribution A amounting to mA, m being the marginal rate on the top bracket of the taxpayer's ordinary income. The total tax saving, as compared to the result if the asset had been sold outright for A would thus be $A(m + g - bg)$ which in favorable circumstances could be greater than A, giving rise to the rather astonishing result that if a taxpayer is desirous of liquidating his investment in an asset with a relatively low basis b, he might actually obtain a greater net realization for himself by giving the asset to an eligible charity than by selling the asset outright and retaining the proceeds. In such cases it is not only more blessed, but more profitable, to give!

Not content with this, some top bracket taxpayers having assets with relatively smaller accrued capital gains made a practice of "giving the gain," i.e., transferring the asset to the charitable organization in a "bargain sale" in return for a payment equal to the basis, entitling themselves to a charitable contribution deduction equal to the excess of the market value over this sale price, and again escaping any assessment of tax on the capital gain. In this case the amount of the tax reduction is $(A - C)(m + g)$ on a gift of $(A - C)$ and the giving can be profitable even when no assets with a very low basis b are available. In its heyday, the charitable deduction loophole for gifts of appreciated capital assets led to such capers as deeding one's collection of objets d'art to a museum or other appropriate institution so that the museum would take immediate title and a deduction would be available, but in many cases arranging informally for the donor to retain the "custody" of the collection, or part of it, until his demise. One case has been reported in which a gentleman retired to a waterfront estate in Florida, had the riparian rights to this estate valued by his friendly assessor, and had his friendly lawyer draw up a deed transferring these rights as a charitable contribution to his alma mater in Iowa. Obviously the prospect of his being bothered by undergraduates camping on his shorefront did not worry him excessively, while conversely the college was not anxious to demur at the transaction in view of the prospects for other testamentary benefits.

In the case of property that is either unique or for which the market is thin, there will, of course, be considerable leeway in establishing the value for which the charitable deduction is to be allowed, and even reasonably respectable and otherwise competent appraisers are unlikely to be completely oblivious to the potential advantages to their future business of leaning towards a generous appraisal when this is to the obvious advantage of all the immediate parties. One hears stories of taxpayers making a rather good thing out of a practice of buying up works of art at relatively modest prices, waiting a suitable period for "ripening," and then donating them to an eligible institution on the basis of an appraisal having an upward bias as great as can pass muster. If h is the ratio by which the appraised value exceeds the realistic market value at which the item could actually be sold for cash, and b is now the ratio of cost to market value, the gift becomes profitable, as compared with market sale, as soon as $hm + g(1-b) > 1.0$.

If the property given was "income property," i.e., property whose sale in the market would normally give rise to "ordinary income" taxable at the full rates rather than at the capital gains rates, the tax reduction would have been $Am(2 - b)$. In many cases, especially where the property is an original creation, the basis is practically zero. Thus the successful artist who found himself in a combined state and federal income tax bracket of over 50 percent (which for 1969 could have been for an income of as low as $25,000 for a single person), by reason of his income from sales to normal buyers, would be in a position to improve his net financial position by giving some of his unsold products to an art museum, taking the charitable deduction for a suitably generous appraisal price rather than holding on to them for the sake of a somewhat problematical future sale. This particular opportunity was closed as of December 20, 1969, by the Tax Reform Act of 1969, to the accompaniment of a final spate of deliveries of such gifts prior to the deadline. "Income property" now provides a charitable deduction only to the extent of its cost, though the full opportunity remains open with respect to capital assets. Also as of December 31, 1969, the "bargain sale" device was shorn of its special attractions by requiring in effect that the transaction be split into a sale of a fractional interest in the property at full value and a gift of the remaining fraction.

EFFECTS OF THE DEDUCTION

One conclusion that seems obvious to the detached observer is that an arrangement that can under special circumstances produce a profit from the making of a gift is going somewhat too far, and indeed the double deduction which creates a substantial tax differential between giving the property directly and the possibly more natural procedure of first selling the property and then giving the proceeds, is of dubious social value. There is nothing especially meritorious in the making of contributions in the form of appreciated property to warrant an especially advantageous incentive in such cases. Indeed, such a practice may place the donee in the unfamiliar role of a liquidator of property in the disposal of which he has no special expertise. If the donor, as a shrewd investor, has determined that sale of the asset is desirable, the delay involved in making the gift and leaving the sale up to the donee may allow the asset to fall in value in the interim. Ordinary avoidance of double counting would seem to indicate that the appropriate treatment in the case of gifts of property is to either allow only the basis of the property as a deduction, or to treat the gift as a realization of the market value, include the appreciation in income, either as capital gain or as ordinary income according to the circumstances, and then allow the full market value to be deducted as a charitable contribution. One might even allow the taxpayer to choose which treatment he prefers, since he can always carry out the transaction implied in the second treatment, and it would be undesirable to compel him to incur the costs involved if he wished to obtain this treatment. Yet even this fairly obvious reform has thus far been successfully resisted, in the case of capital assets (such as securities), by institutions that have engaged extensively in the solicitation of this kind of gift.

Even if one examines the charitable contribution deduction in its straightforward and originally intended form, the effects produced are somewhat open to question. At best, the deduction offers the taxpayer in the 67 percent combined federal, state, and local income tax bracket a two-for-one matching of government contribution toward the gross gift for every dollar of net sacrifice suffered by the taxpayer making the gift, whereas for the lower-bracket taxpayer the matching may be only one-for-five or one-for-six for taxpayers that itemize their deductions. For those using the standard deduction or not paying any tax, largely low-income individuals living in rented housing, no effective matching occurs at all, in the operational sense of making the amount obtained by the donor greater than the net sacrifice made by the donor as a direct consequence of making the gift. The government thus in effect subsidizes the charities favored by the rich to a far greater extent than those favored by the poor. It is not at all clear that this is a healthy bias. In no other area do the wealthy have such a preponderant and explicit influence in determining the manner in which funds indirectly provided by the government are to be allocated.

THE PRICE ELASTICITY OF PHILANTHROPY

From another standpoint, there is grave doubt whether the deduction actually achieves to any detectable extent the intended function of stimulating gifts by individuals, as distinct from merely supplementing such gifts with a government contribution derived from what would otherwise have been tax revenue. If one regards the provision of a sum to the philanthropy as what is being "bought" and the net cost to the taxpayer, after allowing for tax deductions, of providing $1 to the philanthropy as the "price," then the condition that a reduction in this price through the allowance of a tax benefit should increase the net amount "spent" on philanthropy is equivalent to saying that the "price elasticity of philanthropy" is greater than 1.0. For example, if an individual in the absence of any tax benefits would make a contribution of $10,000, the institution of deductibility with a 60 percent marginal rate would have to induce him to increase his contribution to over $25,000 in order for there to be an increase in the net cost of his contribution to him: if he increases his contribution only to, say, $20,000, the net effect is that he has reduced his own share in the gross contribution from $10,000 to $8,000, the remaining $12,000 coming from a reduction in his income tax bill. Such meager indications as there are tend to indicate an elasticity substantially less than 1.0.

One indication is derived from income tax data across income classes for a given year. Table 1 gives some results derived from income tax returns for 1970. Column 16 shows the ratio of estimated net cost of gifts[1] to estimated disposable income.[2] This ratio is remarkably constant over the range from $10,000 to $100,000 of adjusted gross income; it is likely that the behavior

[1] The net cost of gifts is the gross amount of gifts shown in column 14 multiplied by the complement of the estimated marginal rate given in column 13. This in turn is derived by using the rate schedule applicable to joint returns (which account for 85 percent of all itemized deductions) to an estimated average ordinary income given in column 12, obtained by deducting reported capital gains (given in column 6) from net taxable income (column 5) and dividing by the number of returns, the assumption being that in those classes where capital gains are important the alternative tax would be applied and the effective marginal rate would be that on an income exclusive of capital gains.

[2] Estimated disposable income is adjusted gross income (column 7) plus the exempt half of

Table 1. Net Cost of Contributions Relative to Disposable Income, 1970. By Adjusted Gross Income Classes. Returns with Itemized Deductions Only. (Money Figures in Millions of Dollars)

Adjusted Gross Income Class	*Itemizing Returns (M = x1,000)*	*Adjusted Gross Income*	*Net Long-term Capital Gains*	*Tax*	*Apparent Dispos-able Income*	*State and Local Income Taxes*	*Contri-butions*	*Avge. Mar-ginal Tax Rate*	*Avge. Price of Phil-anthropy*	*Net Cost of Contri-butions*	*Ratio of Contri-butions to Dis-posable Income*	*Percent of Returns not Itemizing*	*Percent of Contri-butions made in Property*
(1)	*(2)*	*(3)*	*(4)*	*(5)*	*(6)*	*(7)*	*(8)*	*(9)*	*(10)*	*(11)*	*(12)*	*(13)*	*(14)*
.000– .005	4,444M	16,363	233	823	15,773	155	818	17.13	82.87	678	.0430	82.82	3.8
.005– .010	11,674M	88,983	539	7,659	81,863	1,118	2,740	19.65	80.35	2,202	.0269	47.66	3.4
.010– .015	10,571M	130,004	500	14,598	115,906	2,124	3,204	21.79	78.21	2,506	.0216	25.06	3.7
.015– .020	4,917M	84,053	431	11,399	73,085	1,636	2,000	24.78	75.22	1,504	.0206	11.23	3.7
.020– .025	1,785M	39,480	375	6,107	33,748	912	979	28.13	71.87	704	.0209	6.50	5.2
.025– .030	731M	19,840	343	3,388	16,795	549	502	31.93	68.07	342	.0203	4.92	5.2
.030– .050	806,392	32,974	878	6,838	27,014	1,049	881	39.43	60.57	534	.0197	3.47	8.7
.050– .100	345,059	22,731	1,140	6,513	17,358	1,875	748	52.02	47.98	359	.0207	1.69	19.1
.100– .200	61,818	8,073	945	2,968	6,050	374	396	61.13	38.87	154.0	.0255	1.04	37.6
.200– .500	12,751	3,601	896	1,521	2,976	193	278	65.88	34.12	94.8	.0319	.62	53.4
.500–1,000	1,747	1,172	447	526	1,093	62	131	64.41	35.59	46.6	.0426	.23	59.5
1.000–∞	642	1,419	647	634	1,432	55	215	64.28	35.72	76.8	.0357	.00	74.1

Source: U.S. Internal Revenue Service, Statistics of Income, 1970, part 1, Individual Income Tax Returns.

Col. 2: Page 108, Table 33, Col. 1.
Col. 3: Page 108, Table 33, Col. 2.
Col. 4: Page 114, Table 35, Col 23 – Col 25.
Col. 5: Page 108, Table 33, Col 7 plus Col 8.
Col. 6: (3) + (4) – (5).
Col. 7: Page 123, Table 38, Col. 10.
Col. 8: Page 120, Table 36, Col. 8.
Col. 9: Computed from table 52, pages 158-61, and table 55, pages 168-70, with adjustment for the surcharge specified on page 337.
Col. 10: 100 – Col. (9).
Col. 11: (8) X (10).
Col. 12: (11)/(6).
Col. 13: Page 131, Table 46, Col. 1 / Page 14, Table 4, Col. 1.
Col. 14: Page 127, Table 42, Col. 8/Col. 4.

of this ratio outside this range is as much accounted for by deficiencies in the data as by any inherent difference in taxpayer behavior.[3] If we can take the constancy of this ratio over this range as representative of the entire range (and this range accounts for 65 percent of all contributions), and if we were to assume that the income elasticity of philanthropy were unity, this would imply that the price elasticity is substantially equal to 1.0 over a range of prices from .782 to .359. If we assume the income elasticity to be greater than unity (i.e., philanthropy is a "superior" good), then this would imply that the price elasticity is less than one.

Another indication is given by the analysis of data relating to periods when sharp changes in tax rates have taken place. A recent occasion was the tax reform of 1964, which lowered the top marginal rates from 91 percent to 77 percent, effectively raising the price of giving from 9 percent to 23 percent, an increase of 140 percent in the price, even before considering the effect of the state and local income taxes which would have made the comparison even more striking. Data for contributions are tabulated only for even-numbered years, so unfortunately we do not have data on gifts made to beat the deadline, which in this case might not have been a significant factor, since in December 1963 there was still a great deal of uncertainty as to what actually would eventuate from movements afoot for tax reform. Table 2, however, does appear to indicate an elasticity of less than unity for the upper-income classes: the increase in the price of giving from 1962 to 1964 is associated with what appears to be a noticeable and consistent increase in the proportion of disposable income devoted to the net cost of charitable contributions.[4]

---

realized capital gains (equal to the taxable half given in column 7), minus the federal tax liability in column 9. This can be justified by assuming that for most low-income taxpayers the deductions for property taxes and interest can be considered proxies for the imputed income from home ownership, while for upper-bracket taxpayers any property taxes or interest not representing imputed income can be considered a partial adjustment for other exempt income. Making no allowance for state and local income taxes might be considered a more serious distortion, but this is more than offset by the fact that no allowance for these taxes is made in the calculation of the marginal tax rate that determines the net cost of the gift.

[3] The higher values in column 16 for incomes above $100,000 can readily be attributed to understatement of disposable income on the one hand, owing to the omission of tax-exempt income, unrealized capital gains, and the like, and overstatement of the net cost of gifts made in property rather than cash, which account for over half of all gifts made by taxpayers in brackets above $100,000, but only 5.2 percent of all gifts made by taxpayers in the brackets below $100,000.

[4] Some earlier data bearing on the subject are given in "One Economist's View of Philanthropy," William Vickrey, in *Philanthropy and Public Policy*, Frank G. Dickinson, ed., (National Bureau of Economic Research, 1962), pp. 54-55; also in C. Harry Kahn, *Personal Deductions in the Federal Income Tax*, pp. 73-88, and M. K. Taussig, "Economic Aspects of the Personal Income Tax Treatment of Charitable Contributions," *National Tax Journal* 20 (March 1967), pp. 1-19, which in turn is an abstract of a Ph.D. Thesis, "The Charitable Contributions Deduction in the Federal Income Tax" (Cambridge: M.I.T., 1965).

Table 2. Comparison of Contribution Levels for 1962 and 1964 By Adjusted Gross Income Classes above $20,000

	Taxable Returns with Itemized Deductions													
Adjusted Gross Income Classes ($1,000)	*Disposable Income (Millions of Dollars)*		*Gross Contributions (Millions of Dollars)*		*Price of Philanthropy*		*Net Cost of Contributions*		*Percent of Disposable Income Contributed*		*Average Disposable Income ($1,000)*		*Cumulative Number of Returns*	
	1962	1964	1962	1964	1962	1964	1962	1964	1962	1964	1962	1964	1962	1964
20– 50	19,850	26,552	806.4	987.5	.595	.650	480.2	641.9	2.42	2.42	21.1	24.5	1,089,192	1,248,681
50– 100	5,751	7,983	330.8	401.7	.410	.462	135.8	185.6	2.36	2.32	47.4	60.0	148,219	164,976
100– 500	3,351	4,760	320.8	392.8	.309	.397	99.0	155.9	2.95	3.28	129.8	156.4	26,967	31,879
500–1,000	552	746	56.4	72.9	.305	.374	17.2	27.3	3.12	3.66	686.	755.	1,146	1,433
1,000–∞	715	1,035	91.0	120.7	.287	.368	26.1	44.1	3.65	4.29	2091.	2326.	342	445
(1)	(2)	(3)	(4)	(5)	(6)	(7)	(8)	(9)	(10)	(11)	(12)	(13)	(14)	(15)

Source: U.S. Internal Revenue Service, Statistics of Income, 1962 and 1964, Part 1, Individual Income Tax Returns.
Col. (2): 1962: P. 85, Table 14, col. 2 + p. 87, Table 15, col. 11 – p. 87, Table 15, col. 13 – p. 86, Table 14, col. 17.
Col. (3): 1964: P. 50, Table 15, col. 3 + p. 50, Table 15, col. 19 – p. 50, Table 15, col. 21 – p. 52, Table 15, col. 59.
Col. (4): 1962: P. 85, Table 14, col. 5.
Col. (5): 1964: P. 51, Table 15, col. 53.
Col. (6): 1962: Pp. 110–113, Table 20, average of marginal rates weighted by number of returns, subtracted from 1.00.
Col. (7): 1964: Pp. 76–78, Table 23, average of marginal rates weighted by number of returns, subtracted from 1.00.
Col. (8): (4) × (6)
Col. (9): (5) × (7)
Col. (10): (8)/(3)
Col. (11): (9)/(4)
Col. (12): Col. (2) divided by 1962: page 85, Table 4, col. 1.
Col. (13): Col. (3) divided by 1964: page 50, Table 15, col. 1.
Col. (14): 1962: Page 85, Table 4, col. 1.
Col. (15): 1964: Page 50, Table 15, col. 1.

Analysis from such time series, however, must be considered to have serious difficulties, in that the data for the various years, especially adjacent years, are not really independent. On the one side there is a tendency to establish a steady level of gross support, particularly for ongoing activities, that may persist for a considerable time in the face of substantial changes in the tax incentives, thus leading to a tendency to understate the price elasticity. On the other hand there may be some tendency to transfer contributions from one year to another where differences in effective marginal rates are anticipated, either from a change in the law or changes in the taxpayer's financial circumstances, with a view to maximizing the tax benefits obtainable from a given total of contributions. Such evidence as there is, however, seems to be at least consistent with a hypothesis of a long-term price elasticity of less than one, so that a reduction in the price of philanthropy brought about through tax concessions may result in less, rather than more, net philanthropic effort on the part of the taxpayer.

POSSIBLE EFFECTS OF FORMAL CHANGES

It is quite possible, however, that this net negative effect is in part psychological, depending on the superficial form of the transaction, in that the taxpayer-contributor thinks of himself, as he writes his check, as making a contribution equal to the amount of the check, rather than as making a contribution equal to the net cost, however much aware he may be of the tax consequences of the gift. Quite possibly a different formal arrangement, achieving the same ultimate result, whereby the matching payment is made directly by the government to the philanthropy, rather than indirectly through a rebate of the tax to the taxpayer, would elicit significantly greater contributions from taxpayers, even though there would be no change in the overall logic of the situation. In the United Kingdom, for example, while contributions have generally not been deductible on a year-by-year basis, the effect of a tax deduction can be obtained by a taxpayer entering into a covenant to contribute an annual sum for seven years or more. This is regarded as transferring the original rights on the income from the taxpayer to the beneficiary, the taxpayer becoming a mere channel of payment. The consequence is that in making the payment the taxpayer "withholds" an amount equal to the normal tax and makes out a check for the net cost of his contribution, which he sends to the beneficiary, who in turn applies directly to the Inland Revenue for a refund or credit for the tax so withheld.[5] The payment by the donor of the tax withheld is not handled as a separate transaction but is considered to be included in the tax paid, directly or indirectly, by the donor on his income as a whole.

[5] The degree to which form is often allowed to overcome substance is illustrated by the sucessful defense in the House of Lords by the Duke of Westminster of his use of this procedure to make tax-free payments in lieu of wages to his domestic servants. This practice, however, was disallowed in subsequent cases.

CREDITS AND MATCHING GRANTS IN LIEU OF DEDUCTIONS

In the United States, it has been suggested that as a means of equalizing the degree of matching and incentive as between high- and low-income taxpayers, a credit of a given flat percentage of these contributions be allowed against the tax due, instead of the deduction from income of the amount of the contribution.[6] This still does not take care of the contributions of those not subject to any tax, and retains the emphasis to the contributor on the gross gift rather than the net. There have been many suggestions of providing, as a substitute for the deduction, a direct payment of a matching grant by the government to the eligible recipients of donations from individual contributors. In some proposals the matching would be on a straight proportional basis,[7] in others it would be varied, with the matching percentage being higher for contributions constituting higher percentages of the donor's income. Such a change would have a favorable impact in both of these respects: matching would be the same for high- and for low-income taxpayers, and attention would be focused on the net amount of the gift. There seems a strong likelihood that the gross amount obtained by philanthropy under this method would be increased for any given level of government contribution. Relatively less of the total amount contributed would go to the types of philanthropy especially favored by the wealthy, which from many points of view would seem to be a healthy change.

There is, however, a potential difficulty involved in direct grants to religious bodies that may run afoul of the constitutional strictures against the establishment of a religion that are particularly forceful in the U.S. but which also exist elsewhere. While logically there should be no difference between a payment made directly and a payment channeled through the abatement of a tax to a donor, the form of the transaction has here again turned out to be of paramount importance. The spectacle of embattled strict church-state separationists straining at the gnat of publicly supplied textbooks or bus service to parochial school students, while swallowing the camel of property tax exemption and income tax deductibility for contributions, may appear ludicrous to those accustomed to looking past the form to the substance. Yet even the Supreme Court appears to allow itself to get tangled up in this mixture of historical precedent and formalism. Substantively, even with direct payment of matching grants, it should be possible to maintain that as long as there is no discrimination among alternative religious or secular agencies, there need be no "establishment of religion" such as to contravene the Constitution. Present

---

[6] See Vickrey, *Agenda for Progressive Taxation* (Ronald, 1947; Augustus M. Kell, 1962), pp. 130-31; C. H. Kahn, *op. cit.*, p. 87.

[7] Paul R. McDaniel makes an interesting proposal along these lines in "An Alternative to the Federal Income Tax Deduction in Support of Private Philanthropy," *Tax Impacts on Philanthropy* (Tax Institute of America, 1972), pp. 171-213.

trends, however, leave little ground for hope for an early resolution of the problem along these lines.

One possible way of circumventing this objection might be to retain the deductibility or a tax credit for contributions to religious bodies, while relying on the matching grant as a means of encouraging other kinds of gifts. Even deductibility, if limited to contributions to religious organizations, would be less open to criticism on the ground that the matching rates would vary, since contributions to religious organizations are to a considerable extent concentrated in the lower-income brackets and the differentials would be less extreme. A more indirect scheme might involve asking a taxpayer to list his eligible contributions, including his religious ones, compute a matching grant total based on the total of such gifts, but then distribute this total grant among the non-religious organizations, leaving it to the taxpayer to reallocate his giving in the light of this grant pattern. If taxpayers were fully rational and fully understood the operation of the scheme, this should produce the same end result as a uniform grant to religious and non-religious organizations alike: the religious organizations, though not participating directly in the grant, would benefit indirectly by reason of being part of the basis for the magnitude of the grant and would benefit directly as individuals enlarged their religious gifts and reduced others relatively in the expectation of the resulting grant distribution altering the aggregate balance. While such a provision would avoid any direct contact between state and church, and would certainly involve far less impact of state action on the internal affairs of the church than does for example the exemption from property tax, the very deviousness of the proposal might incline a suspicious court to strike it down. And the indirectness of the benefits to be obtained by the religious organizations under such a proposal might lead them to oppose any change from the present position. There is also the constraint that the amounts received by non-religious agencies must at least equal the amount provided as a matching grant; as it is, some 60 percent of all contributions are for religious organizations, if parochial schools be included, and for many individual taxpayers who normally make nearly all of their contributions to religious agencies, this scheme would compel an expansion of their direct and induced support going to non-religious agencies, a result that could be considered to be inhibiting the "free exercise" of religion.

IMPOSITION OF A THRESHOLD

Another proposal that has superficial similarities with this graduated grant is a proposal to limit the deduction for contributions to the excess over some threshold percentage of income, along the lines of the deduction for extraordinary medical expenses. This will appeal to some as a way of reducing the "tax expenditure" cost of the deduction. If it is advocated on the basis that the

Table 3. Distribution of Contributions by Percentage of Contributions to Adjusted Gross Income, 1970

Contributions Deduction as a percent of Adjusted Gross Income Classes	*Number of Returns (Thousands)*	*Amount of Contributions (Millions of Dollars)*
Over 0, less than 1	7,812	590
At least 1, less than 2	8,233	1,693
At least 2, less than 3	6,275	1,998
At least 3, less than 4	3,690	1,545
At least 4, less than 5	2,121	1,086
At least 5, less than 6	1,312	785
At least 6, less than 7	875	632
At least 7, less than 8	651	515
At least 8, less than 9	512	467
At least 9, less than 10	419	412
At least 10, less than 15	1,107	1,293
At least 15, less than 20	306	498
At least 20	43	82
Over 20, less than 30	147	435
At least 30	128	90
Over 30, less than 40	49	237
At least 40, less than 50	27	168
At least 50	41	245
Over 50	18	121
All returns with contributions	33,634	12,893

threshold level will be such that nearly all taxpayers will be above the threshold, however, it should be pointed out that for taxpayers who actually are above the threshold practically the same tax bill could be produced by leaving the deduction intact and adjusting the rate schedule.[8] Therefore if a justification is to be found for such a measure, it lies in the reduction in compliance and administrative costs achieved by eliminating the item from returns for which it is a trivial amount. Table 3 shows the distribution of gifts by size relative to adjusted gross income. It appears that a threshold of 3 percent of adjusted gross income would eliminate explicit contribution deductions from some 22 million returns annually, or about two-thirds of the returns now showing deductions for contributions. It is not possible to tell how many returns would by this step alone be shifted from the itemizing to the standard deduction category, but

[8] If, for example, the threshold is set at 4 percent of income, exactly the same tax could be produced by using C/1.04 instead of C as the allowable deduction for the contribution, dividing all the bracket levels in the schedule by 1.04 and increasing the various bracket rates from m to 1.04 m, and allowing full deduction of the contribution. Thus if the rate schedule were readjusted to produce the same net revenue after the enlargement of the base by the establishment of the contribution threshold, the result would be to reduce the tax incentive for philanthropy both for gifts above and below the threshold.

off-hand it seems unlikely to be significant, unless indeed combined with other reforms such as the elimination of deductions for property taxes, in which case there would be a strong synergistic effect.

DEDUCTION FOR CONTRIBUTIONS AND FREE EXPRESSION

But whatever is done with respect to gifts to religious organizations, as well as to contributions to the more explicitly public welfare types of charity, there remains a problem in connection with the curious denial of deductions of contributions to organizations if "a substantial part of its activities is the carrying on of propaganda or otherwise attempting to influence legislation." One can sympathize with Congressmen wishing to reduce the lobbying pressures to which they are subject, and even applaud what might be interpreted as a self-denying rule attempting, ostensibly, to curtail opportunities for corruptive campaign favors and contributions. Yet to make the eligibility of an organization to receive deductible contributions depend on whether or not the organization is deemed to be "substantially" carrying on propaganda or attempting to influence legislation is almost inevitably to set the Internal Revenue Service up in the business of censorship, in deciding whether or not any particular degree of expression transgresses the vaguely specified bounds of "substantial." The "chilling" effect of this potential threat on the activities of officers of such organizations can be quite severe, especially as the lines actually drawn often appear extremely arbitrary.

The potential threat has in some cases become very real. For example, the Fellowship of Reconciliation, a pacifist organization with a religious orientation, was for a time removed from the approved list maintained by the I.R.S., but managed to get reinstated; the War Resisters' League, an organization with almost indistinguishable objectives, which maintains its independence of any religious ties, has not been so fortunate. Many organizations have been driven to set up subsidiary organizations to which tax-deductible contributions may be made, with expenditures on what might be interpreted as activities making the organization ineligible being met from other funds: we thus have the N.A.A.C.P.'s "Special Contribution Fund"; the National Sharecroppers Fund has its "Rural Advancement Fund" as its channel for deductible gifts. It is difficult to see what overall social purpose is served by thus replicating organizations.

The problems have in some areas been considerably exacerbated by the provisions of the Revenue Act of 1969 which attempted to check abuses by charitable foundations through self-dealing, accumulation of funds, and other activities tending to negate any genuine philanthropic results. The provisions proscribing direct or indirect political activity by "private" foundations (these being those not meeting fairly stringent qualifications for classification as "public" foundations) again cause such foundations to be rather restrictive with respect to those they will consider for grants, if only because of the additional administrative burden imposed by the checking that becomes necessary to insure against a possible liability for infringement of the law.[9]

Currently, indeed, two attempts are being made to challenge the situation, one on behalf of Taxation with Representation, a public interest organization attempting to represent the public on tax matters,[10] and one on behalf of the U.S. Servicemen's Fund, an organization supporting opposition to the Vietnam War. Admittedly, once one permits contributions to propaganda organizations to be deducted (and it is hard to see how the deduction can be denied or limited without inhibiting free expression), it may be difficult to draw the line between organizations supporting a cause and political parties. Thus one may be driven by the logic of the situation to provide comparable treatment to contributions to political parties, at least, if not eventually to organizations set up to promote individual candidacies. At this point there may arise a difficulty in distinguishing between a contribution *pro bono publico*, support given in expectation of future favorable consideration, and payments more nearly in the nature of corruption or outright bribery. In some cases such payments might be more properly considered a cost of doing business than a voluntary contribution, but whether such a "cost" should be entitled to be deducted in computing income would have to depend on the customs and mores of the jurisdiction involved.

CORPORATION GIVING

While undoubtedly many contributions to philanthropy by corporations have been in effect deducted from the base of the corporation income tax right from the start, whether as business expenses or in the form of free services, supplies, or other facilities provided to philanthropic organizations without cost, it was only beginning in 1936 that explicit recognition was given to the practice of corporate giving through an allowance of a deduction for charitable contributions up to 5 percent of net income. While by some the making of charitable contributions by corporations as such rather than by its shareholders individually was considered a perversion of the purpose of the corporation, involving an *ultra vires* diversion by the directors of funds properly belonging to the stockholders, there were obvious advantages, especially for closely held corporations, in having the corporation make contributions to causes favored by the stockholders, in that in this way the corporation income tax would be avoided, as well as the individual income tax. This became increasingly

[9] See Sydney Howe, "Public Policy Issues and Foundations," in *Tax Impacts on Philanthropy* (Tax Institute of America, 1972) pp. 76-80; Ruth C. Chance, "Operational Effects," *ibid.*, pp. 103-111; Homer C. Wadsworth, "Program Activities," *ibid.*, p. 119; Howard Dressner, Learning to Live with the Tax Reform Act, *ibid.*, pp. 124-25.

[10] *Taxation with Representation News Letter*, June 1, 1973.

important as the corporation income tax, after 1936, became an increasingly substantial additional burden rather than a rough collection at source of a part of the individual income tax. In the case of the more widely held corporations, the collective gift by the corporation to causes with a wide base of support, such as community chests, could also serve as a channel through which the externalities of giving could find a limited degree of expression: stockholders could acquiesce in this form of giving on the ground that in this way they would have an assurance of the comparable contributions of other stockholders to the common purpose which they would not have had had they received a corresponding amount as additional dividends and made the contributions individually. The avoidance of corporate tax plus the assurance of comparable contributions from others could well, for the bulk of stockholders, outweigh the sacrifice of direct control over the amount and distribution of the contribution, even where such contributions would necessarily be limited to causes commanding wide community support or having a special nexus with the operations of the corporation.

SUCCESSION TAXES

Gifts and bequests to philanthropic organizations are deductible without any percentage limit, but subject to the same strictures against legislative or political influence as for the individual income tax in calculating federal estate and gift taxes. Here again, there is little evidence that this produces any net diversion of funds from heirs to philanthropy as against the more obvious diversion of funds from the public fisc to philanthropy, although the data do show a rather more pronounced increase in the proportion of the net disposable estate devoted to the net cost of philanthropic bequests as the size of the estate increases. Some data for returns filed in 1970 are shown in table 4.

Such data must be interpreted with even greater caution than is the case for income tax data. On the one hand one may be somewhat surprised that such substantial amounts show up as charitable bequests when lifetime gifts would avoid not only the estate tax but the income tax as well. Estate tax returns filed during 1970 will have related to deaths occurring largely in 1968 and '69; income tax data for 1964, a suitably earlier period, show that less than 1 in 15 of taxpayers in the $500,000 and over income classes were at all constrained by any of the percentage limitations on the deductibility of contributions. On the other hand, a fairly large proportion of the taxable estate in the top total estate classes is made up of property disposed of during the decedent's lifetime and brought into the estate tax base by various provisions such as those imposing estate taxes on gifts made in contemplation of death or of property in which the decedent retained taxable incidents of ownership, such as a general power of appointment. Such inclusion in the total estate for tax purposes of income not

Table 4. Charitable Bequests in Estate Tax Returns Filed in 1970

	Taxable Returns							Non-taxable Returns			
Total Estate Classes (Thousands of Dollars)	*Number of Returns*	*Disposable Estate (Millions of Dollars)*	*Charitable Bequests (Millions of Dollars)*	*Average Marginal Rate (Per Cent)*	*Price of Charitable Bequest (Per Cent)*	*Cost of Charitable Bequest (Millions of Dollars)*	*Cost as Percent of Disposable Estate*	*Number of Returns*	*Disposable Estate (Millions of Dollars)*	*Charitable Bequests (Millions of Dollars)*	*Charitable Bequest as Percent of Disposable Estate*
(1)	(2)	(3)	(4)	(5)	(6)	(7)	(8)	(9)	(10)	(11)	(12)
0– 60	3,193	– 25[a]	16.1	10.05[b]	89.9	14.5	a	1,079	57	20.1	35.26
60– 80	11,902	770	7.3	10.05[b]	89.9	6.6	0.85	15,325	1,226	31.6	2.57
80– 100	12,562	976	8.3	13.41	86.6	7.2	0.74	10,491	1,037	31.5	3.04
100– 150	22,163	2,364	23.0	18.74	81.3	18.7	0.79	11,570	1,282	48.0	3.74
150– 200	14,440	2,073	25.6	21.34	78.7	20.1	0.97	1,118	146	46.1	31.6
200– 300	12,965	2,491	52.9	26.42	73.6	38.9	1.56	480	82	39.3	47.9
300– 500	8,677	2,492	91.6	29.73	70.3	64.4	2.58	289	90	67.2	74.7
500– 1,000	5,024	2,453	151.6	32.25	67.7	102.6	4.18	121	67	53.4	79.7
1,000– 2,000	1,654	1,510	129.2	36.20	63.8	82.4	5.46				
2,000– 3,000	380	591	72.6	44.03	56.0	40.6	6.88	47	99	68.0	68.7
3,000– 5,000	257	602	100.4	47.9	52.1	52.3	8.69				
5,000–10,000	144	584	137.0	57.7	42.3	57.9	9.92				
10,000–∞	63	712	911.5	74.36	25.6	233.3	32.77				

Source: U.S. Internal Revenue Service, Statistics of Income, 1969, Part 4, Estate Tax Returns.
Col. (2): Page 14, Table 5, col. 1
Col. (3): Pages 15, 17, Table 5, col. 50 (taxable estate) – col. 30 (Lifetime transfers) + col. 47 (marital deduction) + col. 49 (specific exemption) + col. 45 (charitable bequests) – col. 53 (estate tax before credits)
Col. (4): Page 16, Table 5, col. 45
Col. (5): Page 24, Table 13, average marginal rate weighted by number of returns
Col. (6): 100.0 – col. (5)
Col. (7): Col. (4) multiplied by col. (6)
Col. (8): Col. (7) divided by col. (3)
Col. (9): Same as col. (2)
Col. (10): Same as col. (3)
Col. (11): Same as col. (4)
Col. (12): Col. (11) divided by col. (10)

[a]Negative disposable estate due chiefly to tax assessed with respect to lifetime transfers excluded from disposable estate.

[b]Average computed for a combined $0–$80,000 class used for both subclasses.

considered part of the net economic estate is largely responsible for the relatively large amount of charitable bequests in the under $60,000 class and in the non-taxable returns in classes above $150,000. The impact of these returns in the non-taxable return totals for classes between $60,000 and $150,000 is masked to a considerable extent by the inclusion of returns in these figures that are non-taxable chiefly by reason of the marital deduction.

TAX TREATMENT OF CHARITABLE ORGANIZATIONS, TRUSTS, AND FOUNDATIONS

The other major form of fiscal support for charitable organizations consists in granting varying degrees of exemption from taxation to the organization itself. This usually has extended to income tax on net earnings from assets held, of whatever character, and to property taxes on property used directly for the charitable purpose. Other concessions include exemption from certain excises, including in some cases general sales taxes. In the case of religious organizations, these exemptions have sometimes been held to be a corollary of constitutional strictures against impairment of freedom of worship, though the economic logic as distinct from the legal logic of a doctrine of separation of church and state might be held to require, rather, an even-handed treatment free of either extra burden or special privilege. In the case of private schools the exemption has been defended at least in part on the ground that such schools are performing a function that would otherwise devolve upon the public schools at public expense.

Whatever justification these special execeptions may have as a form of subsidy, the fact that the support is specified in this form has adverse effects on the efficient allocation of resources. Churches and schools are encouraged to occupy more real estate and build more lavishly than if the cost of these resources were the same to them as to other enterprises, relative to expenditures on personnel. Organizations are encouraged to occupy possibly less suitable quarters which they can own in fee and thus benefit from property tax exemption rather than renting quarters in a building whose owner would then not be able to obtain a corresponding tax exemption and would have to pass the burden of the tax on in the rent. Storefront churches are discriminated against as compared with more prosperous congregations that can own their own building.[11] Exemption is sometimes granted in capricious and discriminatory ways, in part for historical reasons: the Chrysler Building opposite Grand Central Station is exempt from New York City property taxes, by reason of the ground being owned by Cooper Union, according to a provision peculiar to that

[11] In planning the World Trade Center, the Port of New York Authority made special arrangements to be exempted from taxation on that part of the complex that would be occupied by exempt organizations and agencies such as foreign consulates, government offices, and the like.

institution; Rockefeller Center, built on land leased from Columbia University, enjoys no comparable privilege. And the practice as to how far the exemption will extend to property owned by a philanthropic organization but not directly or exclusively employed in the philanthropic activity varies considerably from one jurisdiction to another. The fact that in some areas the entire exemption might be jeopardized by permitting a partial non-philanthropic use of the property, as for example renting a parking lot for commercial use during the week when it is not being used by parishioners, has led to underutilization of the property.

A more serious issue of recent years has been the degree of exemption from income taxes to be enjoyed by philanthropic organizations. While there has been on the whole no disposition to subject to full taxation under the corporation income tax those organizations genuinely and solely devoted to philanthropic purposes, the fact that many nominally philanthropic organizations have been used to varying extents for tax avoidance and other purposes, sometimes to the neglect of any substantial philanthropic activity, has led to attempt to curb the abuses. The measures that have emerged as a result have in turn had serious impacts, particularly on some of the smaller organizations.

Some of the abuses included the use of the foundation to supply services or amenities to the donor which if secured directly would have to be paid for out of taxed income; management of the assets of the foundation to suit the business purposes of the donor; and accumulation and reinvesting of income so as to build an economic empire rather than accomplishing any immediate philanthropic purpose, with the assets being managed to further the interests of the donor, even though no outright expenditures on his behalf would be made or contemplated for the future. Foundations have been established primarily from a motive of enabling a family to preserve its control over a family corporation, where otherwise large succession duties would require a substantial fraction of the family holdings to be sold to possibly unfriendly interests to pay the tax. By setting up the foundation with shares in the family corporation as its principal asset, large tax liabilities could be avoided and the danger of the accumulation of a controlling interest in the corporation in unfriendly hands averted or at least postponed.

Recent legislation, chiefly the Revenue Act of 1969, has attempted to curb such abuses, but in the process has set up a host of distinctions, requirements, arbitrary lines of demarcation, and penalty taxes that have resulted in an extremely high cost of compliance, at least for the transition stages, which has been a severe burden on all foundations, but especially on the smaller ones, where the legal costs incurred in attempting to ascertain just what their position is have in many cases absorbed significant fractions of the income of the foundation. In theory, at least, directors of foundations have been made personally liable, in some cases where the foundations they control overstep the limits, to penalties that could be of staggering proportions; the extreme caution induced by such provisions can readily be imagined.

The underlying difficulty is that the line between a legitimate function and an abuse is hard to draw on any ground of fundamental principle. A limited amount of accumulation and decumulation of capital fills a legitimate need when the foundation is serving as a conduit, when donor individuals or corporations find it advantageous to make contributions that fluctuate in amount from year to year with income, tax rates, or perhaps capital needs, while outlays in support of programs normally need to be kept more even over time; the reverse relation can also exist when an organization wishes to accumulate reserves to enable it to meet emergencies, as with disaster relief. Reasonable limits which will distinguish this legitimate function and a long-run general accumulation for manipulative purposes are hard to draw. Unless, indeed, current capital valuations are taken into account in the specification of the limits, foundations could, by appropriately selecting investments in growth stocks paying relatively low dividends, accomplish something along these lines without explicitly accumulating income received as a cash flow, though this would tend to restrict trading and might lead to a "locked in" position. The 1969 Revenue Act dealt with this problem by requiring the current distribution of an amount equal to a percentage of capital to be determined annually by the administration, which limits accumulation to cases where the foundation is able to earn considerably more than the stipulated rate. A stipulation in terms of an income inclusive of accrued capital gains would avoid this problem but might pose problems of valuation in the case of assets not having regularly quoted market prices.

Recent provisions for carryover of the contribution deduction in excess of that allowable against current income, plus liberalization of the percentage limits, have eliminated much of the need for such "averaging" action for individuals, though the need still exists with respect to sharp fluctuations of income giving rise to differences from year to year in the marginal rates, as well as for the accumulation of emergency reserves. The general averaging provisions recently introduced are hedged about with so many restrictive provisions as to begin to look like a green whiskers project, though even so some 133,000 taxpayers out of 429,000 in the over $50,000 brackets and 872,000 out of 45,543,000 in the under $50,000 brackets managed to take advantage of the provisions for 1970.

On balance, however, there is much to be said for requiring charitable organizations to expend in current charitable activity at least a given percentage of their capital, either directly or through grants to other organizations. Even so, for foundations currently receiving gifts, it may be difficult to distinguish between capital gifts by individuals and gifts on current account, and tracing funds passing through several organizations complicates matters considerably.

Even more serious are the problems associated with an attempt to distinguish fairly sharply between "private" foundations that could be deemed to be under the control of one or a few major donors, and thus subject to motives other than purely philanthropic, and "public" foundations which either draw a substantial part of their support from small and moderate contributions from a numerous constituency, or are otherwise so constituted as to prevent their being manipulated to serve the private ends of a few taxpayer-donors, and to apply sharply differing regulations to the two types. The distinction, of course, implies constraints on transfers between the two classes of organizations.

OTHER NON-PROFIT ORGANIZATIONS

In addition to explicitly philanthropic organizations there are a number of other non-profit organizations which in varying degrees operate to perform functions that range from the purely commercial to those bordering on the eleemosynary. In size the range is from the credit union operating out of somebody's desk drawer, through the cooperative supermarket, to such institutions as the Metropolitan Life Insurance Company. One immediate problem that arises is what theoretical basis there is for either taxing such entities under the corporation income tax, or for exempting them and thus creating a sharp discrimination between them and ordinary corporations performing the same or similar functions.

Within the general category of "non-profit" commercial organizations practices vary fairly widely. At one extreme the pure co-op may in fact return all profits to member-customers in patronage refunds, and thus be in fact, as well as in name, "non-profit." At the other extreme, many such entities accumulate very large surpluses or reserves, in which no ascertainable individuals may be able to establish an interest sufficiently definite to be converted to liquid form by assignment, transfer, or otherwise. Such reserves thus do not "belong" to anybody. They are, nevertheless, under the control of the officers of the organization, and are presumably accumulated, at least in part, to ensure the continued existence of the organization and the permanence of the salaries of these officers. Normally, the amounts that can be so accumulated are limited by the trading margins that can be imposed, but where competition is limited or imperfect, substantial accumulations can be built up, especially if the organization maintains itself over an extended period of time. Once the accumulation exceeds what can reasonably be required for purposes of assuring continuity of the organization, further accumulation may be used simply for empire building or perhaps to further some general cause. Such situations are one of the odder corners of the economic world, not hitherto subject to much close scrutiny; one possible use may be to serve as a testing ground for concepts that might be able to survive application to more conventional institutions.[12]

[12] An interesting example is found in the mutual insurance companies that write primarily "perpetual" insurance in which the insured pays a capital sum as a premium at the initiation of his coverage which is ordinarily returned to the policyholder at the termination of his coverage. One such company, Mutual Assurance of Philadelphia, with total liabilities of $1.488 million, of which $1.478 million represented premium deposits, had a surplus of over $41 million. Prospective policyholders were promised, if they were accepted, that for their deposit they would be paid a dividend of 4 percent after the first year, 8 percent beginning with the fifth year, 16 percent beginning with the tenth year, and 20 percent in the fifteenth year and thereafter, all of this in addition to insurance coverage. For policyholders continuing their policies for 27 years or longer, this amounts to a cash return of over 10 percent compounded annually, in addition to which they would enjoy insurance coverage for no added outlay. Apparently those who are fortunate enough to be accepted as policyholders fall heir to at least a small part of the income generated by the $28 of surplus available for each $1 of premium deposit. In terms of tax advantage, the policyholder not only benefits from the balloon pattern of dividends, but if the insured property is an owner-occupied residence, he gains from the fact that the income used to provide the insurance is not taxable to him.

*Toward a Theory of the Voluntary Non-Profit Sector in a Three-Sector Economy**

Burton A. Weisbrod

This paper is an exploratory effort to examine the role of a voluntary, "philanthropic" sector in an economy with public and private (for-profit) sectors and with collective-consumption and private-consumption goods. More generally, it seeks an answer to the questions what factors determine which goods will be provided governmentally, which privately in for-profit markets, and which in voluntary markets. The approach is primarily positive, attempting particularly to predict the circumstances under which the voluntary sector will develop, grow and decline. A model will be fashioned in which certain behavioral and organizational constraints limit public-sector and for-profit sector activities and stimulate the voluntary sector; and in which the existence of collective-consumption goods is not sufficient to ensure governmental production or provision. The existence of such voluntary organizations will thus be explained with a minimum of institutional assumptions. In effect, we set forth the logic behind a hypothesis that there are non-governmental, voluntary organizations providing collective goods. Some normative judgments will be reached regarding efficient public policy toward certain types of voluntary organizations.

*This research has received a variety of support: from the Institute for Research on Poverty, pursuant to the Economic Opportunity Act of 1964; from the University of Wisconsin Graduate School; and from Guggenheim Foundation and Ford Foundation fellowships. In connection with various parts of the research I have been very fortunate to be assisted by Jennifer Gerner, A. James Lee, Donna Beutel, and Marc Bendick, Jr. Eugene Smolensky, Mark Menchik, and Donald Nichols provided helpful comments on an earlier draft of this paper.

The analysis presented here is essentially static. There is some consideration, however, of the effects on the distribution of economic activity among the three sectors—government, for-profit, and voluntary—that result from changes in population characteristics and in the level and inequality of income.

The interest that is now developing in organizations variously referred to as voluntary, non-profit, collective, charitable, non-market or philanthropic is overdue, for there is no doubt that a wide array of economic activity is undertaken outside the private profit-seeking sector and outside the public sector. Contemporary economics includes a long-established theory of the private (profit) sector, the rationale for its existence and the mode of its equilibrium behavior; more recently a theory of the public (government) sector has evolved, emphasizing the existence of "public," "collective-consumption" goods for which the private sector is an unsatisfactory production vehicle that is likely to produce sub-optimal quantities.[1] Yet the reality of goods and services that are provided neither governmentally, in the sense of being financed through taxation, nor privately, in the sense of being financed through user charges and operated for "profit," confronts us with a gap in our theories.

But my goal is less ambitious than to explain the existence, let alone the behavior, of all of the many kinds of organizations that are found outside the private-profit and the public sectors. Rather I wish to identify one class of such activities—the provision (financing) of public-type, collective-consumption goods by non-governmental enterprises. Thus, this paper will examine some interrelations between the public sector, the private sector, and the voluntary sector, focusing on the provision of collective-consumption goods outside the government.

We begin with an analysis of governmental behavior. The existence of certain constraints on governments will be seen to create what might be termed government market failure, analogous to the conditions causing private market failures. Development of a voluntary sector will then be posited as an adjustment to the restricted capabilities of these other two sectors.

THE ELEMENTS OF A SIMPLE MODEL OF OUTPUT DETERMINATION IN THE GOVERNMENT SECTOR

To begin with let us assume a society in which

—People behave rationally in pursuit of their individual objectives of utility maximization;

[1] For a useful survey of the varied conceptions of "public" goods, see Peter O. Steiner, "Public Expenditure Budgeting" (Washington, D.C.: The Brookings Institution, 1969).

—A given state of technology and set of production possibilities exists, and these permit production of some collective-consumption and some private-consumption goods;

—Each person's utility is a function of both his private goods and the collective-consumption goods that are available to him;

—Utility functions are not the same for all people.

One question with which we want a behavioral model to deal is: how much of the demand for collective-consumption goods will be satisfied by government. "Satisfied" by a government is defined as financed by a government, no distinction being made between government production (ownership) of some good and provision via purchase or contracting-out—that is, paying a private producer to supply it.[2] Henceforth, the term government *provision* will be used to describe both types of arrangements.

A rule or behavioral assumption is needed for determining how government will finance any given level of output for a specified good, and a rule is also required for specifying how voter demands will influence the level of government provision. Both of these are important and, given the present state of economic understanding, controversial issues. While particular assumptions will be stated shortly, it is desirable to relax the assumptions in order to determine the sensitivity of our results to the particular assumptions. Now, regarding the finance mechanism we postulate:

—any tax (any perhaps user-charge) system may be used by government to finance a particular expenditure program, subject to the constraint that the system does not permit every, or nearly every, consumer to equate the tax he pays with the marginal benefit of the good to him. Such a relatively weak assumption will not permit strong statements about government output levels, and more attention should be given to the implications of more specific requirements, but some interesting conclusions can nonetheless be reached. It should be noted, however, that the assumption is less innocuous than it might appear. It rules out vote trading, selling, or logrolling *if* the effect would be to leave each person with a *net* tax price—net or "bribe"—that is equal to his valuation of marginal output. While such trading activities do occur to some extent and do tend to reduce divergencies between marginal benefit and marginal price among consumers, the combination of information costs, strategic behavior (transaction costs) and, in most instances, legal prohibition (against "selling" votes) sustains significant divergencies.

We turn now to the need for a rule regarding how consumer-voter demands influence decisions by government to supply a good. This has received growing

---

[2] This is not to suggest that the distinction is an insignificant one, but it is not examined in this paper. Indeed, there does not appear to be an accepted theory of the choice between government production and purchase.

attention in recent years but a consensus has not yet been reached.[3] In this paper, however, we begin with the assumption that

—government will supply a quantity and quality of any commodity that is determined by a political voting process. One such process would involve majority vote, according to which the demands of the median voter would determine the outcome.[4] One alternative would be a *weighted*-majority decision rule in which the weight attached to each person's "vote" is some function of the "loudness" of his "squawk" (intensity of dissatisfaction with a given tax-and-provision decision).[5] The latter model might predict that mean, rather than median, demand, determines levels of government provision, and that the dispersion to the right and to the left of the mean might have asymmetrical effects. But these are little more than plausible speculations concerning political processes. For our present purpose we require only that the political process leaves significant numbers of voters dissatisfied with government output and taxation levels.

Summing up: If consumer-voters know the rule by which government will allocate costs among them, their utility functions will generate a set of demand functions for governmentally provided goods which, with the government-supply decision-rule, will determine a level of government provision.

While each of our assumptions may reasonably be questioned as to its realism, there is particular reason to question whether consumer-voters know how the cost of any increased government output provision will be distributed among taxpayers.[6] Nevertheless, it is perhaps reasonable to believe that whatever cost-distribution rule taxpayers expect to be used, few persons expect a rule that

---

[3] See Anthony Downs, *An Economic Theory of Democracy* (New York: Harper and Row, 1957); Duncan Black, *The Theory of Committees and Elections* (Cambridge, U.K.: Cambridge University Press, 1958); James Buchanan and Gordon Tullock, *The Calculus of Consent* (Ann Arbor: University of Michigan Press, 1962); Jerome Rothenberg, "A Model of Economic and Political Decision-Making," in Julius Margolis, ed., *The Public Economy of Urban Communities* (Wash., D.C.: Resources for the Future, Inc., 1965); Roland N. McKean, *Public Spending* (New York: McGraw-Hill, Inc., 1968), especially ch. 9; and Hirschel Kasper, "On Political Competition, Economic Policy, and Income Maintenance," *Public Choice*, Spring 1971, pp. 1-19.

[4] The majority rule approach may produce intransitive orderings. Moreover, since specific issues are generally decided by political representatives, not by voters—at least not *directly* by voters—". . . the link between individual utility functions and social actions is tenuous, though by no means completely absent." [Kenneth Arrow, "The Organization of Economic Activity: Issues Pertinent to the Choice of Market Versus Non-Market Allocation," in Robert Haveman and Julius Margolis, eds., *Public Expenditures and Policy Analysis* (Chicago: Markham Publishing Company, 1971), p. 70.]

[5] Albert Breton posits that individuals are more likely to engage in political activity the greater the difference between their actual and their desired position. ("A Theory of the Demand for Public Goods," *Canadian Journal of Economics and Political Science*, November 1966, pp. 455-467.

[6] For a recent discussion of the issue, see W. Lee Hansen and Burton A. Weisbrod, "Who Pays for a Public Expenditure Program?," *National Tax Journal*, December 1971, pp. 515-17.

(even roughly) equates tax liability with the value of benefits from a marginal unit of the good. This is especially true for the host of governmentally provided goods for which there are no user charges.

The assumption of *non*-benefit-principle tax-pricing is critical to the argument that follows. The reason is that a tax-pricing system that does not equate, for each voter, his marginal tax with the marginal benefit he receives from each collective-consumption good will produce, in general, a level of govenment provision that exceeds what some voters demand and that falls short of what others demand. Not only is such a result non-optimal, as is well known,[7] but as we shall see, its occurrence can be expected to set in motion forces that will influence the aggregate allocation of resources among the three economic sectors. The assumption of non-benefit tax-pricing is quite general, permitting a wide range of tax systems. It rules out only a system that is, in reality, not available anyway, given that little is known about individuals' marginal valuations of particular public goods, and given that the free-rider problem leads people to hide their true valuations, even if they know them, when a benefit-based tax system is known to be used for financing a collective-consumption good.

Figure 1 illustrates a situation in which (a) voter demands for public provision of a specific good vary among the seven persons portrayed, and (b) the tax-finance price rule specifies that costs are borne equally by all,[8] with each taxpayer paying P per unit of output provided by the government. This simple, but unrealistic tax rule is used for its simplicity only; it is not implied by our assumptions. The good may be thought of as a collective-consumption good, although it need not be. Later we will consider briefly the demand for governmental provision of non-collective-consumption goods.

It is apparent from the diagram that, with each consumer-taxpayer paying the same tax, P, per unit of output, a majority of consumers (persons 4-7) would prefer to increase output to the level Q_1. At that level, consumers 1, 2, and 3 prefer to reduce the total tax and the quantity of output, while consumers 5, 6, and 7 prefer to increase both the total tax and the quantity supplied, but they are in the minority. Assuming a majority-vote rule, person 4, the median voter, has his way. In general, however, whether a majority vote or some other rule is operative, in the absence of marginal-benefit taxation the political process of determining an output level is likely to leave some consumers dissatisfied because they are receiving and paying for too much of the good, while others are dissatisfied because they are receiving too little—that is, they would prefer to

[7] Paul A. Samuelson, "The Pure Theory of Public Expenditure," *Review of Economics and Statistics,* November 1954, pp. 350-56.

[8] The horizontal price function assumes implicitly that the cost of supplying marginal quantities of the good (national defense, a park, or anything else) is constant, but this is simply for convenience of exposition and is in no way required.

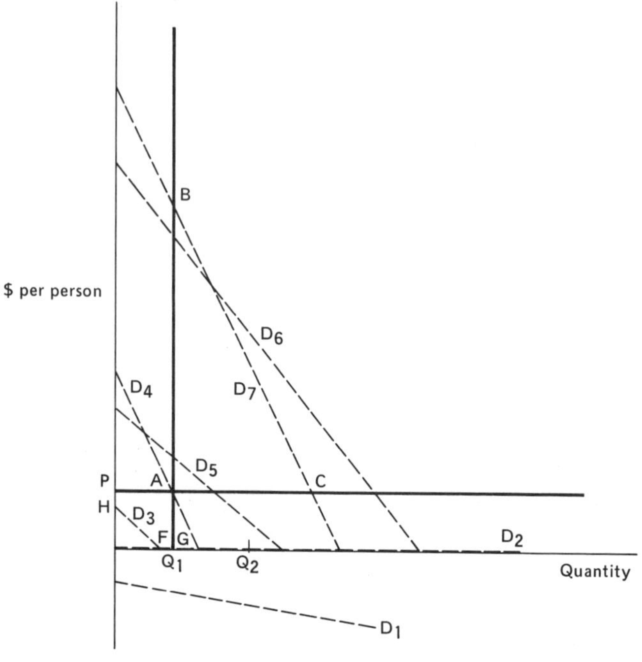

Figure 1

have the total tax payment and output level increased.[9] The relative numbers of the two dissatisfied groups depend, of course, on the particular tax-pricing system and the political decision process. The simple majority-vote rule, for example, would satisfy only the median consumer, and so the population would be split evenly between those who demand more and those who demand less at the prevailing marginal tax-prices.

The *intensities* of individuals' dissatisfactions will also generally vary; for a person who demands *more* than the quantity supplied, the intensity can be measured by the area under his demand curve, above the tax-price curve and to the right of the quantity supplied. For person 7 in Figure 1, this is the area ABC. For a person who demands *less* than the quantity supplied, the intensity of dissatisfaction may be measured, in corresponding fashion, by the area above the demand curve, below the tax-price curve, and to the left of the quantity supplied (PAGFH in Figure 1, for person 3).

---

[9] In this model each consumer is seen essentially as a price taker and quantity adjuster; the tax-price rule, although a variable, is constrained. For a related discussion see Leif Johansen, "Some Notes on the Lindahl Theory of Determination of Public Expenditures," *International Economic Review*, September 1963, pp. 346-58.

REACTIONS OF DISSATISFIED CONSUMERS

With many consumers being either undersatisfied or oversatisfied, adjustments can be expected to occur.[10] Before turning to the nature of the adjustment possibilities, note that the relative numbers of persons who desire any adjustment, and the degree of adjustment desired, depend on the variation in demands at the tax price(s) that each consumer assumes he confronts. Thus, of major importance, in addition to the tax system, is the degree of demand homogeneity of the population. The greater the homogeneity within a political unit—that is, the greater the similarity in income, wealth, religion, ethnic background, education level, and other characteristics influencing demand for any collective-consumption good—the smaller the expected variation in individual demands, and, hence, the smaller the likely degree of dissatisfaction with the politically determined level and quality of output.

There are several adjustment possibilities available to the dissatisfied consumers, including migration, formation of lower-level governments, resort to private market alternatives and to voluntary organizations. Each will be discussed in turn, but the attempt is to describe not a sequential process but

[10] The emphasis in the public goods literature has been on the quantity of the good *supplied* being equal for all consumers. (P. Samuelson, *op. cit.;* J. Buchanan, "Notes for a Theory of Socialism," *Public Choice*, Spring 1970, pp. 29-43, esp. p. 30.) The comparative lack of attention to inequality in *demands* (as portrayed in Figure 1) is, in my view, unfortunate. If some particular national defense expenditure, or some lighthouse—to use two favorite examples of public goods—were demanded by only one person while all other persons were indifferent to them, these goods would presumably be provided in optimal quantities in the private sector. The point is not that such examples are realistic, but only that insofar as the key concern of analysts is the efficiency of private markets—the market-failure issue—the crucial characteristic of a "public" (collective-consumption) good is *not* its technical *availability* to many persons simultaneously, but the number of simultaneous *beneficiaries*—persons into whose utility functions it actually enters.

In Figure 1, for example, the good is, I suggest, *not* a "public good" for person 2, and is not a public good for person 3 in quantities greater than Q_1. Rather than regard a particular good as simply a public good, it is useful to think of women's public goods, water-sports, enthusiasts' public goods, Catholic public goods, "hawks" and "doves" public goods, etc. [Cf. Albert Breton, "Theory of Government Grants", *Canadian Journal of Economics and Political Science*, May 1965, pp. 175-87, who refers to local, metropolitan, state, national, and world goods, but not to the aggregations of consumers (beneficiaries) discussed here.] The figure also illustrates that a commodity can be a public good for some persons—entering all of their utility functions simultaneously—and also a public "bad" for others, such as person 1, entering negatively into their utility functions.

In a recent paper Samuelson has also come to the conclusion that a public good is most usefully defined in utility terms, not in terms of "technological" characteristics of a good. See his "Pure Theory of Public Expenditure and Taxation," in J. Margolis and H. Guitton, eds., *Public Economics*, Proceedings of a Conference Held by the International Economic Association, St. Martin's Press, New York, 1969, pp. 98-123.

The *extent* of benefits to each consumer is a second determinant of the degree of private-market failure. If, for example, a lighthouse entered positively into the utility functions of a number of consumers, but was of trivial value to most, the "few" large demanders might well reach a bargain that led to essentially an optimal level of provision.

rather a general equilibrium adjustment process in which all of these organizational forms for satisfying consumer demands are simultaneously operative.[11]

One option for the dissatisfied consumer is *migration* to another governmental unit in which output and tax-pricing systems lead to an improvement in his economic welfare. The viability of this adjustment option is, of course, considerably greater if local governmental units are being considered than it is if higher-level governments are the focus.[12] In any case, since moving is not costless and since locational decisions reflect many considerations other than governmental outputs and taxes, we can think of the type of situation portrayed in Figure 1 as reflecting the likely situation even after migration adjustments—diverse demands, some "oversatisfied" consumers, and some "undersatisfied."

Beyond migration, the undersatisfied and the oversatisfied consumers do confront somewhat different options. The oversatisfied consumers (persons 1-3 in Figure 1), if they do not move out, will have few options except to bear the burden or else to exert political pressure to alter either the tax-price system or the output-determination system. The undersatisfied consumers, however, have other alternatives, and this paper directs attention to them.

A second adjustment outlet, open to all those who want and are willing to pay for added output, is *to form lower-level governments*. Thus persons 5, 6, and 7 in Figure 1 might organize an additional governmental unit including only themselves, to provide additional units of the commodity in question. They could not entirely avoid the free-rider problem, of course—other persons would use some of their output if they could do so without paying (or paying less than *P*). Neither could the undersatisfied demanders avoid the cost of organizing the new governmental unit. We can expect, therefore, that while (1) some lower-level government supplementation of output will take place—and this is illustrated by parks and libraries, which are provided by federal, state, county, and local governments—at the same time, (2) some undersatisfied demand will remain.

As we consider adjustments in the several economic sectors, it should be noted that because we are considering collective goods, which benefit more than one person simultaneously, the provision of such goods in any one sector may

---

[11] This paper does not explore the possible game-theoretic aspects of decision-making in the three sectors when collective-consumption goods are involved.

[12] This was discussed at the theoretic level by Charles Tiebout, "A Pure Theory of Local Government Expenditure," *Journal of Political Economy*, October 1956, pp. 416-24. See Wallace Oates, "The Effects of Property Taxes and Local Public Spending on Property Values: An Empirical Study of Tax Capitalization and the Tiebout Hypothesis," *Journal of Political Economy*, November-December 1969, pp. 957-71, for a recent empirical examination of the Tiebout model of choice among local governmental units. Jerome Stein, in an analysis of optimal policy toward environmental pollution, has assumed away the issue of heterogeneous demands among consumers by assuming that . . . each locality is composed of identical households. . . ." ("Micro-Economic Aspects of Public Policy," *American Economic Review*, September 1971, p. 534).

well reduce the demand for it in the other sectors. If the good were a "pure" collective good—involving no "congestion" whatever—then an increment of output of the good in one sector would presumably bring about an *equal* decrement in another sector, at least in equilibrium. When the collective good is anything short of pure, however, the provision of an additional unit of output in one sector will not lead to an equal decrease in the level of output provided in another sector.

In addition to migration and formation of lower-level government units, the third and fourth adjustment outlets for the undersatisfied demanders, and the two on which I will focus, are the *private* (for-profit) market and the *voluntary* ("non-profit") markets.

Consider, first, the private market. The currently prevailing view among economists regarding the role of private markets in the provision of public, collective-consumption goods is simply that those markets will produce suboptimal quantities of such goods, and that, therefore, governments may be, and from an allocative-efficiency standpoint should be, called upon to take steps to see that the output level is increased. Implicit in this view is an assumption that the private and the public markets are two alternate organizational mechanisms for providing the *same* good.

PUBLIC-AND PRIVATE-GOOD SUBSTITUTES

This, I believe, is an invalid assumption. As an alternative I suggest that we think of the production-possibility set at a given point in time as including collective-consumption goods and private-good *substitutes* for them, as well as "ordinary" private goods. Thus, for example, the collective good, lighthouse, has a private-good substitute, shipboard radar; the collective good, provision of clean air, has private-good substitutes in air filters and purifiers for home, automobile and place of work; the collective good, stand-by fire department, has a private-good substitute, sprinkler systems; the collective good, generic information (e.g., on drugs), has a private-good substitute, brand-name advertising; and the collective good, police department, has private-good subsitutes that include alarms, locks, guards, and dogs.[13]

To observe that there are often private-good substitutes for collective goods by no means says, however, that they are perfect substitutes. In fact, as the examples just given suggest, these substitutes are generally different in a

[13] Discussing the exclusion principle with regard to collective goods, Kenneth Arrow illustrates the problem with the example of pollution: " . . . it would have to be possible in principle to supply [clean air or water] to one [person] and not the other. . . . But this is technically impossible." (In Haveman and Margolis, *op. cit.*, p. 65.)

But it is *not* impossible. Air and water filters, air conditioning, and bottled water perform precisely this exclusionary function, as do vacations to places "where the sky is not cloudy (or smoggy) all day."

particular and important way, to be discussed shortly, and this difference has a notable implication for any attempt to understand and predict the degree of public sector involvement in the provision of a good.[14]

Observing that there are private-good substitutes for collective goods suggests that it would be useful to study the "industry" comprising (1) each good or service provided by the public sector, plus (2) the substitutes provided by the private sector, plus—for the reason to be explored below—(3) the substitutes provided by the voluntary sector. In a later section of this paper I will report on some early empirical work on such industry studies.

It is presumably true that there is no technological constraint that prevents the private sector from producing collective goods. If that is so, then any observed differences in the "type" of goods provided by the private and the government sectors of an industry are likely to reflect consumers preferences and/or relative prices. From the consumer-preference viewpoint a collective-consumption good is likely to have one important disadvantage compared with a private-good substitute. The disadvantage of the collective good—whether it is governmentally or privately operated—is the lesser degree of individual control that each consumer can exercise over its form, quality and utilization or deployment. Even the classical lighthouse and national defense activities must take particular forms, must be located in particular places, and must be activated and deactivated at particular times and under particular circumstances. Rarely, if ever, will all consumers agree about how any of these decisions should be made, and yet, by the very nature of collective goods, the decisions once made affect all persons. A given lighthouse cannot be located differently for different users, nor can it be turned on and off at different times to satisfy conflicting preferences. (This is to observe once again the heterogeneity portrayed in Figure 1.)

Why, in the face of this disadvantage inherent in sharing, should a good be demanded of government when a private-good substitute exists? One answer is that the private-good substitute may be a very poor substitute—as is the case with national defense, where handguns (private goods) are poor substitutes for such collective goods as hydrogen bombs, and where a social judgment has apparently been made that devastating weapons should not be purchasable by private consumers at any price. In many, perhaps most, other cases, however, where

[14] A striking illustration of the difference between a public-good solution to a problem and a private-good solution is the adjustment to environmental hazards in less-developed areas. Where malaria-carrying mosquitos breed, the public goods, area-wide DDT spraying and swamp drainage, might be used; and among the private-good substitutes are mosquito nets and migration away from the area.

An incisive analysis of the difference between public sector and private sector rationing policies, involving money prices and waiting-time prices, is in Donald Nichols, Eugen Smolensky, and Nicholas Tiedeman, "Discrimination by Waiting Time in Merit Goods," *American Economic Review*, June 1971, pp. 312-23.

private goods are available that can achieve virtually the same objective as the public-good version, the only significant advantage of the public good would seem to be its relative price. That is, some people may prefer to pay for a marginal unit of the public-good version at its associated tax price rather than a unit of the private-good version at its market price. (The particular tax-price system that is used will, thus, affect the number of persons who opt for the public-good or the private-good substitute.)

We can now return to an analysis of the choices open to consumers whose demands for any collective good are undersatisfied through government markets. The consumer who turns to the private-market option is, in effect, choosing an option that often involves a different form of the good in question. He may be expected to select a form which, while providing its owner with greater individual control, does so by providing smaller external benefits to other consumers. After all, if a consumer must bear the total cost rather than share the cost with others, then he will presumably tend to choose a form of the good that maximizes internal benefits, including his individual control, paying little attention to the external benefits that might be provided in greater measure by some other, collective-consumption form of the good.

The point to emphasize is that such a choice may be socially non-optimal, albeit privately optimal in an economy with only two sectors—private and public—and with output in the public sector being constrained. Purchases of private-good substitutes may reflect not simply the interaction of preferences and production costs; rather they can reflect, and, in the situation depicted in Figure 1 actually do reflect, an adjustment to the non-optimal level of provision of the collective good by government.[15] The analysis suggests, at this point, that consumers are likely to be left in non-optimal positions in both private and government markets, being over- or undersatisfied in government markets and making socially inefficient choices in private markets.

THE VOLUNTARY SECTOR

This brings us to a rationale for the development of voluntary non-profit organizations.[16] The reasoning above suggests the hypothesis that a class of voluntary organizations will come into existence as *extra-governmental providers*

---

[15] A vertical summation of the seven demand curves in the diagram would intersect with the commodity cost curve, $7P$, at quantity Q_2, the output level that would be Pareto optimal if tax prices were set equal to marginal valuations of each consumer. While the optimal output exceeds the "actual" in this illustration, this would not be the case under some other political-decision rule.

[16] For a useful introduction to some issues in this area, see William Vickrey, "One Economist's View of Philanthropy," in *Philanthropy and Public Policy* (New York: National Bureau of Economic Research, 1962).

of collective-consumption goods.[17] They will "supplement" the *public* provision (which can be zero) and provide an alternative to the *private*-sector provision of private-good substitutes for collective goods.[18]

If the voluntary organizations do in fact provide collective goods, they may be expected to confront financial problems, given the free-rider problem. However, since all the alternatives available to undersatisfied demanders also involve inefficiencies, it may be worthwhile (that is, efficient) to form and maintain voluntary organizations as a "second best" solution.[19]

This exposition has seemingly implied that the initial response to demands for collective-consumption goods is sought in the public sector, with subsequent adjustments reflecting dissatisfaction with that response. Such a sequence may or may not be accurate as a description of real-world behavior—although a little evidence on this will be cited later—but in any case the sequencing is only an expositional convenience. Although the public sector has some clear advantage in the provision of collective goods, it may also have a disadvantage in the form of organizational costs.[20] When the differential costs of organizing economic activity in the various sectors (and at various governmental levels) are considered—

---

[17] Eli Ginzberg, *et al.*, discuss a wide range of "non-profit" organizations. The authors observe that "Many non-profit organizations perform functions that are identical or closely allied to those performed by government. In fact, many governments weigh carefully whether to establish or expand certain activities under their own aegis; whether to seek to accomplish their goals by relying on non-profit organizations; or whether, as frequently happens, to do part of the work themselves and to look to non-profit organizations to do the rest." [Eli Ginzberg, Dale L. Hiestand and Beatrice J. Reubens, *The Pluralistic Economy* (New York: McGraw-Hill Book Co., 1965), p. 23.]

On the relationship between the activities of non-profit and private for-profit organizations, however, Ginzberg, *et al.*, are not in agreement with the analysis in this paper. They state: "The key difference between the private sector and the not-for-profit sector is not in the economic activities which they undertake, but in whether they are organized in order to seek a profit from their efforts." (*Ibid.*, p. 30.) These authors make no distinction between collective-consumption goods and their private-good substitutes.

[18] If it is true that there exists a non-public voluntary sector that provides collective-consumption goods, as do governments, then it really is ". . . a shame that public goods are called 'public'." (Otto A. Davis and Andrew B. Whinston, "On the Distinction Between Public and Private Goods," *American Economic Review*, May 1967, p. 372.

[19] Our emphasis on the similarity of outputs of the government and voluntary sectors, and on the qualitatively different outputs of the private-sector substitutes, may be contrasted with the dichotomization presented by James Buchanan and Gordon Tullock. They emphasize the distinction between *government* provision and "private," where the latter includes both for-profit and "voluntary, but cooperative" organizations (Buchanan and Tullock, *op. cit.*, p. 50). The similarity of voluntary, "philanthropic" activities and the activities of the "free market" is also expressed by Robert A. Schwartz who states that individual philanthropic efforts "supplement the functioning of the free-market system. . . . ," rather than supplementing the outputs of public markets, the emphasis suggested in the present paper. (Schwartz, "Personal Philanthropic Contributions," *Journal of Political Economy*, Nov.-Dec. 1970, p. 1291.)

[20] For a theoretical analysis of organizational costs, related to both population heterogeneity and the nature of political decision rules, see J. Buchanan and G. Tullock, *op. cit.*, esp. p. 115.

a factual matter about which little is known—it is no longer apparent in which sector the initial response to collective-good demand will occur. It is likely, however, that the government sector will *not* be the first to respond to consumer demands for collective goods. The reason is that demands by all consumers do not generally develop simultaneously, and so the political-decision rule will at first determine a zero level of government provision, leading the undersatisfied demanders to non-governmental markets.

Not all governmentally provided goods and services have a significant collective-consumption component. Publicly provided employment services and library provision of current best-seller novels (but not research materials), for example, are not easily explainable as responses to this source of market failure.[21] Why governments provide non-collective goods is a matter deserving further scrutiny, and we will only touch on the question here. One potential justification for public provision of a private-consumption good is the saving in private-market transaction costs (or enforcement costs) in cases where there is widespread agreement regarding the quantity of an individual-consumption good that each consumer wishes to consume (or wishes others to consume). As long as tax bills are being paid to finance govenment provision of collective goods, there may be advantages to adding to the bill a sum to finance the "minimum" level of a private good that the political majority prefers. While more study is needed of the rationale for government provision of goods with little or no collective character, it is important to note that governments do provide them. For if this is the case, then the voluntary sector, if it is indeed providing collective-consumption goods, as has been hypothesized in this paper, will be found to be more prominent in supplementing those government activities having the "largest" collective-consumption component. By contrast, we may expect that the *private*-good activities of government will be supplemented to a relatively greater extent in the private for-profit sector.

With a collective-consumption good and substitutes for it being provided in two or even three economic sectors, there is no easy answer to the question of whether such a good is likely to be provided in optimal, sub-optimal, or super-optimal total quantities. What is needed is a more general theory that goes beyond the *private* market's tendency to underprovide collective-consumption goods and explains the public and voluntary markets' supplemental activities.

PRIVATE- AND PUBLIC-GOOD SUBSTITUTES, SOME DYNAMICS

Up to this point we have assumed that the set of collective-consumption and individual-consumption goods from which consumers could choose was given

---

[21] James M. Buchanan has recently focused attention on "the effects generated by governmental organization of the supply of goods and services that are largely if not wholly 'private,' that is, fully divisible into separate and distinguishable units of consumption." "Notes for an Economic Theory of Socialism," *Public Choice*, Spring 1970, p. 29.

exogenously. Now we will drop the static assumption of a predetermined set of goods, instead examining some determinants of what is included in the set. Specifically, is there a basis for predicting that in the course of time the menu of collective-consumption goods will expand more, or less, rapidly than the menu of private goods? What determines such changes?

It was stated above that a major distinction between public goods and their private-good substitutes is the greater individual control offered by the latter and preferred by consumers generally. Granted such a difference it would seem likely that if consumers at a given level of income are found to be purchasing a particular ratio of a public good to its private-good substitute, then at sufficiently higher income levels that ratio is likely to fall, as demand shifts in favor of the private goods. This is not to say that the income elasticity of demand for any collective good is necessarily negative at some income levels. We suggest the following hypotheses: at "very low" income levels the income elasticity of demand for a given collective good is positive and large; as income increases people shift expenditures from a pattern in which *neither* a collective good *nor* a private-good substitute is purchased to a pattern that includes *some* collective goods. And as incomes rise further, the demand for collective goods rises, but at some point the private-good substitutes will come to be bought instead of the collective good. (This point may differ, of course, for different goods.) That is, the income elasticity of demand for collective goods may be positive but lower than that for private-good substitutes at sufficiently high levels of income. Thus, the relationship between the level of per capita income and the relative size of the government sector is likely to be that of an inverted *U*.[22]

SOME BITS OF EVIDENCE

This brief section provides a number of scraps of "evidence" on the notions presented above. None of the evidence, individually or in total, is offered as "proof" of the propositions we have discussed. Rather, they are intended to be suggestive of the types of research that would be useful in order to better understand the role of voluntary organizations in a three-sector economy that also includes government and private for-profit sectors.

---

[22] Cf. "Wagner's Law" which, though variously interpreted, predicts that the public sector will grow with per capita income. For the original exposition, see Adolf Wagner, *Finanzwissenschaft*, Leipzig, 3rd edition, 1890; for discussions in English see Richard M. Bird, "Wagner's Law of Expanding State Activity," *Public Finance*, No. 1, Vol. 26, 1971; and Bernard P. Herber, *Modern Public Finance: The Study of Public Sector Economics* (Homewood, Ill.: Richard D. Irwin, Inc., 1971), pp. 371-81.

1. Private-Good Substitutes for Collective Goods

We now consider the effects of relaxing the initial assumption of an exogenously determined set of collective and of private goods. If the hypothesis is correct that beyond some level of income for any given person collective goods are demanded in preference to private goods, then, as such an income level is approached by increasing numbers of persons, we should expect an increase in the amount of private-market resources devoted to research and development on private-good substitutes. Thus, the set of private, individual-consumption goods that are available would expand in response to increased incomes. This may be one of the factors explaining (a) the growing number of inventions to provide home and business security—in addition to the expanded provision of the traditional collective good, police protection; (b) the development of home garbage disposers, incinerators and, now, trash compactors as substitutes for the more collective good, trash collection; and (c) the development of electronic air filters as substitutes for cleaner air in the environment.

In more general terms, there are many other examples of how increased incomes are reducing consumers' relative demands for "shared" goods, which they can utilize only under particular conditions and at particular times—e.g., urban mass transit and public libraries—and are increasing demands for non-shared goods that are fully under the individual's control—e.g., private autos and paperback books. I do not suggest that the distinction between shared and non-shared goods is synonymous with the distinction between collective-consumption and individual-consumption goods. Nevertheless, there is a relationship: collective-consumption goods, except for the pure case, do require sharing.

2. A Fragment of Historical Evidence on Voluntary Provision of Public Goods

Our analysis concerning undersatisfied demanders of collective goods and their relationship to voluntary organizations portrays the latter as non-governmental providers of collective goods that are normally identified with governments. Historical events provide one test of our view, which implies that before a political majority comes to demand government provision, the minority that demands governmental provision of a good will be undersatisfied and will turn to voluntary organizations. Thus, *provision by voluntary* (non-profit) *organizations is hypothesized to precede governmental provision historically*. It is noteworthy, therefore, that in 16th-century England, where governmental provision of any civilian goods or services was very modest, private "philanthropies" (voluntary organizations) were providing funds for such wide-ranging public, collective activities as schools, hospitals, non-toll roads, fire fighting apparatus, public parks, bridges, dikes and causeways, digging of drainage canals, waterworks, wharves and docks, harbor cleaning, libraries, care of prisoners in jails, and charity to the poor[23]—in short, for the gamut of non-military goods that we identify today as governmental responsibilities. Such voluntary-sector giving even included support for such noble charitable causes as "houses for young women convinced of their folly.[24] At the same time we are told that private interests "sought to prod the central government to carry forward needed projects . . . "[25]—behavior that we would anticipate since collective-type goods were involved.

The relationship between governmental and voluntary provision of goods has also been noted by historians of Elizabethan England. "The various philanthropic activities, which we have been reviewing [including highways, police charity, hospitals and schools] were supplemented in some important respects by the corporate action of the towns."[26] Whether the public sector "supplemented" the voluntary, or vice versa, is, I believe, an insignificant distinction.

Note that it is quite consistent with our theoretic model that the level of politically determined governmental provision of a collective good can be zero even though a large minority (or even a majority, if a political-decision rule other than majority vote is used) has positive demands. If the undersatisfied demanders turn to the voluntary sector, as is likely, then this sector will develop first. Later, perhaps in response to economic development, the number of positive demanders might increase and so the government sector would become a provider of the good involved. Thus, in general, we might expect the voluntary sector to precede the government sector in the provision of collective goods.

A historical perspective on public-sector activities raises the question of to what extent any observed changes in the relative size or scope of government are the results of changes in the magnitudes of variables—e.g., incomes—or changes in the magnitudes of parameters—such as those mirroring attitudes toward the "appropriate" role of government. Both, of course, may be important. The view (hypothesis) being set forth here, however, is that the varying roles of government over time, as well as across countries, are not a consequence of exogenously determined "attitudes" toward government; rather that such attitudes are themselves endogenously determined by changes in incomes, in other demand variables and in the state of technology and factor prices. Depending on stages of development and on population demand characteristics, a different role for government can be expected.

---

[23] W. K. Jordan, *Philanthropy in England, 1480-1660* (London: George Allen and Unwin, Ltd.), 1959, *passim.*

[24] Robert Nelson, "An Address to Persons of Quality and Estate, Ways and Methods of Doing Good," published in 1715, cited by B. Kirkman Gray, *A History of English Philanthropy* (London: Frank Cass and Company Limited, 1905), p. 95.

[25] Jordan, *op. cit.*

[26] Gray, *op. cit.*, p. 25.

3. Financing Voluntary Provision of Collective Goods

If our identification of voluntary organizations with the provision of public, collective goods, is valid, we should expect these organizations to confront finance problems. Indeed, because they share with private-sector firms ". . . the absence of the coercive and compulsive powers of government," Buchanan and Tullock have grouped those two types of organizations, terming them "voluntary groups" and distinguishing them from governments.[27]

It is important, however, to distinguish between any differences among organizations in the types of their *outputs*, and differences in the methods of their *finance*, although the two are not entirely independent. Our emphasis here is on the nature of outputs, and on this basis the similarity of government and voluntary organizations is significant, as is the difference between both of these and the private for-profit organizations. The free-rider problem associated with collective goods does lead us to expect that non-governmental providers of such goods face a financial obstacle.

Upon further study, however, it turns out that voluntary organizations do employ "coercive and compulsive powers," just as do governments, although the penalties are social rather than governmentally sanctioned fines or imprisonment. While pressures to "donate" to the United Fund, Red Cross, Cancer Society, or private colleges are (sometimes) somewhat more subtle than the pressure to pay one's taxes, the difference is one of degree, not of kind.[28]

There are several plausible reasons why people may give to a voluntary organization when there is neither compulsion of law nor any apparent *quid pro quo*. One is the social pressure just noted.[29] A second, very closely related to the first, is captured by the recent conception of Pareto optimal redistribution—individuals' utility functions may be such that they derive benefit from either the act of giving or from seeing someone else benefited.[30] That is, the *apparent*

---

[27] James Buchanan and Gordon Tullock, *op. cit.*, p. 49.

[28] At the theoretical level this similarity has been discussed by Thomas R. Ireland and David B. Johnson, *The Economics of Charity* (Blacksburg, Virginia: Center for the Study of Public Choice, 1970).

[29] John Stuart Mill recognized that societal reinforcement could serve as a possible inducement to people to incur costs for which there was otherwise little or no private benefit. Although arguing that ". . . it is a proper office of government to build and maintain lighthouses . . . [since] no one would build lighthouses from motives of personal interest . . . .," and that few people would undertake scientific research without government support, he also mentioned the possibility that "great public spirit" might motivate some persons to undertake activities that are "of great value to a nation." [John Stuart Mill, *Principles of Political Economy*, Vol. III, (Toronto: University of Toronto Press, 1965), p. 968.]

[30] See Harold Hochman and James Rodgers, "Pareto Optimal Redistribution," *American Economic Review*, Sept. 1969, pp. 542-57; Robert A. Schwartz, "Personal Philanthropic Contributions," *Journal of Political Economy*, Nov.-Dec. 1970, pp. 1264-91; and T. Ireland and D. Johnson, *op. cit.*

lack of a *quid pro quo* may be misleading. A "donor" to a voluntary organization may derive satisfaction from the act of giving to a "worthy" cause. Also he may benefit from the gratitude, esteem and plaudits of his neighbors and fellow citizens—rewards which to some extent even show up as financial returns and act to internalize what would otherwise be external benefits to the donor.

Sometimes the benefit from giving is quite direct and in a private-good form; thus a giver may receive a tangible gift in return for his "donation." One organization offers a "free" road atlas for a $3 donation; in other cases the donor may have his name inscribed on a plaque or even on a college library or hospital wing.[31]

The question of *why* people like such social reinforcement rewards and, hence, are willing to pay for them is an important matter of utility-function determination that economists have avoided too long. Utility functions are not determined entirely by forces exogenous to the economic system, and even if they were, economic analysis could still contribute to understanding the process of their formation. In any case, there can be no doubt that there are very many transactions in the economy that involve no binding *quid pro quo*—there are many things that people do which, like supporting voluntary organizations, bring little or no clear and certain reward. One example is truly voluntary giving to charity or to a blood bank.[32] Another is the support by young people for old age pensions through the social security system, support which appears to hinge on the hope and faith that future generations of young people will be willing to finance the retirement of the aged just as the current generation of young people is doing. It is by no means obvious why young people have such faith, but apparently it is a real force influencing actions. It seems to apply not only to retirement pensions, but also to the support for public eduation. There appears to be a "social compact" such that each generation of adults agrees to support the education of the younger generation.

4. The Logic of Public Subsidy for Voluntary Giving

We have seen in Figure 1 that of the seven (groups of) people portrayed, only three demand more than Q_1 level of provision at the price P. A fourth, however, consisting of people such as person 4, would derive *some* positive benefit from additional output. It might be expected, therefore, that a majority of voters would favor a government program that financed, in addition to Q_1, a *part* of the cost of output in excess of that quantity. Given consumer awareness of the free-rider problem and its likely resolution in diversion of non-government

[31] Note that income-tax deductibility of such "donations" would never be a sufficient inducement for giving, as long as marginal tax rates confronting an individual were less than 100 percent.

[32] The market for human blood is discussed in the most thought-provoking book by Richard Titmuss, *The Gift Relationship* (London: George Allen and Unwin, 1971).

resources from collective goods to private-good substitutes, a political majority of voters would be rational to agree not only to *full governmental* financing of some output but also to *partial* government subsidy for some additional *non*-governmental provision of collective goods.

Such a subsidy could take various forms, being an explicit grant or a tax subsidy. Both, in fact, are employed. The voluntary hospital industry in the United States, for example, receives *partial* government support through outright cash grants from the federal government for construction, through the Hill-Burton Act, and also benefits from the income-tax deductibility of private contributions to voluntary non-profit hospitals. By contrast, the public hospitals are financed *fully* by government.

It is noteworthy that such governmental subsidies, and in particular the income-tax deductibility subsidies, are extended only to some of the non-governmental organizations that provide goods that are also provided governmentally. In general, only organizations in the health, education, charity, and religious areas can qualify for such government subsidies—not, by contrast, the non-governmental organizations that either do, or might, provide trash collection, roads, fire or security services, or other services that have counterparts in the public sector. It would seem that the magnitude of the subsidy ought to depend—from the standpoint of allocative efficiency—on the severity of the free-rider problem—that is, on the magnitude of external benefits that would be generated by individuals' private decisions to purchase (or supply) the good. If we were correct in arguing above that governments provide some non-collective-consumption goods, it would follow that subsidies would be widely supported (and would be efficient) only for the non-governmental providers of *collective* goods, and not for the non-governmental providers of private goods that substitute for collective goods.

Under current federal income-tax law, there are only two "levels" of such subsidization through the deductibility route: either zero, with gifts and grants to the organization not qualifying for tax deductibility, or full deductibility. (Of course, the importance of the latter from the *giver's* viewpoint depends on his marginal tax rate and whether he itemizes his deductions.) While a binary subsidy schedule would surely not be economically efficient under conditions of perfect information, it *could* be a reasonably good rule-of-thumb basis for setting subsidies to stimulate non-governmental provision of public goods.

How good is it? How effective is it? I make no attempt here to answer these questions carefully. While further study is needed, it seems that the kinds of activities for which private giving does qualify for tax deductibility do have a larger public-good component than is the case for other activities—that is, they enter the utility functions of more persons and enter more "importantly." If this is so, then there is at least some efficiency basis for the voluntary-donations deductibility feature of our tax system.

5. Heterogeneity of Demand

Just as the model sketched above predicts that there will often be private-market or voluntary-market supplementation of governmental provision of goods, so it also predicts that there will be little or no undersatisfied demand—and, hence, little or no extra-governmental provision—if all consumer demands are essentially the same. One testable implication of this proposition is that if two political units (e.g., countries) differ in the degree of "heterogeneity" of their populations—in the degree of income inequality, diversity of cultural heritage or other demand-determining variables—the unit with the lesser heterogeneity will, *ceteris paribus*, have a lower level of private and voluntary-sector provision of collective-type goods or their substitutes.[33] In short, that country will tend to have a relatively larger public sector. Conversely, in a country, or smaller political unit, with great *in*equality in the level of individuals' demands for collective goods, the level of private and voluntary-sector supplementation of public-sector provision will be larger and the public sector will be relatively small.[34]

It follows that one should not be surprised to find that the governmental "provision" (that is, support) of, say, church activities—which have a significant public-good component for persons of that faith but not for others—is apparently great in countries where virtually the entire population shares one religion (e.g., Spain and Ireland). Similarly, it is not surprising that the public provision (financing) is far lower in a country such as the United States, where religious preferences (including atheism) are far more diverse; it seems likely that no religion in the U.S. could win the support of a majority of voters to the cause of substantial public financing of its activities.

If our hypothesis is correct and the heterogeneity of demand for collective goods influences the degree of supplementation in private and voluntary markets, then the relative size of the government sector would be expected to be a function of that heterogeneity. As one test of this hypothesis an analysis has been undertaken of determinants of the changing relative size of the total non-defense government sector (federal, state, and local) in the U.S. for various

[33] The influence of "subcultures," defined by homogeneity of ethnicity and income, on voting behavior is examined in James Q. Wilson and Edward C. Banfield, "Public-Regardingness as a Value Premise in Voting Behavior," *American Political Science Review*, December 1964, pp. 876-87.

[34] The relationship between population heterogeneity and degree of public-sector activity has also been considered in terms of the costs of organization; the greater the heterogeneity, the larger the prospective costs of organizing through political markets relative to the costs of organizing private firms. (See Buchanan and Tullock, *op. cit.*, especially Ch. 8.

For an interesting paper describing the variation in size of public sectors among a number of countries, and attempting to explain it by "ideological differences," see Anthony King, "Ideologies as Predictors of Public Policy Patterns: A Comparative Analysis," paper presented at Meeting of American Political Science Association, Chicago, September 1971.

years over the time period 1929-1969.[35] Explanatory variables in the model include, as proxies for heterogeneity of demand, the variances in income, age, and education, and measures of diversity of religion, race, and urban-ness; *mean* or other average values (e.g., percent of population that is urban) for these six variables were also included. Of particular interest are the variance measures, for our model suggests negative signs for them. That is, it predicts that government (non-defense) expenditures as a percentage of total GNP will be a negative function of the variation in demand for collective-consumption goods, and we are taking heterogeneity of population characteristics to reflect such variation.

The regression model we used is handicapped by having only 10 degrees of freedom (24 observations and 13 independent variables); nonetheless, our findings, while not overwhelming, are rather encouraging. First, inclusion of the heterogeneity measures actually increases the significance levels of the variables reflecting mean values. Second, the F-ratio is extremely significant (.0000 level). Third, of the six heterogeneity variables, five were negative, as hypothesized. Only two of the five—religion and race—were significant, however, a result that may reflect the multi-collinearity and the relatively small number of degrees of freedom. Variance in income, for example, had the anticipated negative relationship with the relative size of the government sector, but the coefficient was significant at only the .33 level.

Further analysis of time-series data would be useful in order to test for the impact of population heterogeneity. Similarly, cross-country comparisons of the size of the government sector would be useful. Lack of data on dispersions of demand variables, however, is an obstacle to such studies.

6. Industry Analyses—the Market Niches of the Public, Private, and Voluntary Sectors

The emphasis on the respective roles of the private and voluntary sectors vis-à-vis the public sector has led me to a new type of "industry study." Each service provided by governments (at this stage no distinctions between *levels* of government are being made) can be usefully thought of as a portion of an industry that also may include a voluntary and a private for-profit sector.

One principal hypothesis is that in such industries in which the government is providing essentially a *private* good, the undersatisfied demand will be manifest principally in the private for-profit sector, and the voluntary sector will be comparatively small. Similarly, if the government services are substantially *collective*, then supplementation will tend to be in the voluntary sector, with the private for-profit sector being relatively small.

Several small-scale industry studies for the U.S. are now under way to shed light on this hypothesis—the hospital industry, the library industry, and the

[35] In this work I have been aided by Jennifer Gerner.

employment-service industry. Findings to date will be briefly summarized below. Other studies are planned for the education, fire, police-security, information-research and possibly other industries.

The hospital industry is a very complex, multi-product industry. Measured by expenditures, it is 22% public, 73% voluntary, and 5% private for-profit. Much of what any hospital does involves provision of *private* services, but some outputs—such as medical care for the indigent, cancer research programs, and the stand-by availability of intensive-care units, open heart surgery facilities, and 24-hour emergency rooms that charge prices below profit-maximizing levels—appear to be of a collective-good type, benefiting many potential users simultaneously.[36] I have attempted to test the propositions that public and voluntary hospitals provide essentially identical services, while for-profit hospitals less commonly provide the kinds of collective goods just noted.[37] Data are limited but our tentative conclusion is quite supportive of our hypotheses regarding the roles of the three sectors. Consider emergency departments in small hospitals (under 50 beds), for example: in 1969, 80.3% of public hospitals and 78.5% of non-profit hospitals had such a department (a statistically insignificant difference), but only 58.7% of the private hospitals (less than the public and voluntary percentages at the .05 level of significance). In general, for all of the six hospital-size classes, each of the 21 hospital services that we had previously identified as of the collective type were provided predominantly in public and voluntary hospitals, as expected, while each of the nine services identified as private-type were provided predominantly in the private, for-profit hospitals, again as expected.[38]

We have found that private hospitals are significantly less likely than public or voluntary hospitals of similar size to have a social work department, a family-planning service, an organized outpatient department, a teacher-intern-

[36] This form of "option demand" was discussed by Burton Weisbrod, "Collective-Consumption Services of Individual-Consumption Goods," *Quarterly Journal of Economics*, August 1964, pp. 471-77. See also subsequent comments in the *Quarterly Journal of Economics* by M. Long, May 1967, pp. 351-52; C. Lindsay, May 1969, pp. 344-46; D.R. Byerlee, August 1971, pp. 523-27; and C. Cicchetti and A.M. Freeman, III, August 1971, pp. 528-39. Much of the debate has concentrated on whether an option demand would be present if the seller were a perfectly discriminating monopolist. Since real-world sellers are limited, however, in the knowledge required for such discrimination, and in addition seldom have substantial monopoly power, the option demand (or consumer surplus, in the case of zero uncertainty or of risk neutrality) will tend to be greater than zero for such stand-by services as those considered in the hospital industry.

[37] In this hospital study I have been assisted by A. James Lee.

[38] For further discussion and analysis of our findings concerning the three sectors of the hospital industry, see Burton A. Weisbrod and A. James Lee, "A Model of Demand for Collective Goods, as Applied to the Hospital Industry," paper presented at the Conference on Medical Economics from an Industrial Organization Viewpoint, Northwestern University, May 19-20, 1972 (mimeo).

ship program or a cancer research program, to name some of the collective-type services studied. If there were no difference between the "collective" (government plus voluntary non-profit) and the for-profit hospitals with respect to frequency of provision of these various services, we would have expected to find that each service was equally likely to be found in either class of hospitals. In fact, however, this was decidedly not the case. Thus, our findings to date do tend to confirm the hypothesis that the collective and for-profit hospital sectors do differ in the extent of their provision of "collective-type" services.

Similarly, we have compared the relative frequency with which various services are found in the governmental and the voluntary hospitals. The hypothesis is that there will be no difference between these two sectors. We have found, after controlling for hospital size (as was also done above), that 60 percent of the services were provided with greater relative frequency in the government hospitals and 40 percent in the voluntary hospitals. This 60-40 split is significantly smaller than the 78-22 split found between the combined government-voluntary hospitals and the for-profit hospitals; this suggests that, as expected, the governmental and voluntary hospitals are more like each other than they are like the for-profit hospitals. Nevertheless, the 60-40 split is still significantly different from 50-50 (at the .05 level) and this does not support the hypothesis that the governmental and the voluntary hospitals are the same.

Further study and the search for better data seem to be warranted. We have barely scratched the surface of the research effort that is required to discern the differences in outputs by type of hospital, since we have not considered community size, the *total* supply of hospital services in the "market area," or a variety of demand-side variables.

In the case of libraries, data have thus far been exceedingly difficult to find concerning the relative size of the three sectors.[39] One might guess, *a priori*, that the stand-by services of a research library have a significant collective-good component, whereas the provision of current best sellers is essentially a private good, entering the utility function of only the person who holds it at the moment. This being so, we would expect the bulk of the *public* library services—which do *not* consist of current best sellers—to be supplemented in the *voluntary* sector, while the private-good services of the public libraries are supplemented in the *private* sector. Both appear to be the case. There are, in addition to libraries of "private" universities (voluntary, in our terms), various "non-profit" libraries such as the John Crerar Library in Chicago and the Pierpont Morgan Library in New York City. There is a private for-profit sector, too; small and diffuse, it consists of the rental libraries that specialize in the private good, current best sellers; these libraries can be thought of as supplementing the level of public provision for persons who do not want to wait weeks or months to obtain today's favorite books.

---

[39] In the library work I am being assisted by Donna Beutel.

The most appropriate way to define any industry is always a problem, given the availability of close substitutes, and this is certainly the case for libraries. There is a question as to whether it is useful to define an industry to include only *rental* activities; the availability of books for outright purchase is, of course, a close substitute for library books—a private-good substitute.

Turn now to the employment-service industry.[40] Government employment services appear to provide an essentially private service in matching a worker with an employer. This being so, we would expect that persons seeking to supplement this government service, seeking a higher-quality or faster service, would turn to the *private* market, there being little rationale for attempting to organize in the voluntary sector. Indeed, given the apparently small collective-component of employment services, and the variation in the extent to which people wish to use formal employment services, we expect the size of the public sector to be small. Again, our early findings support the expectation. In a study of hiring by 75 Chicago firms in the period 1960-63, it was found that among both blue-collar and white-collar workers, almost 98 percent found their jobs through *private*-market channels—including referrals by other workers, direct firm applications, advertisements and employment agencies; nearly 2 percent found their jobs through the *public* employment service; and only about one-half of one percent, through the *voluntary* sector, including agencies of churches and charities.[41]

Our hypothesized difference between the types of good provided publicly and privately—between the collective-consumption good and the private-good substitute—is confirmed again in the employment-service industry. *All* employment agencies obtain job-market information as part of their activities. "Unlike a public intermediary, however, private agencies quite naturally endeavour to keep this information on vacancies and workers confidential. . . . Thus, . . . private agencies *restrict* the flow of information in the market."[42] By so doing, they can convert a collective good, of the type provided by government employment services, into a private-good substitute. Such information restriction, however, while privately rational, is socially inefficient.

Conclusion

To summarize: first, the expectation is that supplementation of public-sector provision of any good will either be overwhelmingly voluntary or overwhelmingly private, depending on whether the publicly provided good is

---

[40] In the employment-service project I am being assisted by Marc Bendick, Jr.

[41] Computed from data in Eaton H. Conant, "An Evaluation of Private Employment Agencies as Sources of Job Vacancy Data," in *The Measurement and Interpretation of Job Vacancies*, A Conference of the National Bureau of Economic Research (New York: National Bureau of Economic Research, 1966), pp. 519-47.

[42] *Economic Council of Canada*, *Eighth Annual Report*, Ottawa, September 1971, p. 189.

primarily a collective or an individual good. In addition to the extent of "collectiveness" of the governmentally provided good, the relative size of the voluntary and private sectors in any industry will depend on the state of technology—specifically on the closeness of private-good substitutes for collective goods and on the relative production costs.

Second, in a model attempting to explain the relative size of the government sector in some industry or for some country, a significant variable is likely to be the heterogeneity of demand—the smaller the heterogeneity the smaller the non-governmental sector. In a simple majority-vote model without vote-selling, the greater the undersatisfied demand—that is, the demand in excess of the median—the larger will be the combined private and voluntary-sector outputs, and, hence, the smaller the proportion of industry output that is governmentally provided, for that is determined solely by the median. In another model that, for example, weighted voters by intensity of preference, the resulting predictions would differ quantitatively; yet we would still expect that greater variation in consumers' demand would lead to relatively greater extra-governmental provision and a relatively smaller role for the public sector.

The analytic approach suggested here points to a number of testable propositions, involving historical, international, and three-sector industry studies (governmental, for-profit, and voluntary). While a number of suggestive pieces of evidence from preliminary studies have been presented in this paper, much more study is needed, both positive and normative, of the interrelated roles of the governmental, private, and voluntary sectors of the economy.

Toward a Behavioral Theory of Philanthropic Activity

Bruce Bolnick

I

Much of the all-too-scarce literature on the economics of philanthropy is devoted to analyses of the effects of philanthropic or charitable activity[1] on interesting economic phenomena. This genre of the theory is typified by the analysis of income redistribution presented by Hochman and Rodgers[2]: assuming that utility functions contain interpersonal arguments (e.g. that an increase in Jeff's income will benefit Mutt to some extent), redistribution can be considered as an optimality problem. David Johnson has carried this approach even farther, examining the patterns of exchange generated under a variety of assumptions about the form of interdependent utility functions.[3] By assuming that philanthropic activity yields utility, these writers have rendered such behavior susceptible to the traditional tools of economic analysis; benevolence represents a special case of the general theory of consumer choice, posing no formidable challenge to the basic theory.

But at the same time, a more fundamental issue is uncovered: What types of motivation underlie philanthropic activity? Until this issue is confronted,

[1] We will use the term "philanthropy" interchangeably with "charity" and "voluntarism." All will refer to the act of choosing to donate funds, services, or goods to other individuals, or to organizations or the public weal, without direct economic *quid pro quo*.

[2] Harold M. Hocnman and James D. Rodgers, "Pareto Optimal Redistribution," *American Economic Review*, September 1969.

[3] David B. Johnson, *The Fundamental Economics of the Charity Market* (1968 dissertation, University of Virginia). See Part III.

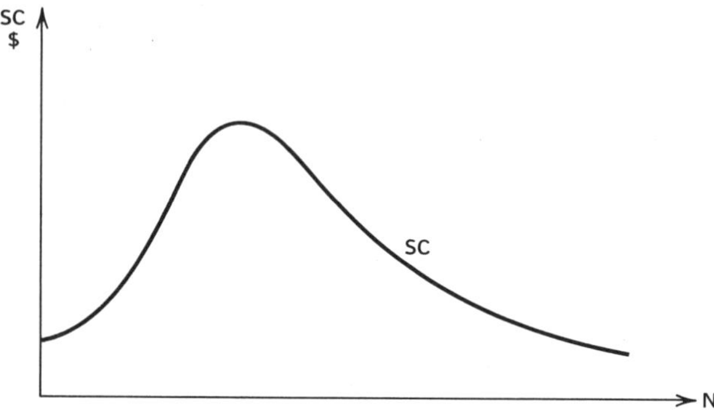

Figure 1

economic theory will find it difficult to explain why charity succeeds in financing project *X* but not project *Y*, or to understand the nature of the social interdependence usually assumed to lie at the root of charitable behavior. While it is logically unassailable to add benevolence to the utility function in order to assess its impact on equilibrium or optimality conditions, this approach is unsatisfying as a behavioral theory. One would hope that social scientists can do more than add an arbitrary form of interdependence to the utility function to illuminate the origins of philanthropic behavior. Especially considering the apparent irrationality of this behavior[4]—the philanthropist is assumed to gain utility from the act of foregoing consumption opportunities without receiving a *quid pro quo*—a more systematic analysis of underlying motivation is called for.

A few attempts have been made to explore the behavioral basis of philanthropic or charitable activity. One notable attempt to construct a model of philanthropic behavior (or "voluntarism") has been provided by David Johnson.[5] Johnson's basic hypothesis is that individuals will donate to a charity only to avoid "societal costs" in the form of social pressures, religious beliefs, and psychic unpleasantries. If each individual's contribution is small in relation to the aggregate philanthropic effort, the free rider psychology would ordinarily preclude success of the "charity market." Where this is so, philanthropic activity must be placed in the hands of the "political market" instead. Only a selective cost imposed on each individual can overcome the compelling logic of the free

---

[4]This characterization is made by Mancur Olson. In his introduction to *The Logic of Collective Action* (Cambridge: Harvard University Press, 1965) he states that only "altruistic" or "irrational" individuals will forego their self-interest to provide for the common good. Also Musgrave, in his *Theory of Public Finance* (New York: McGraw-Hill, 1959) in effect argues that the assumption that individuals will behave cooperatively is "unrealistic and inconsistent with the premises of all other phases of economic analysis." See p. 12.

[5]David Johnson, *op. cit.*, Part IV.

rider; in Johnson's model, the societal costs serve this function. Specifically, the societal cost is generated by invective aimed at the tightwad, discounted by a factor representing the likelihood that others will detect his selfish behavior. Since both of these factors are a function of the size of the community (*N*), the societal cost (*SC*), translated to dollar equivalent, can be described as a function of *N*, as shown in Figure 1.[6] For any *N*, the height of *SC* shows how much the individual will be willing to allocate to philanthropic activity, such as the provision of a public good through voluntary cooperation.

In summarizing his model, Johnson concludes that "the height of the societal cost function depends upon the folkways and mores of the community, the type and quantity of the public good, and the social position and wealth of the individual in question."[7] This is a superb statement of the many factors influencing individual behavior. But unhappily none of these factors had systematically entered Johnson's model, except one—the quantity of the public good, which was introduced in a way unrelated to the height of the societal cost function. That Johnson understands the complexity of the behavior is clear from his conclusion. Equally clear is the fact that his model does not explain how these complex factors affect motivation and action.

Another interesting discussion of philanthropy has been provided by Vickrey.[8] In analyzing the interdependencies which might give rise to charitable redistributions of income, Vickrey suggests that individuals in a social structure will relate themselves to others in a definable way. In particular, he proposes that individual *A* tends to empathize with others of a similar status, favoring those slightly below himself. On the other hand, *A* will tend to feel a rivalry with those of similar or slightly higher status. Aggregating these factors and discounting by *A's* assessment of the marginal utility of income for various income groups, Vickrey arrives at the relationship drawn in Figure 2, showing the net benefit to *A* of a contribution to augment the income of others. The horizontal axis shows income classes (Y_A being *A*'s own status group), and the vertical axis represents a utility measure (with 1.0 being *A's* own marginal utility of income). Thus in the range *VW*, *A* will receive net benefit by giving voluntarily.

Although Vickrey has gone further than most economists would be willing to go in describing social interrelationships which might motivate behavior, one cannot be too satisfied with his model. Aside from any analytical difficulties, it seems that all of the interrelationships which are suggested are based more on introspection than on a systematic probing of social interaction. That his model

---

[6] The hump is the result of Johnson's specification of the two elements of *SC*: the disutility of invective will be an upward sloping function of *N*, with a negative second derivative; the probability of detection will be downward sloping with a negative, and then positive, second derivative.

[7] Johnson, *op. cit.*, p. 149.

[8] William Vickrey, "One Economist's View of Philanthropy," in Frank G. Dickinson, ed., *Philanthropy and Public Policy* (New York: National Bureau of Economic Research, 1962).

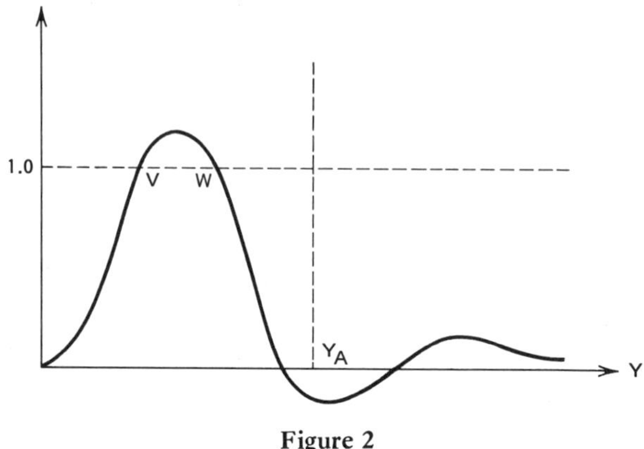

Figure 2

is either significantly incomplete or misspecified is conceded by Vickrey himself, who cites empirical evidence contradicting his finding that charity will, in general, be directed toward a redistribution of income in favor of lower (but not lowest) income groups.

Still, to the extent that he tries to identify underlying motivations based in social and psychological relationships, Vickrey has broken the ice, leading the way to a plunge into what Margolis has called "the murky waters of political sociology."[9] As Frank Dickinson states in his summary of a 1962 conference on philanthropy, "the inapplicability of the whole mechanism of value theory was clearly recognized again and again by the economists present."[10] As we have just seen, attempts have been made to understand philanthropic behavior by moving beyond the traditional focus of value theory, examining the influence of important social variables on people's motivation. What has been glaringly neglected, however, is reference to the results uncovered by behavioral scientists concerning precisely those important social variables and their effects on motivation. The task to which we now turn is one of trying to replace the common ad hoc specifications of interdependency with an explicit analysis of the theories of the behavioral sciences. Assuming only that social psychologists and their like are as honest and thoughtful as economists, the incorporation of their theories to the discussion of behavior should at worst do no harm.

II

In order to develop a behavioral theory of voluntarism, we must examine the types of motivations which affect individual decision-making when man is

---

[9] Julius Margolis, "A Comment of the Pure Theory of Public Expenditure," *Review of Economics and Statistics*, November 1955, p. 348.

[10] Dickinson, *op. cit.*, p. 112.

placed into a social context; i.e. when "economic man" is transformed into "social man." As an introduction to social behavior, this section will first explore the channels of influence and types of motivation which affect the individual in small groups. Then we will see that "non-economic" motivations in such groups have commonly been acknowledged by economists, though these factors are usually assumed to disappear as group size grows. Thus we must inquire into the basic differences between small and large groups to understand this disappearance. Finally, we will see how social motivations can, in fact, persist in large groups, traditional assumptions to the contrary notwithstanding.

Before proceeding, a few disclaimers are in order regarding the use to be made of the received knowledge of social psychology. First, many assertions will be made below concerning social influences, relationships, cognitions, and motivations. All will be drawn from established positions of behavioral and social theory. My concern being the application of these principles and hypotheses to the economic problem at hand, I lay no claim to establishing new insights into that theory. Further, I do not intend to imply that there is unanimous agreement among behavioral scientists concerning social processes. If we constrained ourselves to only those hypotheses which are uniformly accepted or have been proven valid, given the state of the science we should have little to work with. Thus the assertions to be unveiled should be regarded as what they are—hypotheses of behavior, with varying amounts of supporting evidence and varying degrees of acceptance. Where possible I shall refer to supportive experiments which have corroborated various hypotheses, but no proofs or definitive answers should be expected.

Specific reference to experiments is also important because of a technical problem which arises in trying to combine isolated hypotheses into a general analysis of behavioral motivation. It must be noted that many of the experiments alluded to below are not strictly applicable to the problem of voluntarism, in that they test behavior with regard to symbol acts rather than referent acts, i.e. expressed attitudes rather than behavior. Just because individual *A* says, in an experimental situation, that he agrees with individual *B*, one cannot conclude that, in a behavioral context, he would in fact act in a manner consistent with this statement. The relationship between such symbol acts (statements) and their referent acts (corresponding behavior) depends on a complex blend of social, psychological, and situational factors[11] which are beyond the scope of this paper. In the same way that the application of economic models to real situations involves utilization of data which only approximates the desired variables, the experimental evidence supporting many behavioral hypotheses often tests only approximations to the actual relationships

[11] This relationship is one of the basic points of inquiry in Ulf Himmelstrand, *Social Pressures, Attitudes, and Democratic Processes* (Uppsala: Almquist & Wiksells, 1960).

in which we are interested. Therefore brief reference to supportive tests is necessary to facilitate a proper evaluation of the extent to which this technical problem affects the applicability of the behavioral theories.

Finally, it is important to make clear that what is sought below is an understanding of basic social processes and relationships which affect individual behavior, and which might motivate philanthropic activity. The analysis to be undertaken is by no means meant to be an exhaustive survey of the field of social psychology. An anthropologist attempting to introduce principles of economics to the problem of capital formation in a primitive tribe (such as irrigation ditches, kivas, fortifications, bows and arrows) might refer to elementary ideas such as present-future trade-offs. More complex models such as putty-clay vintage technology concepts would probably be overlooked. Similarly, a more sophisticated application of social psychology to the theory of philanthropy awaits future discussion.

"Two or more persons engaged in any kind of a relationship with each other constitute a group."[12] That individuals generally belong to at least one group is obvious from even the most casual observations. The need to engage in some kind of relationship with others follows from a variety of motivations, based on the assumption that individuals seek satisfaction, gratification, self-identification, and pleasure. Aside from the possibility that man is endowed with a social "instinct," the individual learns from infancy that association with others aids in the satisfaction of needs, and provides satisfactions in and of itself such as approbation, security, and love. To the extent that man is a stimulus seeking organism, social situations provide stimuli. Further, contact with others is a necessary part of self-identification, and evaluation of one's attitudes, activities, status, and opinions.[13] Thus relationships are sought. In effect, the individual is buying rewards at the cost of a degree of conformity and compatibility.[14]

Most social gratifications are provided by "small groups" or "primary groups" which involve face-to-face personal contact among members. These groups may be "formal," such as an office staff, or "informal," such as a group of neighbors. A further distinction can be made between "affect-oriented" groups, in which the relationship among members is itself the major object of group activity, or "achievement-oriented" groups, in which interaction is related to task performance.

The basic unit of a primary group is the "dyad," or the contact between two individuals. On this simplest level of social influence, the avoidance of

---

[12] Henry Clay Lindgren, *An Introduction to Social Psychology* (New York: John Wiley & Sons, Inc., 1969), p. 247.

[13] *Ibid.*, see ch. 2. Also see Leon Festinger, "Theory of Social Comparison Processes" in Herbert H. Hyman and Eleanor Singer, ed., *Readings in Reference Group Theory and Research* (New York: Free Press, 1968).

[14] This formulation is stressed by John W. Thibaut and Harold H. Kelley, *The Social Psychology of Groups* (New York: John Wiley & Sons, Inc., 1961).

dissonance is a fundamental facet of a relationship. This gives rise to the "consonance" or "balance" theory of social relations.[15] Concerning each issue relevant to the relationship, a triangle of cognitions exists for individual *A*: his evaluation of individual *B*, his perception of *B's* position or opinion, and *A's* own opinion. Social balance is the state achieved when *A's* evaluation of *B* conforms to the differences of opinion or attitude. Thus if *A* is attracted to *B*, but their positions differ, dissonance is created. Similarly if *A* agrees with *B*'s position, but dislikes *B*, the dyad is out of balance. The magnitude of the dissonance is a function of the perceived discrepancy of opinion, the importance of the issue to *A*, and the importance of the dyad to *A*. This last factor can be called the "cohesiveness" of the dyad from *A's* point of view. Such dissonant situations create what Newcomb has called a "strain toward symmetry,"[16] or a tendency toward consonance. This strain will generally act upon the weakest link of the triangle of cognitions, producing either a change in *A*'s opinion of *B* as an individual, a change in *A's* opinion about the issue, or a change in *A's* perception of *B's* opinion about the issue. An example of the evidence supporting this theory of consonance is an experiment by Horwitz, Lyons, and Perlmutter[17] concerning influence in discussion groups: "Questionnaire responses showed that there is a close relationship between the degree to which a member likes the originator of an assertion, and the member's tendency to agree with the assertion. Further, a member perceives liked members as agreeing with his evaluation of the assertion, and disliked members as disagreeing."[18] This balance hypothesis does not imply that one of the links of the triangle *will* in fact be altered, only that there are pressures in this direction. In this context, Back has shown that highly cohesive dyads showed a greater tendency to move toward agreement than did less cohesive dyads.[19] But in general frictions exist which might result in an equilibrium being reached without complete resolution of all dissonance related to the issue in question.

Given that we are talking about a dyad, it must be asked whether *B* will tend to influence *A* or whether *A* will tend to influence *B*. Clearly a mutual interaction is present. The results will depend on the relative desires to continue the relationship, the relative importance of the issue to each, and the perceptions of one another's positions. Defining "power" as the ability to influence the

---

[15] See Robert E. Lane and David O. Sears, *Public Opinion* (Englewood Cliffs: Prentice Hall, 1964), ch. 5. Also Joseph E. McGrath, *Social Psychology: A Brief Introduction* (New York: Holt, Rinehart & Winston, 1964), ch. 5. And Thibaut and Kelley, *op. cit.*, ch. 5; Lindgren, *op. cit.*, ch. 7. The basic hypothesis is usually attributed to Theodore Newcomb.

[16] Theodore Newcomb, *The Acquaintanceship Process* (New York: Holt, Rinehart & Winston, 1961); cited in Lindgren, *op. cit.*, ch. 7.

[17] M.W. Horwitz, J. Lyons, and H.V. Perlmutter, "Induction Forces in Discussion Groups," *Human Relations* 14, 1951, cited in Thibaut and Kelley, *op. cit.*, ch. 5.

[18] *Ibid.*, in Thibaut and Kelley, *op. cit.*, p. 77.

[19] Kurt W. Back, "Influence through Social Communication, "*Journal of Abnormal and Social Psychology*, 1951. Cited in Thibaut and Kelley, *op. cit.*, ch. 7.

behavior of the other member of the dyad, it is rare that power will be exactly equal between the two individuals. To some degree, power-dependence relationships often characterize dyads, affecting not only the direction of influence, but even the expectations of the direction of influence. In a relationship of this sort, the dependent might expect to be led, and the leader might expect to function in that role. "It is more feasible for a person of generally high power to maintain consistent values and attitudes than one of low power. This is a consequence of the greater influence of the former upon the values that the pair come to share. Thus the powerful person is better able to keep the values with which he enters the relationship, these being consistent with the standards that exist in his other relationships."[20] Concerning these expectations, Hoffman and Maier have demonstrated that people in a position of leadership will try to influence others in experimental groups.[21] Sometimes leadership is established by the ability of one member to control the rewards accruing to the other, either psychic or material.[22] Alternatively, power might be established because of differing evaluations about the importance of maintaining the dyad as a functioning relationship. Finally, since the result of the strain toward symmetry will depend on the perceptions each member has of the other's attitudes, the outcome will depend vitally upon communications. One possible circumstance, similar to Schelling's strategy of "commitment,"[23] is that one member might express a point of view on an issue, forcing the other to agree or to create dissonance. If *B* clearly perceives *A's* position without clearly expressing a position himself for *A* to perceive, it is likely that *B*, rather than *A*, will adjust to achieve consonance. This sort of behavior might be expected where power-dependence role expectations exist within the dyad. All of these considerations show that, while mutual interaction is, indeed, present, the direction of influence and the extent of influence on a given issue may not be indeterminate.

Given that the dyad strives toward a resolution of dissonance, we are still not in a position to conclude that this facet of social interaction can affect actual behavior. We must consider the possibility that *A* might pay lip service to *B's* attitude to achieve social consonance; i.e. *A* can achieve social balance

---

[20] Thibaut and Kelley, *op. cit.*, p. 119.

[21] L. R. Hoffman and N. R. F. Maier, "Valence in the Adoption of Solutions by Members of Homogeneous and Heterogeneous Groups," *Journal of Abnormal and Social Psychology*, 1961. Cited in Lindgren, *op. cit.*, ch. 15.

[22] Thibaut and Kelley, *op. cit.*, ch. 7. It is interesting to note that the authors use a variation on game theory to demonstrate a matrix of outcomes accruing to the dyad members. The variation is based on the recognition that there is imperfect information about one another's strategies, that perceptions change, and that the rewards and costs over time are endogenous to the game.

[23] Thomas Schelling, *The Strategy of Conflict* (Cambridge: Harvard University Press, 1960). See ch. 2.

through hypocrisy. While this might occur, social psychologists, notably Festinger,[24] suggest that this creates a more subtle form of dissonance with which *A* must then cope—a psychological inconsistency, or "cognitive dissonance." This creates a cognitive equivalent of the strain toward symmetry which, depending on the importance of the dyad, the magnitude of the discrepancy, the relevance of the issue to *A*, and a complex of other factors, might be resolved by an actual change in *A*'s opinion in the direction of that put forth by *B*. Thus the theory of cognitive dissonance: if *A* dislikes *X* and yet is induced to do what *X* wants or to support *X*, his attitude toward *X* reacts in a favorable direction. Festinger and Carlsmith have shown experimentally that students assigned the task of convincing others of an assertion which the former knew to be false, actually changed their own attitudes to reduce the dissonance built up by the role conflict.[25] Often the easiest way to reconcile a divergence between attitude and behavior is to change one's own attitude. In this way, *B's* influence over *A* in terms of the dyadic relationship can cause *A* to internalize a value or attitude.

In summary, the hypotheses basic to this model of interpersonal influence are twofold: first, that individuals gain rewards from social relationships; and second, that consistency and avoidance of dissonance are significant motivating factors. On this very elementary level of social relations we can see that behavior can be motivated by "non-economic" variables, including social rewards and psychological consistency. The force of these non-economic motivations becomes more pervasive as we complicate the analysis by expanding the scope of the social context first to small groups, and finally to influences in a large community.

In generalizing to social pressures in primary groups the conclusions regarding influence in dyads remain intact, except that we must now consider the mutual interaction of a larger number of individuals. Within the small group we can talk of the establishment of group "norms," and then of the pressures which operate upon members of the group to conform to these norms.

Through group interaction processes, including communications, flows of influence, and task performance, a group will establish "norms" concerning relevant issues. A norm can very generally be defined as a "standard of behavior,"[26] and can refer to a frame of reference, a prescribed "right" attitude or behavior toward an issue or object, affective feelings regarding "right" behavior, or a set of sanctions, both positive and negative, within the group.[27]

---

[24] Leon Festinger, *A Theory of Cognitive Dissonance* (New York: Harper and Row, 1957). Cited in Lindgren, *op. cit.*, ch. 7. Also in Clifford T. Morgan and Richard A. King, *Introduction to Psychology* (New York: McGraw-Hill, 1966), pp. 613-16.

[25] L. Festinger and J.M. Carlsmith, "Cognitive Consequences of Forced Compliance," *Journal of Abnormal and Social Psychology*, 1959. Cited in Morgan and King, *op. cit.*, p. 614.

[26] Morgan and King, *op. cit.*, p. 579.

[27] McGrath, *op. cit.* See ch. 11.

Norms are defined with varying degrees of precision or ambiguity depending on the relevance of an issue to the group.

Within the group, pressures to conform to these norms are created by what Thibaut and Kelley call "norm sending" activity,[28] which is defined to include both the amount of communication generated concerning the norm, and the clarity with which the norm is embodied in these communications. The effectiveness of norm sending regarding an issue relevant to the group is then a function of a variety of group and individual characteristics. In particular, the intensity of norm sending will vary positively with factors such as the amount of interaction within the group, the familiarity among group members (depending on group size and group history), the homogeneity of opinion within the group, the salience of the issue in question, and cohesiveness, or attractiveness to the members, of the group. This last factor, cohesiveness, depends in turn on considerations such as the affect feelings within the group, the prestige of membership, and the congruence of individual and group goals. The intensity with which these pressures to conform are perceived by individual group members depends on such factors as the amount of discrepancy of opinion and the skewness of opinion variation, the amount of communication directed at the individual, and the individual's receptivity to the norms and communications. In addition, personality factors such as the need for affiliation, ego-centrism, self-esteem, and hostility, will bear upon the individual's receptivity to these pressures to conform.[29] The set of factors mentioned here is not exhaustive, but serves quite well to illustrate the complexity of the interaction and influence.

That group influences do, indeed, affect behavior has been demonstrated by a number of experiments. Sherif has shown that "individuals in ambiguous situations are inclined to depend on one another for clues or suggestions about the course of action to take," and to carry over this effect of group consensus to behavior outside the group.[30] Asch has demonstrated that group pressures, even in an ad hoc group of no importance to the individual, overwhelmed objectivity in judging line lengths.[31] More striking to the economist is Homan's result that individuals in a work group conform to internal group norms regarding a fair day's work even at the expense of maximizing earnings, given a piece-meal wage structure. Group cohesiveness proved more important than economic rewards.[32] In still another experiment, Schachter has found that greater cohesiveness in small

---

[28] Thibaut and Kelley, *op. cit.* See ch. 13.

[29] See Lane and Sears, *op. cit.*, ch. 4. Some of these relationships have been mathematized by Herbert Simon in *Models of Man* (New York: John Wiley & Sons, Inc., 1957), to show how modelling can clarify hypotheses and lead to insights about equilibrium states and dynamic feedback processes of social interaction.

[30] Muzafer Sherif, *Psychology of Social Norms* (New York: Harper's, 1936). Cited in Lindgren, *op. cit.*, p. 96.

[31] S. A. Asch, *Social Psychology* (Englewood Cliffs: Prentice Hall, 1956). Cited in Lindgren, *op. cit.*, ch. 6.

groups led to less tolerance with deviants and more communication aimed at those deviating from conforming behavior.[33] In general, experimental evidence strongly supports the hypothesis that group interaction and pressures to conform are significant factors in motivating individual behavior.

As with dyadic behavior, however, the question of who does the influencing and who gets influenced is vital to an understanding of flows of influence through social groups. Clearly the group does not take a referendum on all relevant issues with the majority or median attitude being adopted and internalized by all. Rather the establishment of norms concerning attitudes, behavior, values, and sanctions is determined by a more complex form of interaction. Similar to the case of a two-person group, patterns of leadership generally characterize the group structure, with strong influences over group processes and group development. Just as the formation of the group leads ordinarily to the establishment of norms through interaction, communications, and expectations, so does the interaction of a number of individuals commonly result in implicit subjective status relationships within the group. This does not mean that a status system is imposed; instead, a consensus about status develops as the group interacts over time.[34] The leadership role which evolves involves not only the ability to influence others in the group, but also the expectation on the part of others that the leader will try to influence their behavior. The degree to which a leader's actions "are regarded as significant, relevant, and important by others" is called his "prestige."[35] The extent to which he is able actually to influence behavior of others is his "power."

It is interesting to note that something not dissimilar to free-rider psychology might guarantee that the non-leaders will adjust to the attitude of the leader. If each individual expects the others to accept the leader's attitude then he might decide to agree himself, even if, in fact, the non-leaders as a group would prefer to back the leader down. While it might be in the interests of the group (less the leader) to maintain its previous attitude, the perceived self-interest of each member could lead to the result that the leader successfully influences the group's norm.

What characteristics will a leader possess? Ordinarily the role of leadership will be filled by a member who is characteristically salient, intelligent, and well-accepted by the group. A most important attribute of leadership, however, intimately related to the role expectation of attempting to influence others, is

---

[32] G. C. Homans, "Group Factors in Worker Productivity," in Proshansky and Seidenberg, eds., *Basic Studies in Social Psychology* (New York: Holt, Rinehart & Winston, 1965). Cited in Lindgren, *op. cit.*, ch. 15.

[33] Stanley Schachter, "Deviation, Rejection, and Communication," *Journal of Abnormal and Social Psychology*, 1951. Cited in Lindgren, *op. cit.*, ch. 15.

[34] Thibaut and Kelley, *op. cit.*, p. 230.

[35] Lindgren, *op. cit.*, p. 291.

deviancy.[36] Leaders (and marginal group members) will conform least to group norms because leadership necessitates introducing new attitudes and opinions. Dittes and Kelley have experimentally shown that those with the highest levels of acceptance within the group are generally those who feel the least pressure to conform to established norms.[37] Noting that individuals in ambiguous situations rely on group consensus to establish norms, Vidulich and Bayley have shown that high status members are more readily accepted as models.[38] Thus leaders are key figures in social learning, having visibility and prestige within the group. Further, Page has demonstrated that the influence which a leader has on an individual can be increased by paying more attention, or directing more communication to that individual, to bring about a change of attitude.[39] The power of the leader to introduce new norms and the extent to which deviancy on his part is tolerated by the groups are, of course, not unlimited. Since the leader will have a strong interest in the vitality and solidarity of the group he is unlikely to threaten its cohesiveness through excessive deviancy.[40] Still, within a fairly flexible range, the ability and willingness of the leader to influence the group and to introduce new attitudes and opinions is generally apparent.

Can anything be said about who, in any given group, might be endowed with the prestige and concomitant power of the leadership role? Much evidence exists which correlates leadership in small groups with general status in alternative social contexts; prestige within a group is distributed not independently of social position and social class in the community at large.[41] "If group members differ in their general social status, there may be tendencies to organize and assign roles that are 'fitting' . . . for each status. Thus decision-making and leadership functions are likely to be sought by high-status persons. If, in the external social organization, these persons have power, lower status persons may acquiesce to this role differentiation."[42] Evidence to support this relationship between group status and general social status includes experiments by Bass and Wurster, who show that "high officials in a company exhibit more leadership in temporary, initially leaderless, discussion groups, than do officials of lower rank."[43] And

[36] *Ibid.* See ch. 15.

[37] J. Dittes and H. H. Kelley, "Effects of Different Conditions of Acceptance upon Conformity to Group Norms," *Journal of Abnormal and Social Psychology*, 1956. Cited in Lane and Sears, *op. cit.*, p. 31.

[38] R. N. Vidulich and G. A. Bayley, "A General Field Experimental Technique for Studying Social Influence," *Journal of Social Psychology*, 1966. Cited in Lindgren, *op. cit.*, ch. 15.

[39] E. B. Page, "Teacher Comments and Student Performance," *Journal of Educational Psychology*, 1958. Cited in Lindgren, *op. cit.*, ch. 15.

[40] O. J. Harvey and C. Consalvi, "Status and Conformity to Pressures in Informal Groups," *Journal of Abnormal and Social Psychology*, 1961. Cited in Lindgren, *op. cit.*, ch. 15.

[41] Lindgren, *op. cit.*, ch. 15.

[42] Thibaut and Kelley, *op. cit.*, p. 286.

[43] B. M. Bass and C. R. Wurster, "Effects of Company Rank on LGD Performance of Oil Refinery Supervisors," *Journal of Applied Psychology*, 1953. Cited in Thibaut and Kelley, *op. cit.*, p. 287.

Thibaut and Kelley suggest that "association with people of higher status yields certain kinds of rewards not available from people of lower status."[44]

It is important to note at this point that none of the hypotheses being discussed lead to determinate results or fixed behavioral consequences. We are examining, instead, what are only tendencies in social situations, not certainties and rules of social interaction. In fact, we can regard the results of social interaction as stochastic sets of behavior, rather than uniquely defined behavior, for two fundamental reasons. First, the entire set of significant variables is clearly more complex than can be easily described by a manageable decision function. And second, even given a complete list of factors affecting the rewards and costs to an individual in his social context, his behavioral decision may not be uniquely defined because of the nature of his decision calculus.

Regarding this last point, it has been argued that models of economic man, the maximizer, attribute too much knowledge and ability to individuals as decision-makers. An excellent discussion of alternative, and presumably more realistic notions of decision-making has been provided by Simon,[45] who develops the notion of "bounded rationality." His task is "to replace the global rationality of economic man with a kind of rational behavior that is compatible with the access to information and the computational capacities that are actually possessed . . . ."[46] Given the limitations of man as a calculator, and the need to keep information-gathering costs and decision costs to acceptable levels, an individual may well truncate the search for maximum net rewards, and settle for a satisfactory solution. He would then choose to behave in a way which will yield an acceptable payoff rather than an optimal payoff, where "acceptability" is determined by some "aspiration level" which might be a flexible standard, varying with the ease of attainment. In general, behavior will not be uniquely determined by the information concerning costs and rewards. Only an acceptable behavior set is definable. Beyond that the decision will depend on the order in which alternatives are considered and by feedback effects on the aspiration level. Unless those two factors can be specified, the outcome of the decision process will not be uniquely determined. The decision function will at best describe the probability of a given satisfactory decision being chosen.

Once the individual is placed in a social context, with non-economic motivations and non-maximizing decision mechanisms being acknowledged, we can begin to understand how decisions which the traditional economic theory would consider to be "irrational" might be explained. If gratifications can be had outside the world of economic goods, and if decision-making capacities are indeed bounded, then it would not be surprising if observed behavior did not conform to traditional value theory, which is normally based on a *quid pro quo*

[44] Thibaut and Kelley, *op. cit.*, p. 48.

[45] Herbert Simon, *op. cit.*, especially chapters 14, 15 and the introduction to Part IV.

[46] *Ibid.*, p. 241.

exchange with the goal of maximization. Although, as Boulding[47] has suggested, social motivations can be added to the utility function to preserve the form of value theory, it is important to keep in mind that the motivations anchored in social relationships are quite distinct from the motivation anchored in consumption preferences. We can include in the latter class philanthropy which is atomistically motivated; i.e. valued as a consumption good. This type of "altruistic" behavior is implicitly the focus of Hochman-Rodgers' type stories.[48]

In fact, "non-economic" motivations in small groups have commonly been acknowledged by economists dealing with voluntarism. For example, Boulding[49] recognizes that an individual is likely to contribute to the support of a group if he identifies with its cause; but as the size of the community increases, this necessary sense of identification becomes more "tenuous." "In large, heterogeneous, and anonymous communities in which the individual loses the sense of face-to-face contact with other members, it is almost always necessary to reinforce philanthropy with coercion."[50] Similarly, in Johnson's societal cost model,[51] social pressures will become less prominent as N increases. The most outspoken advocate of this distinction between behavior in large and in small groups is Mancur Olson[52] who acknowledges that individuals may act in violation of their economic self-interest in the special case of a small group, where interpersonal effects are strong. In large groups, it is possible that "altruistic" or "irrational" individuals will act in the group interest, but to Olson this phenomenon is usually of no practical importance. Non-economic behavior can be induced by selectively applied social pressures; but such forces work only in groups small enough to permit direct individual interaction.

In general we find a cognizance of social pressures which can potentially induce non-economic behavior. But only in small groups, where interpersonal influences are sufficiently potent, will such pressures function effectively. Let us turn, then, to a more scrutinizing appraisal of large groups to see if this simple conclusion can be justified.

A large group, or secondary group, differs basically from a primary group in that face-to-face contact is not characteristic of the relationship between all members. A large group can be an organization, such as a labor union, a community, a distinguishable sector of society, such as an economic class, or a

---

[47] Kenneth Boulding, "Notes on a Theory of Philanthropy," in Dickinson, ed., *op. cit.*, p. 61.

[48] Compare this result with Musgrave's criticism of Hochman-Rodgers in his comment on "Pareto Optimal Redistribution" in *American Economic Review*, December 1970. Musgrave argues that Hochman and Rodgers fail to distinguish between that part of redistribution which is by choice and that part which is in fact coerced.

[49] Boulding, *op. cit.*, p. 62.

[50] *Ibid.*

[51] Johnson, *op. cit.* See Part IV.

[52] Mancur Olson, *The Logic of Collective Action* (Cambridge: Harvard University Press, 1965).

society as a whole. Although any collection of individuals with a common function, characteristic, or value can be formally considered as a group, we will be concerned not with "categorical groups" such as blondes, but only with functioning communities. That non-economic motivations are insignificant within these large groups may at first glance seem true by definition: as Boulding has envisioned, the individual in such a group "loses" the necessary "sense of face-to-face contact with other members." Unfortunately this simple and elegant result cannot be depended on, because large groups are more complicated than the definition suggests.

New York is a large group. Yet it is certainly more than a collection of individuals with the characteristic that some pairs are not in direct face-to-face contact. Indeed it is difficult to think of New York without implicitly or explicitly thinking of the neighborhoods, the firms, the community organizations, the schools, the softball teams, the political parties, the social strata—in short all of the subgroups which give New York its vitality and identity. To say that a large group is characterized by loss of face-to-face contact does not imply that such relationships exist nowhere within the large group. Depending on the interrelationships of the subgroups (which do involve direct personal effects) within the large group, it is possible that channels of influence might exist even in a large, heterogeneous, and anonymous community. To illustrate, imagine a firm having three distinct subgroups—managers, foremen, and production workers. Even though managers and production workers may have no direct contact, channels of personal influence can exist because of the obvious linkages between the subgroups. Only in a large group which is not composed of a complex of primary subgroups can we be sure that social pressures derived from face-to-face contact will not find channels of influence throughout the group. But because personal contact of some sort is necessary for the group to function, and because individuals within large groups will seek out personal relationships in the form of primary subgroups (which alone can provide certain forms of satisfaction), it is clear that the simple designation "large group" is nothing more than a formal category embodying complex personal interrelationships. In short, a large group is composed of a set of interrelated small groups; thus social pressures may well exist to enforce norms within the large group, although the strength of social sanctions and the clarity with which the norms are transmitted to each individual will depend on the linkages in the chain of primary groups.

That the substructure of large groups may have an important influence on the behavior of group members can be demonstrated by reference to Almarin Phillips, who has applied this type of social model to the problem of market structures.[53] Realizing that interdependence among firms is a significant aspect of market behavior, Phillips focuses attention on the "market group," not on

[53] Almarin Phillips, *Market Structure, Organization, and Performance* (Cambridge: Harvard University Press, 1962).

the individual firms within the group. His theory of interfirm organization relies upon a complex form of interdependence which does not require the concentration of production among a few large firms, or "simple oligopoly." In his model of "linked interdependence," an industry may be characterized by many firms, but each firm identifies only a few close rivals and conceives of the rest as an amorphous group. Citing Henderson's theory of duopoly, Phillips quotes: "there may be thousands of grocers, yet each grocer will be intimately affected by a very small number of neighboring grocers."[54] Thus oligopolistic behavior can exist even with a large group of sellers. "That is, it may be incorrect to assume that as the number of firms increases, interdependence tends to disappear and that rivalry approaches. . . competition."[55] Although simple oligopoly can statistically be shown to affect only a limited number of industries, Phillips suggests that some form of linked interdependence may be more ubiquitous. Because the large group is composed of interrelated small groups, interdependence effects can motivate characteristic small group behavioral forms within the large group. It is not enough that a group be large to discount the impact of small group pressures.

Another consequence of the multiplicity of groups within a community is that we must modify our conception of individual motivation. We have examined the channels of influence, and some important variables which affect the strength of pressures to conform within a small group. Now we must complicate things by admitting that an individual usually belongs to more than a single small group. Thus it is not enough to examine the pressures to conform within a single group. The individual must reconcile diverse pressures and influences in forming an opinion or choosing a course of behavior. To achieve a satisfactory resolution of dissonance necessitates the weighing of many complex and even contradictory social factors.

Fortunately we need not be totally dismayed by the morass of complications which we have encountered. Certain analytic hypotheses regarding tendencies of motivation and behavior can still be salvaged. First, for many individuals, the most efficient solution to conflicting social pressures is to compartmentalize one's values and respond in a different way to each set of social influences.[56] Where this is possible, behavior may still respond to motivations within any primary group. To the extent that compartmentalization is used, behavior will depend on the relative salience of different group memberships at any one time. Thus if pressures exist at the office to give to a charity, but the individual's bowling buddies disdain such softheartedness, he may give at the office and not mention it on Wednesday night. A multiple

[54] Alexander Henderson, "The Theory of Duopoly," *Quarterly Journal of Economics*, November 1954. Cited in Phillips, *op. cit.*, p. 23.

[55] Phillips, *op. cit.*, p. 23.

[56] Thibaut and Kelley, *op. cit.*, p. 119.

exposure of this sort might lead to problems of self-consistency, but where an optimal solution cannot readily be found, an imperfect behavioral response must be accepted as satisfactory.

A second hypothesis which survives our complications involves the effects of status. Consistency of attitude is more readily retained for a high status individual than for a low status individual because of the former's ability to influence the norms of the groups to which he belongs. Thus we can expect that a norm generated by high status groups in a community will tend to be more readily transmitted through the chain of group linkages than will a norm originating in lower status groups.

Finally, where we are confronted with multiple group membership, we can expect that the effectiveness of pressures to conform to a norm in group *X* will depend on the extent to which the individual's attitudes are important for maintaining consonance in groups *Y* and *Z*. This can be called the "social anchoring" of the attitude in question. Himmelstrand has theorized that the social anchoring of an attitude is a fundamental factor in determining whether a given norm will be translated into behavior.[57] In general, pressures to conform to a norm for which there is no counteracting social anchoring will more likely be effective than they will when such countervailing forces exist.

So far we have acknowledged only one form of social influence which can affect individual behavior—the influences within primary groups originating in the basic need for rewarding, consonant social relationships. These direct interpersonal influences are not the only source of social motivation which enter an individual's decision calculus in the context of a large group. In fact an individual may be strongly influenced by groups of which he is not a member, and by individuals with whom he has no personal contact. An individual may be motivated not only by the direct social pressures which we have been discussing, but also by identification with certain persons or groups, whether or not these relationships involve direct contact.[58] Any group to which an individual refers himself in forming an opinion or in making a decision, be it a membership group or non-membership group, can be called a "reference group." "The point to be stressed is that the links in the interpersonal chain do not have to be forged exclusively via direct social relations."[59] Whereas a membership group can impose sanctions, the referent power of any group over attitudes is limited by the strength of the individual's identification with the group, and his need for reference norms. But that power is nonetheless real.

Reference groups serve two distinct functions for the individual—first as sources of norms for behavior and attitudes, and second as sources of social

[57] Himmelstrand, *op. cit.* See ch. 1, section 2.

[58] See Lane and Sears, *op. cit.*, ch. 4.

[59] Hyman and Singer, *op. cit.*, p. 3.

comparison.[60] For the latter function an individual is likely to refer himself to status groups which are neither far above nor far below his own, and will very likely refer heavily to groups of which he is a member. But for normative references, "the individual chooses a normative reference group so that . . . he can feel himself part of a more favored group."[61] Because higher status groups often have high salience, and because one's aspirations often anticipate upward mobility, "individuals identify with advantaged groups and thereby gain gratification," especially in a society where mobility is perceived or is stressed.[62] In practical terms this means that "every editor, politician, banker, capitalist, employer, clergyman, or judge has a following with whom his opinion has weight. He in turn is likely to have his own authorities. The anatomy of collective opinion shows it to be organized from centers and subcenters, forming a kind of intellectual feudal system."[63] The basic drive which is manifested in such identifications, according to Festinger's hypotheses, is the need for self-evaluation based on comparison with others.[64] As with direct social pressures, behavior can be motivated by rewards anchored in social linkages of this nature.

Important empirical evidence has been gathered to support these contentions concerning flows of influence through reference identifications. Merton, in analyzing the influence structure of a community, found that distinct opinion leaders, or "influentials," existed who served as "reference points" (i.e. loci of reference identification) within that large group.[65] Some influentials derived their power from close ties to people in the community. In these cases referent influence would flow through the same channels as the chain of primary group influences which we described above. Others, who maintained a degree of social distance from the populace, derived their influence through prestige based on skills, education, and occupation—in general through imputed status rather than a network of close personal relationships and primary group contacts. In both cases, the influentials were commonly looked to in decision-making by the people of the community.

In a second study, Eisenstadt[66] has demonstrated empirically that reference orientation serves as a mechanism of social control and is closely linked to leadership and communication. Reference norms are especially important in

---

[60] See H. H. Kelley, "Two Functions of Reference Groups," in Hyman and Singer, *op. cit.*

[61] Hyman and Singer, *op. cit.*, p. 13.

[62] *Ibid.*, p. 14.

[63] E. A. Ross, *Social Psychology* (New York: Macmillian, 1908). p. 348. Cited in Hyman and Singer, *op. cit.*, p. 121.

[64] Leon Festinger, "Theory of Social Comparison Processes," in Hyman and Singer, *op. cit.*

[65] R. K. Merton, "Patterns of Influence: Local and Cosmopolitan," in Hyman and Singer, *op. cit.*

[66] S. N. Eisenstadt, "Studies of Reference Group Behavior," in Hyman and Singer, *op. cit.*

"situations in which an individual is called upon to perform some civic duty, participate in a drive, etc."[67] Eisenstadt's experiments with immigrants to Israel showed that, in ambiguous situations, individuals expect communications involving norms and that these communications come from people in positions of leadership.

Reference groups, however, are not unique. An individual will ordinarily have a set of reference groups. In any given situation the potency of the norms of each reference group depends both on the absolute importance of that group to the individual, and on situational salience.[68] Kelley has demonstrated experimentally that artificially increasing the visibility of a latent reference group (in his experiment, the Catholic Church) tended to influence attitudes in the direction of Catholic norms, among Catholics being tested.[69]

Having analytically distinguished influences based on reference group identification from influence grounded in the need to participate in consonant, rewarding social relationships, it is important to acknowledge that the interaction between these two sources of influence can be a powerful factor in the dissemination of norms. Research involving this more complex flow in influence in large groups is very scarce, but some results have been provided by Katz and Lazarsfeld.[70] In examining the effects of advertising, the writers show that although only a few individuals may actually be affected by these communications, many others are affected by those few through personal contacts, resulting in a two-step flow of influence. A similar pattern can be expected where the communications involve norms concerning attitudes and behavior instead of product advertising.

Thus, within a large group, where most previous models assumed that social pressures were unimportant as compared to economic motivations, we have found that social pressures are not necessarily diluted to the point of impotence. In fact they may even be pervasive. Through direct social pressures existing in the small groups which function within the large group, and through pressures derived from identification with significant reference groups and reference individuals ("influentials" or "opinion leaders") within the large group, channels of influence can be maintained even as group size increases. Behavioral models based solely on assumptions of economic rationality and economic motivation are apt to fail to explain behavior within these social contexts.

One last building block remains before the sociological foundation of our behavioral model is complete. Up to this point we have examined influences which

---

[67] *Ibid.*, p. 421.

[68] Hyman and Singer, *op. cit.*, p. 121.

[69] H. H. Kelley, "Salience of Membership and Resistance to Change of Group Anchored Attitudes," in Hyman and Singer, *op. cit.*

[70] Elihu Katz and Paul F. Lazarsfeld, *Personal Influence* (Glencoe: Free Press, 1955). Cited in Ch. IV of Neil Smelser, *Sociology of Economic Life* (Englewood Cliffs: Prentice Hall, 1963).

can affect individual attitudes and behavior in a given situation. But the range of norms to which the individual might respond and the range of attitudes which the individual might value can be narrowed by acknowledging the role of social learning in establishing and anchoring attitudes and values.

Culture can be defined as the "overriding system of values, beliefs, norms, artifacts, and symbols that have been developed by a society and are shared by its members."[71] Those norms which are of particular importance to the culture can be called the "cultural core values." Some societies might stress education; others may value physical prowess; still others might honor piety. These values influence an individual's attitude set because of the fact that his personality, i.e. the characteristic and distinctive traits of the individual,[72] is developed through a process of social learning, or socialization. This process begins in infancy, and continues through one's formal education and into adulthood, being the aggregation of the types of social influences which we have been exploring. Thus "the development of individual motivation is . . . a process of the internalization of social norms and not . . . the independently given basis of social processes and social values..[73]

Now that we have examined explicitly the received wisdom of social psychology in an attempt to identify and to understand the types of motivations which underlie behavior, we are prepared to assemble the various parts into a generalized behavioral theory, and to relate this theory to the observed phenomenon of philanthropic activity. Before proceeding, though, let us briefly review the major hypotheses which we have uncovered in our search. Fundamentally, we have found that "non-economic" influences can significantly affect individual behavior, even in large groups. An individual will respond to direct pressures to conform to norms of various primary groups within the large group, in order to gain gratifications which are provided by harmonious primary group relationships. And because of the basic need for external sources of reference by which the individual can evaluate and define his status, behavior, and attitudes, indirect pressures to conform to norms of various reference groups are created. Thus one's social environment can be described as a constellation of primary relationships and reference orientations, which interact with one's personal attitude set acquired through an ongoing social learning process. These social variables can be considered as affecting the costs and rewards facing the individual in any given situation. Given this set of costs and rewards, in addition to the costs and rewards from economic considerations, a decision will be made about a course of action, within the limitations of man's bounded rationality.

---

[71] Lindgren, *op. cit.*, p. 205.

[72] Morgan and King, *op. cit.*, p. 205.

[73] Talcott Parsons and Neil Smelser, *Economy and Society* (London: Routledge and Kegan Paul, Ltd., 1956), p. 32.

These are the "murky waters" of sociology. We shall now try to apply them to the problem of philanthropic behavior.

III

Given a mode of behavior B, concerning which individual i must make a choice, his decision calculus can most generally be described by a stochastic function of four variables: D, the direct social pressures perceived; I, the indirect social pressures from identification with reference groups; E, the economic utility of B for the individual; and C, the objective cost of doing B. Thus the probability (Pr) of individual i choosing to do B can be written as:

$$Pr(B) = F(I,D,E,C).$$

Let us examine each part of this equation carefully in the light of the behavioral hypotheses we have developed.

In our context, B is a behavioral norm prescribing a contribution to a charity, a philanthropic act, or even a vote in favor of governmental philanthropy. As we have argued above, the behavioral outcome for any given values of functional variables is most suitably described by a probability operator rather than a determinate solution. The individual is not able to calculate perfectly the utility of B, the values and costs of social relationships, or the precise opportunity cost of using scarce personal resources for B. These limitations on human rationality have led us to the adoption of a satisfying decision mechanism. If the relationship of the social and economic rewards to the social and economic costs is satisfactory, B might be chosen. However, the choice to do B will depend on an aspiration level, which might vary endogenously, and on the order in which alternatives are considered. If an alternative action is equally satisfactory, the first course of action considered will be chosen and B might be ignored. Where the situation is stimulated by a suggestion or pressure to do B, this action might well be considered fully. Thus when an office associate walks up to i and confronts him with a request for contributions, he not only increases the situational salience of the norms concerning B and this set of social pressures, but also creates a situation in which B will be seriously considered as a use of i's personal resources. But because of the uncertainties of specifying how i perceives I, D, and even E, the uncertainties of the order in which alternatives are considered, and the uncertainties associated with the nature of the aspiration level—because of these uncertainties the choice can most generally be left as a stochastic function of the relation of rewards to costs.

Turning to the strength of pressures to conform to the norms concerning B, we find that I is an aggregation of a set of I_j, $j = 1,2,\ldots,J$, where J is the number of reference groups referred to by individual *i*. The strength of the pressures to conform to the norm of each reference group *j* will depend on the prestige and salience of group *j*, the amount of communication and clarity of information received by individual *i* concerning *B* from each group *j*, the extent to which the norm of group *j* regarding *B* conflicts with or corresponds to socially anchored norms (including cultural core values), and the strength of individual *i*'s identification with group *j*. In addition, the extent to which *B* represents an ambiguous behavioral situation will affect the extent to which individual *i* will rely on reference groups for prescriptions of behavior.

Similarly, *D* will be the aggregation of a set of D_k, $k = 1,2,...K$, where *K* is the number of primary groups to which individual *i* belongs. The importance that *i* attaches to the pressure within each group *k* will depend on the value of relationship *k* to the individual, the amount, clarity, and salience of norm-sending activity within *k*, as perceived by *i*, and the deviation between these received norms and established norms for individual *i*. Unlike reference identifications, which are important only to the extent that the individual searches for a behavioral norm due to uncertainty as to proper behavior, these direct pressures will be brought to bear even if the behavioral situation is unambiguous to *i*. Because he belongs to these small groups and values these relationships, he will have to reckon with such pressures. Note that the set $\{j\}$ and the set $\{k\}$ need not be mutually exclusive; i.e. some membership groups may function as reference groups as well.

The economic utility, *E*, that individual *i* will receive from *B* is, for any normal consumption good, a simple function of his preference set. The utility level will depend on *i*'s tastes, including the possibility that he gets utility from altruistic behavior *per se.* Since attitudes and personality, including preferences and tastes, are shaped (though not necessarily determined) by the process of social learning, we can expect that individual *i* will value, to some extent, philanthropic causes which correspond to cultural values. It is likely that he will get some positive utility from seeing schools, hospitals, or welfare provided to the community at large. In addition he will certainly value any direct benefits which accrue to him or to others with whom he identifies. Thus he will value public education positively if he has children to educate. In general, depending on the nature of the good or service being provided by philanthropic activity—its value in terms of internalized cultural norms, and its value in terms of the distribution of actual benefits—*i* will receive a certain level of utility from having the good provided. In discussing these factors we are not ignoring the free-rider problem. Indeed it may be true that individual *i*'s contribution has a negligible impact on the aggregate supply. Still the utility measure is relevant to his behavioral decision: we can expect that *i* will be more *likely* to contribute to a charity if its object is a good or service which he values highly.

Two complications do arise, however, in dealing with philanthropic activity.

First, preferences may be endogenous to the system of social interaction because communications received regarding *B* may change the information content of *i*'s evaluation of the object of this charity effort. To the extent that perceived communication contains new, relevant information, we must be concerned with *i*'s preference ranking at the time the decision is made, and not with some exogenously determined, pre-established ordering.

Second, since we are dealing with philanthropy at the source of its financing, i.e. the individual donor, the actual level of the good to be supplied, and therefore the amount of utility which *i* will derive from the project, is not specified at the time the decision is made regarding *B*. Therefore we can expect that the probability that others will contribute will be an important variable in determining the expected utility accruing to *i*. This is one reason why pledges may be more useful than straightforward requests for contributions; if the individual knows that he need not pitch in a penny unless others contribute a sufficient amount, the expected utility of the project will be higher and the risk factor correspondingly lower.

The final argument in our decision function is *C*, the cost of behavior *B*. In normal consumption decisions, the cost is a parameter provided by the market. However where *B* is a voluntary contribution, the level of *C* must be decided on by the individual. The reason that we have not specified the decision function as a probability distribution over *C* is that the cost is not unambiguously a dependent variable determined by *I, D,* and *E*. In fact, if *i*'s primary relationships prescribe that he contribute a "fair share," the level of *D* may be dependent on *C*. Furthermore, to the extent that *i*'s utility *E* includes an altruistic motive, the value of *E* may depend on the size of *C*. Also it is possible that the size of *i*'s contribution will affect the likelihood that others contribute, again affecting *E*.[74] Taking account of all these variables, individual *i* will make his choice about *B* based on a satisfactory level of net rewards, considering the social gratifications and costs as well as the economic utility and expense of his action.

We can see that the traditional theory of economic choice is a special case of our present generalized model. In particular, in the absence of any social pressures, $Pr(B)$ will collapse into a function of *E* and *C* alone; and where *E* and *C* will be known with certainty, the probability operator will degenerate into the form $Pr(B)=1$ when $E > C$, and $Pr(B)=0$ when $E < C$, assuming that the costs and benefits are measured in the same units. This special case of our model differs from the traditional neo-classical model of consumer choice in one vital respect: the former models effectively determine all consumption choices, the entire consumption bundle, simultaneously. Given the utility function and the income constraint, individual *i*'s consumption bundle is uniquely determined. In

[74]Note that this is Vickrey's "contagion effect" in his article "One Economist's View of Philanthropy," in Dickinson, ed., *op. cit.*

our model, on the other hand, we deal with a single decision. Where there is no uncertainty and perfect knowledge, the two approaches will give the same result. But in a world of imperfect knowledge and uncertainty, still assuming no social pressures, the stochastic model which describes the relevant factors for a single decision will be more fruitful in many applications. Many decisions are in fact taken serially, and situational factors, including the order in which the decisions are made and even whims can be very important. If Mr. Jones goes to a sporting goods store at the beginning of the month, he may very well come home with a new spinning reel. If he goes at the end of the month, he just might forego that pleasure in deference to his bank balance. Further, if we allow social motivations to creep in, the fact that Smith just bought a reel might become relevant and change this decision. The salient situational factors at the time the decision is made may be important in explaining behavior. A model which determines the entire set of consumption decisions simultaneously cannot take these factors into account.

Having systematically examined the motivations underlying the behavior of "social man," and having condensed this information into a general behavioral model of decision-making, we can now briefly apply these developments to the specific issue of philanthropic behavior. For example, assuming the existence of an organization to direct and administer a charity drive, we can expect this group to generate communications to the community at large. Depending on the status of this organizational core and the amount of norm-sending generated, there will be a tendency for members of the community to contribute. These individuals in turn will generate chains of primary group pressures, tending to induce more contributions. In addition, the members of the organizing group will each generate a chain of primary group pressures, the strength of these pressures varying with the prestige of the initiators. Through these channels of influence, much of the community will be exposed to direct and/or indirect social pressures to contribute to the charity, and will base their decisions upon the strength of these pressures, the utility derived from giving to the particular project, and the cost of choosing to contribute. Thus, while traditional pubic-goods theory would assume voluntarism to be improbable whenever any individual's contribution will be negligible in relation to the whole, where traditional theory would consider a theory of voluntarism to be "unrealistic and inconsistent with the premises of all other phases of economic analysis,"[75] we have seen that it is not unrealistic to expect "social man" to engage in philanthropic activity.[76]

IV

Recognizing that a satisfactory understanding of philanthropic activity requires a broadening of economic behavioral models to include social and psychological motivations, we have tried to approach this issue by reference to the received knowledge of social psychology. In doing so we have seen how individuals can seek gratification not only from economic transactions, but from social interaction as well. In fact, "social man" might rationally accept economic costs in order to maintain gratifying, consonant social relationships. Realizing further that social man possesses only limited capacities for decision-making, we were able to show that "non-economic" behavior need not be irrational behavior.

But we should not conclude without noting that the relevance of the behavioral sciences to economics is not limited to the issue of philanthropy. Indeed this issue is merely a convenient showcase for demonstrating the need for more inclusive behavioral models in economic theory. However complex or "murky" the realm of social psychology may be, it is doubtful that economists will be able to develop satisfactory models of stabilization policies, investment behavior, consumption choices, or even market structures without taking a step in this direction.

REFERENCES

Arrow, Kenneth, *Social Choice and Individual Values* (New York: John Wiley & Sons, Inc., 1963).

Buchanan, James, "Cooperation and Conflict in Public Goods Interaction," *Western Economic Journal*, March 1967.

---

[75] Richard Musgrave, *Theory of Public Finance* (New York: McGraw-Hill, 1959), p. 12.

[76] Using our behavioral analysis we can also illuminate the issue of political philanthropy. In particular, why might individuals vote in ways not consistent with their economic self-interest? It has been suggested by many economists* that man is basically bi-furcated"; when acting in the market he expresses pragmatic decisions, but in voting on social questions he expresses his interpretation of moral imperatives. From our model we can go beyond reference to some metaphysical "ought" which pervades political choice without affecting market decisions. We can hypothesize that individual behavior might well be different in the two spheres of choice because of a differential effect of one's social milieu. Given that $Pr(B) = F(I,D,E,C)$, it is quite possible that mundane consumption decisions are little affected by I or D, while these social factors are more important to decisions of a political nature. The rewards and costs relevant to political decisions may be qualitatively quite different from those bearing weight in every day consumption choices. In short, man need not be "bifurcated" to act in his own traditionally defined self-interest in some instances, and in the public interest in others; in both cases the same underlying motivations may be at work, with only the strength of certain variables being altered.

*This idea is confronted by Kenneth Arrow, *Social Choice and Individual Values* (New York: John Wiley & Sons, Inc., 1963); J. G. Head, "On Merit Goods," *Finanzarchiv*, March 1966; James Buchanan, "Politics, Policy, and Pigovian Margins," *Economica*, March 1962; and Margolis, *op. cit.*

———, *The Demand and Supply of Public Goods* (Chicago: Rand-McNally, 1968).

———, "Politics, Policy, and the Pigovian Margins," *Economica*, March 1962.

Dickinson, Frank G., *Philanthropy and Public Policy* (New York: National Bureau of Economic Research, 1962).

Head, John G., "On Merit Goods," *Finanzarchiv*, March 1966.

Himmelstrand, Ulf, *Social Pressures, Attitudes, and Democratic Processes* (Uppsala: Almquist & Wiksells, 1960).

Hochman, Harold M., and James D. Rodgers, "Pareto Optimal Redistribution," *American Economic Review*, September 1969.

Hyman, Herbert H., and Eleanor Singer, eds., *Readings in Reference Group Theory and Research* (New York: Free Press, 1968).

Johnson, David B., *The Fundamental Economics of the Charity Market* (Ph.D. dissertation, University of Virginia, 1968).

Katona, George, "On the Function of Behavioral Theory and Behavioral Research in Economics," *American Economic Review*, March 1968.

Lane, Robert E., and David O. Sears, *Public Opinion* (Englewood Cliffs: Prentice Hall, 1964).

Lindgren, Henry Clay, *An Introduction to Social Psychology* (New York: John Wiley & Sons, Inc., 1969).

Margolis, Julius, "A Comment on the Pure Theory of Public Expenditure," *Review of Economics and Statistics*, November 1955.

Morgan, Clifford T., and Richard A. King, *Introduction to Psychology* (New York: McGraw-Hill, 1966).

Musgrave, Richard, "Pareto Optimal Redistribution: Comment," *American Economic Review*, December 1970.

———, *Theory of Public Finance* (New York: McGraw-Hill, 1959).

Olson, Mancur, *The Logic of Collective Action* (Cambridge: Harvard University Press, 1965).

Parsons, Talcott, and Neil Smelser, *Economy and Society* (London: Routledge and Kegan Paul, Ltd., 1956).

Phillips, Almarin, *Market Structure, Organization, and Performance* (Cambridge: Harvard University Press, 1962).

Schelling, Thomas, *The Strategy of Conflict* (Cambridge: Harvard University Press, 1960).

Simon, Herbert, *Models of Man* (New York: John Wiley & Sons, Inc., 1957).

Smelser, Neil, *The Sociology of Economic Life* (Englewood Cliffs: Prentice Hall, 1963).

Thibaut, John W., and Harold H. Kelley, *The Social Psychology of Groups* (New York: John Wiley & Sons, Inc., 1961).

Comment

Amartya Sen

William Vickrey has presented a penetrating analysis of the U.S. fiscal system related to philanthropy and has made a number of well-argued suggestions for reform. I have only a few comments. First, the opaqueness of the tax refund system may, in fact, be part of its attraction to donors in so far as a relatively small net contribution is made to look like a much larger donation. This fact would not affect Vickrey's expectation that a tax reform which makes things less opaque should, if implemented, increase total donation, but it is of relevance in explaining the continuation of the present tax system and the pressures that are likely to counteract Vickrey's reform scheme. It seems useful to distinguish between the normative question of the desirability of a tax system and the empirical question of the genesis and survival of that system. Vickrey's attention is concentrated on the former, perhaps appropriately for this conference, but the political questions surrounding the growth and persistence of the current system in America would have to be studied in the context of the possible implementation of the Vickrey reforms.

Second, on the subject of charitable contributions directly by corporations (rather than by the individual shareholders), Vickrey is right in pointing out that this provides a guarantee to each shareholder that others are contributing also. One can distinguish between two types of psychology here, viz., "I would be happy to contribute this much if I am assured that others would too" and "I would not like to contribute as much given the other shareholders' contributions, no matter what they are, but I would be agreeable to contribute that much as a price for persuading the others to make similar contributions." From the formulation that Vickrey gives, emphasizing the role of the "assurance" that others would contribute, it would appear that he has the former type of interdependence in mind, whereas the latter type of interdependence—in the familiar "Prisoner's Dilemma" form—would also provide support for such a procedure. In fact, in the latter case the system of direct giving by corporations cannot be replaced by a voluntary agreement among shareholders; whereas in the former case it can be, since no one would have the desire to break the assurance given by each to the others (and an unenforced agreement would be an "equilibrium point").

Burton Weisbrod's interesting study of the equilibrium between the different sectors, and in particular his analysis of the relationships between the provision of public goods and that of substitute private goods, have emphasized the substitutability between classes of public and private goods. While he is concerned with developing a model "in which certain behavioral and organizational constraints limit public-sector activities and stimulate the voluntary sector," that is not necessarily the historical direction of causation. Frequently the inadequacy of private goods to meet a public need would lead to an eventual development of an appropriate public good when political and social charges permit such a development. The historical relationship between public and private sectors is indeed very complex, and Weisbrod's model concentrates, naturally enough, on a limited aspect of it.

My main difficulty with Weisbrod's paper lies in the fact that it does not go much into operation of the voluntary sector. He demonstrates why a demand for voluntary supply may exist, but not how this is to be met since a "Prisoner's Dilemma" type of problem is present here. Weisbrod refers to the "free-rider problem," which is a special case of this, and points out that there are "pressures to donate" and also that people may actually enjoy giving. This is fine as far as it goes, but there is a need to explain the psychology of voluntary giving in circumstances where the "pressures" are weak. An explanation of giving in terms of enjoyment of giving could be tautological. In voluntary community services, or in the provision of labor in a commune, a complex interrelationship holds between each person's activities, his expectations of others' actions and his notions of his responsibility. Each person may prefer not to contribute given the contribution of others, leading to a classic "Prisoner's Dilemma" situation, but nevertheless an implicit moral code might rule out individual rationalistic calculations and produce a voluntary "equilibrium" involving appropriate actions.

Some of the political controversies of recent years, e.g., the Chinese debates on the "cultural revolution," have been concerned with this range of issues. The spectacular feature of the "Prisoner's Dilemma" is that individualistic rational calculations produce an inoptimal outcome. If I_1 and I_0 stand respectively for a particular person contributing a unit of labor and not contributing it, and R_1 and R_0 for others contributing labor or not, and if a typical preference ordering (in descending order) is I_0R_1, I_1R_1, I_0R_0, I_1R_0, then I_0R_0 is the only equilibrium (and is the result of "dominant" strategies on the part of each person), whereas everyone prefers I_1R_1 to I_0R_0. The scope for an enforceable contract requiring each person to do I_1 exists in principle, but in some cases enforcement may be very difficult, e.g., in guaranteeing intensive communal work on the part of each person. If, however, people acted *as if* their ordering were I_1R_1, I_0R_1, I_0R_0, I_1R_0, and expected others to do R_1, then they will end up in I_1R_1, which will be superior to I_0R_0 even according to their "true" ordering. The economic relevance of cultural reorientation relates directly to this fact and raises important questions of freedom and moral code.

Bruce Bolnick's paper is concerned with a related set of issues. He dismisses the hypothesis that man may be basically "bifurcated" and develops a behavioral theory of philanthropy such that "individual behavior may be different in the two spheres of choice because of a different effect of one's social milieu." It would appear that Bolnick's "social man" would not hold the preference ordering underlying the "Prisoner's Dilemma"—not for long anyway—thanks to the social milieu. This would certainly be a way of escaping the "Prisoner's Dilemma" problem. But what remains to be seen is how special a case this is and whether the processes of value formation that Bolnick describes are likely to be fairly generally observed. This undoubtedly remains an interesting area for further work.

Index

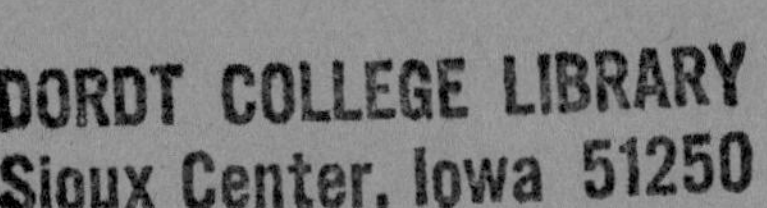